MW00583939

The Politics of Purity

The Politics of Purity

Harvey Washington Wiley and the Origins of Federal Food Policy

Clayton A. Coppin and Jack High

Ann Arbor

THE UNIVERSITY OF MICHIGAN PRESS

Copyright © by the University of Michigan 1999
All rights reserved
Published in the United States of America by
The University of Michigan Press
Manufactured in the United States of America
⊚ Printed on acid-free paper
2002   2001   2000   1999   4   3   2   1

No part of this publication may be reproduced,
stored in a retrieval system, or transmitted in any form
or by any means, electronic, mechanical, or otherwise,
without the written permission of the publisher.

A CIP catalog record for this book is available
from the British Library.

Library of Congress Cataloging-in-Publication Data

Coppin, Clayton A.
    The politics of purity : Harvey Washington Wiley and the origins
of Federal Food Policy / Clayton A. Coppin and Jack High.
        p.   cm.
    Includes bibliographical references and index.
    ISBN 0-472-10984-7 (cloth : alk. paper)
    1. Food law and legislation—United States—History.   2. Food
industry and trade—Law and legislation—United States—History.
3. Competition, Unfair—United States—History.   4. Wiley, Harvey
Washington, 1844–1930.   I. High, Jack C.   II. Title.
KF1900.C67   1999
344.73'04232—dc21   99-13530
                                                                CIP

To James Harvey Young

Contents

Acknowledgments

Various scholars have critiqued parts of this work over several years. We particularly thank Robert Cuff, Don Lavoie, Robert Tollison, Richard Vietor, Suzanne White, Donna Wood, James Harvey Young, participants in the Empirical Workshop at George Mason University, participants in the Public Choice Seminar at George Mason University, and participants in the Business History Conference at the Huntington Library, Pasadena, California.

Part of chapter 1 appeared as Jack High, "Can Rents Run Uphill?" *Public Choice* 65 (1990): 229–37. Chapter 6 was previously published as Clayton Coppin and Jack High, "Umpires at Bat: Setting Food Standards by Government Regulation," *Business and Economic History*, 2d ser., 21 (1992): 109–17. An earlier version of chapter 7 appeared as Jack C. High and Clayton Coppin, "Wiley and the Whiskey Industry: Strategic Behavior in the Passage of the Pure Food Act," *Business History Review* 62 (summer 1988): 286–309. We thank the editors of those journals for permission to incorporate previously published material.

Colin Day, Ellen McCarthy, and the staff at the University of Michigan Press were most helpful in improving the style and seeing the book through production. Pat Carda of Wellesley, Massachusetts made numerous editorial improvements to the manuscript.

Finally, we gratefully acknowledge financial support from the Lynde and Harry Bradley Foundation, the Earhart Foundation, the Charles G. Koch Charitable Foundations, the David H. Koch Charitable Foundations, and the Claude R. Lambe Charitable Foundation. Without their generous support, we would have been unable to complete the research.

Introduction

Regulating Competition

Every day millions of U.S. consumers, selecting from a rich variety of options, must decide what to eat for dinner. The meal and the method of decision vary widely. The U.S. Army solves the problem of choice by regimen—liver on Wednesday, meat loaf on Thursday, fish on Friday. Most persons use more creative methods of choice, with a wider variety of results. Some browse at the grocery store until something strikes their fancy; some select organically grown vegetables in tune with their environmental beliefs. Some, like diabetics, have special dietary requirements, while others, concerned with nutrition, favor oat bran and broccoli. Habit, too, influences our decisions. A study by the National Academy of Science found that most people ignore advice to eat healthier foods. People eat what is familiar, such as meat and potatoes, even when they know that bean sprouts and tofu are healthier.[1]

Even larger than the variety of foods among which consumers choose is the variety of claims made for the food. These claims add to the difficulty of deciding what to eat, a subject that is often in the news. *Time* magazine, in a cover story on misleading labels, believes that food labels dupe consumers. The solution, says *Time*, is government regulation: "The government could clear up some of the confusion on supermarket shelves and help Americans become healthier consumers." *Time* lauds the efforts of the Food and Drug Administration's former commissioner, David Kessler, who, says *Time*, has an "utterly novel vision that consumers should be able to tell what they are ingesting by reading what is written on food labels."

The vision may seem novel to *Time*'s reporters, but the idea is as old as food regulation itself. The Pure Food and Drugs Act, which was passed by Congress and signed into law on 30 June 1906, regulated food labels. It declares a package or label to be misbranded if it bears "any statement, design, or device regarding such article, or the ingredients or substances contained therein, which shall be false or misleading in any particular." The *Time* article unwittingly demonstrates that eighty-five years of regulation by the federal government has not solved the problem that the law was intended to solve. In fact, the complaints voiced in *Time* are the same complaints voiced by journalists nearly a century ago.[2]

Lack of results is not the only consequence of food regulation in the United States. Different government agencies release conflicting information about food. A *Newsweek* cover story pointed out that the surgeon general recommends a low-fat diet with a minimum of meat, milk, and cheese, while the Department of Agriculture recommends a higher consumption of meat and dairy products.[3] Not only has food regulation resulted in contradictory recommendations, it has also suppressed information. When the American Heart Association proposed putting their symbol on foods that were beneficial to the heart, the Food and Drug Administration objected, saying that "third party endorsements are not in the interest of consumers . . . They are likely to contribute to consumer confusion and to mislead the consumer." Here, too, the modern government bureau carries on a tradition. In 1910 regulators prevented the White Cross, a private organization whose purpose was to promote purity, from certifying foods. Thus the effort of government bureaus to maintain a monopoly on food certification goes back to the beginnings of food regulation in America.[4]

Consumers apparently desire a simple, reliable symbol that indicates a food is safe. According to *Newsweek,* even non-Jewish consumers examine food packages for the circled "U," which signifies that food is kosher. Although the symbol merely indicates that the food complies with religious laws, consumers use it as a signal of nutritious or safe food.[5]

The debates over food labeling have almost always invoked health or fraud. Advocates of regulation usually claim that it is intended to insure the health of the consumer or to prevent him from being duped. Occasionally, however, another issue will surface. David Kessler, commissioner of the Food and Drug Administration, said that the "purpose of the FDA's review of the food label is to make sure all food companies are competing on a level playing field." He added, "One company should not be allowed to gain a market advantage over another company by promoting its product as something it is not."[6]

Everyone lauds a level playing field, but achieving it is apparently a peculiar business. It involves more than prohibiting false labels; it sometimes means prohibiting true ones. A product like Crisco, which is vegetable fat, cannot claim that it is free from cholesterol, even though it is. On the other hand, a package of beef with the highest fat content is labeled "USDA Choice" by the Department of Agriculture. The dairy industry advertises the wholesomeness of its products, despite the high fat and cholesterol content of milk and butter. From the standpoint of health or of fraud, it would be difficult to rationalize these labeling practices; they are comprehensible only if we understand that government agencies are, as Kessler says, regulating competition. Even so, the level playing field of regulated competition must appear oddly tilted to the makers of vegetable shortening.

Analyzing food and drug laws as the regulation of competition throws a different light on the subject. We find that *health* and *honesty* and *the public interest* are vague and elusive terms, more serviceable as rhetorical devices than as practically achieved goals. Such rhetorical devices find ready use by contestants in the process of regulated competition. The study of regulated competition also enables us to discern more clearly the particular interests that actuate the regulatory process.

By tracing out the effects of regulated competition, we are led to the commercial, political, and bureaucratic interests that are benefited or harmed by regulation. These interests attempt to shape regulation to their advantage. This book examines the origins of food and drug regulation in America, the Pure Food and Drugs Act of 1906, as the result of regulating competition in the food industry.

Harvey Washington Wiley

The central figure in the passage of the Pure Food and Drugs Act of 1906 was Harvey Washington Wiley, Chief of the Bureau of Chemistry in the Department of Agriculture. He drafted most of the law, gave extensive testimony to Congress on its behalf, lectured tirelessly of its virtues, and built a coalition of businesses, bureaucrats, and politicians to support it. His influence was so great that the law was frequently called the Wiley Act. After the act was passed, Wiley served as chief administrator of the law until 1912. In this capacity, he laid the foundation for food regulation in the United States for the twentieth century.

Wiley was a forceful personality who contributed to the development of agricultural chemistry. Quite apart from his connection to food legislation, his work in chemistry makes him a notable figure in American science. Moreover, his personal life was eventful and intriguing, and it sometimes overlapped with his official life. His honeymoon, for example, was spent at the adulteration trial of Coca-Cola, a trial that he worked long and hard to bring about.

Of necessity Wiley is the centerpiece of our study, but this not a biography of him. We are concerned only with his involvement in food legislation. There is no biography to which we can refer the reader to get a full view of Wiley's life. Oscar Anderson's *The Health of a Nation* and James Harvey Young's *Pure Food*, like our study, concentrate on Wiley's regulatory activities. A more complete view of Wiley is offered in William L. Fox's doctoral dissertation, "Harvey W. Wiley: The Formative Years." Fox covers Wiley only up to 1903 but nonetheless provides insight into his life and activities outside the Bureau of Chemistry. Fox's work is essential to a full understanding and judgment of Wiley.

Fortunately for the historian, Wiley kept detailed records of his life, including letter press copies of his outgoing personal correspondence and a voluminous amount of incoming correspondence. In total, it amounts to nearly three hundred boxes, which are now in the Manuscript Division of the Library of Congress. In addition to these records, there are large amounts of official correspondence and records in the National Archives. Few historians writing on food regulation have made extensive use of these materials; most have used them selectively and relied on the comprehensive research of Oscar Anderson for their understanding of Wiley. Anderson researched most of the Wiley materials. However, as will become evident in the course of our narrative, he palliated Wiley's involvement with commercial interests. Anderson portrays Wiley as a dedicated reformer, at times conspiratorial and overzealous, but who nevertheless promoted the welfare of the consuming public. Anderson dismisses Wiley's critics in much the same way that Wiley did, by portraying them as cheaters and food dopers. The image of Wiley as a dedicated reformer was created during the crusade to pass a national pure food law. Wiley himself worked tirelessly to project that image, and he was helped by sympathetic reporters and paid press agents. This image has been one of the most enduring legacies of food regulation in America. Wiley's claims, that he regulated in the public interest and that his opponents were captured by special interests, have gained a wide currency among scholars of regulation. Even Gabriel Kolko, who has done more than anyone to encourage historians to look for the special interests behind regulation, has repeated Wiley's claims.

Wiley's reputation has endured even while the regulatory agency that he fathered has tarnished. Critics have charged that food and drug regulators were captured by the interests that they were supposed to regulate. Wiley escaped this criticism partly because he himself originated the charge that the agency was captured by unscrupulous business interests. Almost from the moment of its passage, Wiley claimed that the Pure Food Act was being subverted by corrupt government officials. These officials, said Wiley, served the interests of those who wanted to cheat and poison the public. Consequently, he is praised both by those who think that the Pure Food Act served the public interest and by those who think that it was captured by business interests.

Approaching the Pure Food Act as a law that regulated competition reveals a rather different picture of Wiley. Instead of a champion of purity, we see him working hand in glove with firms that benefited from his enforcement of the pure food law. Wiley helped these firms gain a competitive advantage over their rivals. Nor did the benefits of cooperation accrue merely to the business firms. Wiley himself was engaged in a difficult competitive struggle to maintain the size and importance of his bureau. His involvement with commercial firms helped propel him into national prominence and gave him a powerful pulpit to strengthen his bureau and expand his influence. At the same time, Wiley's involvement with business firms placed him in conflict with other government officials, especially the secretary of agriculture, James Wilson. Much of Wiley's conflict with his superiors resulted from his commercial favoritism.

The influence of business firms on the passage of the Pure Food Act has begun to attract notice in recent years. Donna Wood's *Strategic Uses of Public Policy* is particularly valuable in drawing attention to ways in which firms used legislation to gain a commercial advantage over their rivals. James Harvey Young incorporated commercial self-interest into *Pure Food*, his overarching history of the federal food law's passage. Young's treatment is especially important, because the breadth and depth of his scholarship are so impressive. Although Wiley's commercial favoritism has been pointed out by critics since the turn of the century, it is only in the past few years that this interpretation of the food law has gained a respectable currency.[7]

State Food Officials

The enactment and the early implementation of the 1906 food law were not simply a matter of overcoming unscrupulous opposition, as the public interest interpretation of the law has often maintained. Wiley's version of a pure food law was vigorously opposed by many respectable persons who simply wanted a different law. Governmental opposition was centered in the Association of State Food and Dairy Officials, an organization with a frustrating propensity to change its official name. After several annual meetings where the organization's name was repeatedly altered, one official quipped that the current meeting was the most successful in years, simply because the association had not changed its name. We will avoid confusion by referring to the group as the National Association of State Food and Dairy Officials, even though its name may have been different at a specific time.

The association was formed by food officials who sought uniformity in state laws. Many of these officials favored national legislation, but could not agree on the administrative mechanisms of a national law. Some members advocated establishing a new agency headed by a national food commissioner who would regulate food shipped in interstate commerce. Others saw little need for a regulatory agency at the national level; they believed that a law allowing states to regulate all foods entering a particular state would be sufficient. Still others wanted to put authority for regulation in Wiley's Bureau of Chemistry. The organization became a microcosm of the debate over a national food law. These debates reveal that the greatest conflict was not over regulation per se, but over who would regulate and how.

State food officials with a different vision of a national food law were not less honest or dedicated than Wiley. Many had worked to regulate food on the state level for many years. They saw Wiley as an interloper interested in increasing his power and prestige at their expense. Some resented the attention and admiration Wiley received in the national press, while their own contributions went unrecognized. Many were aware of Wiley's commercial ties and believed that he was corrupting their organization. They resisted Wiley's influence over their association, and they criticized his denunciation of those who opposed him as agents of dishonest businesses.

Those who opposed Wiley have been banished to the margins of the history of food regulation and dismissed as the supporters of unscrupulous business. This is an inaccurate portrayal of many of these men. To be sure they sometimes favored local over national control, but it does not follow that they were dishonest or corrupt or even necessarily wrong.

Buried in the disputes over federal regulation is a conflict between local and national food companies. In various ways, federal regulation conferred competitive advantage on national firms. This conflict was not resolved with the passage of the 1906 law, but its significance has been overlooked, because the public interest and capture theories created a dichotomy that left little room for these interfirm controversies. We take these controversies to be an integral part of the history of food regulation. We analyze regulation as the outcome of two distinct competitive processes, one that takes place in the market, the other in the polity. While food companies used regulation to earn profits or avoid losses, government officials used it to gain power and prestige in the bureaucracy. The interaction of commercial and bureaucratic competition produced the Pure Food and Drugs Act of 1906 and set the course for future food regulation. We believe that this study provides new insights into the nature of food regulation in the United States and hope that it will encourage those interested in regulation to look beyond the rhetoric of public interest to the more substantial issues found in regulated competition. In these issues will be found the powerful forces that create and sustain government regulation of economic life.

CHAPTER 1

The Theory of Economic Regulation

This study, while primarily historical, relies heavily on the economic theory of regulation, for several reasons. Economic theory aids our understanding of regulatory events. Even when motivated by concerns for health, purity, or other noble causes, regulation will produce economic effects. Legislators, administrators, and managers will not be indifferent to these effects; a firm or agency or politician that stands to gain or lose financially by regulation will almost certainly try to influence it. The history of regulation is richer if it includes the economically self-interested activity of individuals, firms, and bureaus. A second reason we rely on economics is that it can provide historical guidance. Theory can sometimes alert the historian to evidence that she might otherwise overlook or misprize; an awareness of economic effects can aid the search for documents and meaning.

Theory can also help us to answer that most unsettling of historical questions: So what? One of history's purposes is to distinguish what is general and permanent in human action from what is particular and transitory. If history is to be something more than entertainment, its narrative will convey enduring lessons. Tying historical research back into theory forces the historian to ask himself how his narrative fits into the general principles of human action, and thus into the general lessons of concrete historical episodes.

There is another reason that we have joined theory and history together in one study: history improves theory. As disciplines, the theory of regulation concentrates on the abstract features of regulatory behavior, and the history of regulation focuses on its concrete manifestations. It is possible, of course, to study either the abstract or the concrete features alone, but integrating the two disciplines helps keep the theory consistent with the stories and thus anchors theory in actual events. This has been especially apparent during the last few decades, when the theory of economic regulation has been repeatedly revised to take account of new historical evidence. This study is no exception; we also have found it necessary to revise the theory of regulation in order to bring it into line with the historical record.

Because this work has been so influenced by economic theory, we have thought it best to make the theory explicit. To do so, we briefly recount the history of regulation theory. Approaching theory this way reveals interconnections between theoretical and historical research. At least in America, the history and economics of regulation display strong similarities and have developed along roughly parallel lines.[1]

The Development of Regulation Theory

From the Progressive Era through the 1950s, historians and economists usually depicted regulation as government's necessary and beneficial response to market failure. According to this view, regulation was imposed on an unwilling business community by government officials committed to serving the public interest. So, for example, historian Arthur S. Link wrote that "there was a progressive movement on the national level, which took form in attempts to subject railroads, industrial corporations, and banks to effective public control." Similarly, economist Claire Wilcox, speaking of the growth of natural monopolies, wrote that "Government was, therefore, compelled to intervene to safeguard the public interest."[2]

Beginning in the 1960s, however, historians and economists began to doubt that public interest could adequately explain the emergence of regulation. In his influential *Triumph of Conservatism*, Gabriel Kolko argued that "the dominant fact of American political life at the beginning of this century was that big business led the struggle for the federal regulation of the economy." The growing historical evidence that businesses supported and benefited from regulation led economist George Stigler to formulate a commercial self-interest theory of regulation. According to Stigler's theory, regulation is an exchange between politicians and businessmen, both of whom benefit as a consequence. As a rule, Stigler believed that "regulation is acquired by the industry and is designed and operated for its benefit."[3]

Kolko and Stigler had a profound impact on the history and theory of regulation. Their work stimulated research but also controversy, from which an increasingly complex interpretation of regulation has emerged. Under pressure from historical evidence, the economic theory of regulation has gradually evolved from a capture theory to one that gives due prominence to conflicting business interests and to political and bureaucratic influences.

Business Interests and Regulation

Although it is impossible to deny the Kolko–Stigler thesis, that businesses have sought out and benefited from regulation, it is also true that regulation has not always been desired by the regulated industry. R. H. K. Vietor, for

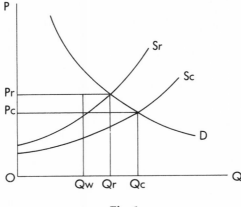

Fig. 1.

example, has documented the railroads' almost unanimous opposition to the Hepburn Act of 1906, which nevertheless passed and which expanded the rate-making powers of the Interstate Commerce Commission. The historical evidence shows that regulation is not always captured by the regulated industry. If the theory of economic regulation is to be generally applicable to historical facts, the Stigler model, which is a capture theory, has to be modified.[4]

At the same time, historians have found that businesses do not usually constitute a monolithic interest group, even in the same industry. Morton Keller has drawn attention to the "roiling diversity" of interests that influenced regulation, and Ralph W. Hidy has emphasized the "divisions of opinions, postures, and actions within firms, industries and other groupings" in the making of public policy. A general theory of regulation will have to account for conflicting commercial interests.[5]

Economists James Buchanan and Gordon Tullock have developed a theory to account for regulatory conflict within an industry. They recognize that regulation does not affect all firms equally; some firms can gain a competitive advantage at the expense of others. For example, if regulation imposes more costs on inefficient firms than it does on efficient firms, then some inefficient firms will be driven out of business. Fewer firms will mean less output and higher prices, which may benefit the firms who remain in business. This situation is shown in figure 1. Equilibrium price and output—P_c and Q_c—are shown by the intersection of the demand curve D with supply curve S_c, which is a long-run industry supply curve that has been drawn under the assumption that there is no regulation. Each point on the supply curve represents a firm, so that the firms with lower costs are represented by the leftward part of the curve and firms with higher costs are represented by the rightward part of the curve.

Curve S_r shows the industry supply curve after regulation is imposed. The vertical distance between S_r and S_c represents the cost of regulation to each firm. The larger distance between the curves as we move rightward implies that higher cost firms are more hurt by regulation than are lower cost firms. Some higher cost firms, those between Q_r and Q_c, will be driven out of business, thus restricting output to Q_r and raising price to P_r. All firms that remain in the industry will get a higher price for their output. However, because of the regulation, they also will incur higher costs of production. Point Q_w represents a critical divide. All firms to the left of Q_w will gain more from the higher price than they lose from the increased cost of regulation. For all firms to the right of Q_w, the increased costs of production outweigh the gains from a higher price. Thus, on a strictly monetary calculation, the firms to the left of Q_w will favor regulation, and the firms to the right will oppose it. This can lead to intraindustry conflict over regulation.[6]

Although the Buchanan–Tullock analysis incorporates opposing interests within the same industry, it implies that firms with lower costs of production will favor regulation and firms with higher costs of production will oppose it. The history of regulation has not always shown this to be true. For example, the mandatory use of coal scrubbers was opposed by western coal companies and supported by eastern coal companies. The eastern companies prevailed even though they had higher costs of production than the western companies.[7]

Figure 2 depicts a situation in which this kind of outcome will occur. In the graph, D represents industry demand and S industry supply. Again we assume that each point on the supply curve represents a particular firm, so that firms with lower costs of production are represented by the lower part of the supply curve, and firms with higher costs are represented by the higher portion of the curve. Regulation that restricts the output of the lower cost firms will raise prices, which will benefit the firms in which output is not restricted. In the graph, (P_c, Q_c) shows competitive price and output before regulation and (P_r, Q_r) the restricted price and output after regulation. Q_d represents the amount by which output is diminished. The firms that suffer from the restrictions will lose profits equal to the heavily shaded area in the graph; the remaining firms will increase their profits by the amount shown in the lightly shaded area of the graph. On the assumptions that firms are guided solely by monetary considerations and that those who can pay the most for regulation will win, higher cost firms will defeat lower cost firms in regulatory battles as long as the lightly shaded area is greater than the darkly shaded area.[8]

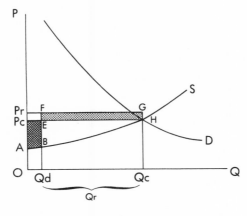

Fig. 2.

Bureaucratic Entrepreneurship

From public interest to industry capture to business's use of regulation as a competitive weapon, the history and economics of regulation have developed more or less in tandem. There is yet another parallel development between theory and history that calls for some elaboration, because this development helps us to understand regulation generally and the history of food regulation in particular. Although business interests are important to regulation, they are not always its driving force. Leadership for regulatory change often originates within the political sector.

The deregulation of airlines is a particularly clear example of this. The immediate impetus for deregulation came from Senator Edward Kennedy. In the spring of 1975, when he held hearings on deregulation, the airlines were adamantly opposed to it; Delta Airlines even claimed, using a kind of Orwellian logic, that the attempt to deregulate "promised more regulation and perhaps eventual nationalization."[9] Obviously, regulatory reform was not embraced by the regulated industry. Rather, change was initiated from within the political sector, and, after Alfred Kahn was appointed chairman of the Civil Aeronautics Board, from within the regulatory agency itself.[10]

Near the end of his study of three successful public figures, historian Eugene Lewis coined the term *heroic bureaucrat,* an oxymoron that calls to mind a salient feature of American bureaucracy. Despite an image of dull routine, bureaucracies, commanded by individuals of unusual talent and dedication, often display fierce rivalry and dynamic growth. Enterprising bureaucrats have changed American social life. They have influenced the food we eat, the clothes we wear, the environment we work in, the schools

our children attend, the terms we trade on, and our political processes. They
have built huge organizations with budgets that run into the hundreds of
millions of dollars and with control over land, labor, and capital that rival
the resources of successful business leaders. The bureaucratic entrepreneur
is no less a force of American life than the business entrepreneur.[11]

For all this, the bureaucrat has not been particularly studied as an
entrepreneur, especially in that quarter of academia where he should naturally command attention—the economics department. Modern economic
theory is nearly devoid of entrepreneurship studies. As economist William J.
Baumol has said, "Look for him [the entrepreneur] in some of the most
noted of recent writings on value theory, or in neoclassical or activity analysis models of the firm. The references are scanty and more often they are
totally absent. The theoretical firm is entrepreneurless—the Prince of Den-
mark has been expunged from the discussion of Hamlet."[12]

Although economists have developed an impressive literature on bureaucracy, they have paid little explicit attention to entrepreneurs. Yet bureaucratic entrepreneurship is central to the origin and growth of bureaus.
Norman Frolich, Joe Oppenheimer, and Oran Young call it the "missing
link" in analyzing the evolution of bureaucracy. Certainly, the history of
American bureaucracy cannot be understood apart from the competitive
process set in motion by entrepreneurs within the political system.[13]

Entrepreneurship is perhaps best defined as "acting man exclusively seen
from the aspect of uncertainty inherent in every action."[14] In economic
theory, entrepreneurship refers not to particular individuals, but to an aspect of action or decision making. It emphasizes the complexity and uncertainty that surround human action, and the economic advantage of foresight
and sound judgment. "Entrepreneurial talent," writes Israel Kirzner, "con-
sists in peering into an unknown future and arriving at an assessment of the
relevant features of that future."[15]

Usually, entrepreneurship is studied as it applies to the theory of markets. The pursuit of entrepreneurial profit sets in motion a competitive
process that, taken as a whole, determines the production, allocation, and
consumption of economic goods. However, the meaning of entrepreneurship is not tied to any particular economic system. Joseph Schumpeter has
pointed out that private property is not essential to entrepreneurial activity.
Both Frolich and Eugene Lewis developed a theory of public or political
entrepreneurship. Mark Casson has pointed out that the meaning of entrepreneurship is "institution free," and Ludwig von Mises, who put the entrepreneur at center stage in economic theory, has written, "In using this term
[*entrepreneurship*] one must never forget that every action is embedded in
the flux of time and therefore involves a speculation."[16] Entrepreneurship is

present in the actions of politicians and bureaucrats as well as those of businessmen.

Bureaucratic entrepreneurs are appointed government officials who exercise creativity, alertness, judgment, and persuasion in attempting to increase their control over scarce resources. This definition emphasizes that bureaucrats need not passively accept their environment, even though they operate in a world of rules and routine. They can actively try to change the law in order to increase their bureau's budget and their control over it.[17] Government officials, as economist Fred McChesney notes, are not "mere brokers redistributing wealth in response to competing private demands, but ... independent actors making their own demands to which private actors respond."[18]

Because entrepreneurs operate in an uncertain environment, they can fail as well as succeed. The very complexity that makes alertness and judgment valuable in economic life implies that some failure is inevitable. Some bureaus will expand their control over resources, and some will lose their control. Although a bureau does not operate according to monetary profit and loss as business firms do, bureaus are subject to the discipline of survival within a competitive process.

To increase the resources under their control, bureaucratic entrepreneurs must win the approval of legislators because, at least in the U.S. system, the immediate source of the bureau's funds is the legislature. In the sense that they raise and allocate tax funds, legislators provide the immediate demand for the activities of the bureaus. Legislators themselves, however, are only intermediaries; they require the votes of their constituents to hold office. Raising and allocating tax funds ultimately requires implicit approval of the electorate. Demand for the services of the bureau thus runs from the voters through politicians (especially those whom the actions of the bureau can help or hurt) to the members of the bureau. The bureaucratic entrepreneur can, therefore, increase his budget by influencing voters, or elected officials, or both.[19]

This same reasoning applies to the rules and regulations that govern the activities of a bureau. Elected officials pass the laws that create bureaus and their missions, but these officials must do so with an eye turned toward their constituents. If bureaucratic entrepreneurs want to change the rules that govern them, they must influence voters or elected officials. The hierarchy of bureaus creates chains of officials who influence the rules of the bureau and the allocation of resources. While decisions within the hierarchy usually will be vital to the entrepreneur's success, the principles determining success or failure remain the same: the voters, through elected officials, hold ultimate authority over the rules and budgets that govern bureaus.

The ability of bureaucratic entrepreneurs to influence voters, while not essential to success, can be a powerful weapon. As economist Gary Becker has noted, "voter preferences are frequently not an *independent* force in political behavior. These 'preferences' can be manipulated and created through the information and misinformation provided by interested pressure groups, who raise their political influence partly by changing the revealed 'preferences' of enough voters and politicians."[20] The opportunities to influence preferences usually are greater in political than in commercial life. For one thing, because each vote has only a minor influence on the outcome, voters have less incentive to be informed than consumers.[21] For another, the truth or falsity of particular claims is more difficult to ascertain in political life than in private life.[22] This is one point at which public interest enters the theory of economic regulation. The various sides of a regulatory dispute will invoke the rhetoric of public interest to support their views. This rhetoric is a powerful weapon in the struggle to shape preferences, attract votes, and control regulation. However, because the claims of public interest rhetoric are so difficult to evaluate, they often are exaggerated and contradictory, much like the rhetoric in political campaigns. The correspondence between the effects of regulation and the claims used to justify it is often tenuous.

The competitive process within bureaucracy has other similarities to and differences from the competitive processes of markets, similarities and differences that will not concern us here.[23] We simply want to emphasize that entrepreneurs in a bureau will compete to increase their control over scarce government resources. Whether motivated by public purpose or private gain, these entrepreneurs will set in motion a competitive process that is essential to understanding bureaus in general, and regulatory agencies in particular.

From 1890 to 1910 competitive growth is particularly evident in the federal government, especially in the scientific bureaus of the Department of Agriculture. Historian A. Hunter Dupree has described the ideal type of scientific bureau of this era. It was, according to him, organized around a problem, had an ongoing appropriation that did not have specific requirements, and had a stable staff of scientists from various disciplines. It had strong relations with the appropriate congressional committees, and, for security, it was connected with an outside group that could represent the bureau's interests and lobby on its behalf. This kind of bureau would be well situated to win in the competitive struggle for resources.[24] There were several bureaus in the Department of Agriculture during these two decades that conform to Dupree's vision of the ideal bureau. The Bureau of Plant Industry, the Forest Service, and the Bureau of Chemistry all grew rapidly as the result of the entrepreneurial efforts of their respective chiefs, Beverly Galloway, Gifford Pinchot, and Harvey Washington Wiley. Galloway brought under his control various small units to form the Bureau of Plant Industry, which provided services to American farmers. Galloway's success lay in his ability to define specific services that his bureau could provide to farmers, who then became a powerful outside constituency for the bureau. As a result, Galloway became an outspoken advocate for the problem-centered approach to government bureaus.[25]

Gifford Pinchot of the Forest Service has long been recognized as the leader of the conservation movement. He successfully garnered the support needed to transfer the National Forest Service from the Department of Interior to the Department of Agriculture. By providing governmental services to logging companies, mining companies, cattle farmers, and other interested groups, he acquired their support for his plans to manage the national forests. He developed a publicity system that kept his actions in the public eye, and he cultivated the support of President Theodore Roosevelt. Pinchot was a highly successful bureaucratic entrepreneur until the Ballinger affair led to his dismissal by President Taft.[26]

After some groping about, Harvey Washington Wiley captured the pure food movement and used it as the basis for expanding his bureau. Like the other successful entrepreneurs in the Department of Agriculture, he identified a problem and marshaled a powerful outside constituency to help him build his bureau. His entrepreneurial bureau building is a crucial element in the history of food regulation.

Interpretations of the Pure Food Act
The historical interpretation of the Pure Food and Drugs Act of 1906 has followed that of regulation generally. The act is usually presented as public interest legislation. According to this view, the law was promoted by Wiley, the American Medical Association, public-spirited organizations such as women's groups, legitimate businesses, and a majority of Congress. The leaders of the pure food movement, and Wiley in particular, are portrayed as morally upright, solicitous of the health and welfare of the consumer, and opposed to shoddy products and fraudulent labelling. This interpretation was advanced by Wiley himself, by the influential journalist Mark Sullivan, and by historian Oscar Anderson. Those opposed to the act are portrayed as corrupted businessmen and politicians, including Nelson Aldrich and other Old Guard senators.[27]

A second interpretation of the food law is that special interests captured it for their own purposes. Wiley's *History of a Crime Against the Food Law* argued that unscrupulous businesses such as the whiskey rectifiers, Coca-Cola, and Monsanto corrupted the secretary of agriculture and other powerful officials, who then thwarted congressional intent.[28] The capture of the regulatory agency has become a theme of food regulation. The 1930s saw the appearance of the first of the guinea pig books, *100,000,000 Guinea Pigs,* by Arthur Kallett and F. J. Schlink. They argued that the food industry controlled regulation with little interference from the regulators. In the 1970s a Nader Group study sounded the same theme, which can also be heard in the 1992 conflict between the Food and Drug Administration and the Department of Agriculture over food labeling; the department is charged with being a tool of the meat and dairy lobby.[29]

An important step forward in the interpretation of the Pure Food and Drugs Act was taken by sociologist Donna Wood, who vividly recounts the conflicts between business interests during the passage of the act. These conflicts, she points out, were not between honest and dishonest producers, as the public interest theory suggested, but rather between legitimate business interests that were intent on using regulation to gain an advantage over their competitors. Wood calls this activity "the strategic use of public policy," which was essential to the passage and early enforcement of the act. The various historical interpretations of federal food regulation have been woven together nicely by James Harvey Young in *Pure Food,* his most comprehensive work on food and drug legislation.[30]

As vital as business interests were to the passage of food regulation, they are only part of the story. The other part is Wiley himself. When Wiley was appointed chief of the Bureau of Chemistry in 1883, he took over a small group of ten professional employees and a budget of under $50,000. When he resigned in 1912, the bureau employed over 600 and its budget exceeded $1,000,000. Throughout his tenure, Wiley was engaged in a struggle to increase the size and importance of his bureau. He was only modestly successful until he decided to pursue food regulation. His decision to devote his bureau to securing a food law was an entrepreneurial choice that was crucial to his success.[31]

Conclusion

Public interest, capture, business conflict, and bureaucratic entrepreneurship—the main elements of the economics of regulation—are evident in our historical interpretation of the Pure Food and Drugs Act. Throughout the study, theory has guided our interpretation of the facts; for example, in sifting through Wiley's voluminous correspondence, we were sensitive to the effects of Wiley's actions on the gains and losses of particular firms. This sensitivity to commercial interests resulted in a reading of the Wiley papers that is substantially different from that of Oscar Anderson and other advocates of the public interest interpretation.

To be guided by theory, however, does not mean to be ruled by it. When the flow of events did not correspond to the theory, we did not attempt to force it into a set of concepts that was ill suited to sensible interpretation. Instead, we revised the theory. There are two notable instances of this. First, the firms with lower costs did not prevail over the firms with higher costs in regulatory competition, as theory of regulation implies. This was especially evident in the whiskey industry, but it was also true for other products, such as catsup and baking powder. Thus we were forced to rethink the theory to see if it was possible for higher cost firms to win these battles. The second and more important instance in which the history did not fit into the existing theory was the role played by Wiley himself. As almost all historians of the pure food law have emphasized, Wiley was an independent force in the passage and early enforcement of the act. To account for the central role played by Wiley, we incorporated bureaucratic entrepreneurship into the economic theory of regulation. This incorporation enabled us to give the governmental side of regulation due prominence. Regulators exercise leadership, plan strategically, and compete with others for budgets and for influence over the regulatory process. Within the machinery of government they seek out and exploit opportunities for prestige, power, and wealth. Their actions are fully as important to regulatory outcomes as the profit-seeking actions of business firms. In our view, the passage and early enforcement of the 1906 Pure Food and Drugs Act is best understood as a competitive process in which business, political, and bureaucratic interests pursued their particular aims.

CHAPTER 2

The Way We Ate

The Pure Food and Drugs Act of 1906 reflected two broad trends of American life at the turn of the century: the move toward urban life and increasing federal regulation of the economy. The transformation of the United States from an agrarian to an industrial society changed the way in which people ate. Food became something to be purchased rather than something to be home-grown. Like so much else in the United States of the late 1800s, meat and potatoes increasingly fell into the market nexus of specialized production and exchange. The "gale of creative destruction," as Joseph Schumpeter called it, worked its way into the food factory, the dining room, the government bureau, and the popular press with the rise of specialists on health and nutrition. The combined effects of new technology, new food products, new competition, uncertain consumers, food experts, and government officials combined to produce the Pure Food and Drugs Act of 1906.[1]

New Technologies, New Foods, New Competition

As an increasing number of families moved from the farm to the city in the late 1800s, the food industry in the United States responded by developing new technologies and producing new goods. By 1900 mass distribution in the form of chain stores, which had grown up in the post–Civil War period, was well established. The Great Atlantic and Pacific Tea Company had stores from coast to coast by the turn of the century. Large firms that integrated mass production with distribution had begun to appear in the 1880s and 1890s. American Sugar Refining, Pillsbury, H. J. Heinz, Campbell Soup, Borden, Swift, Armour, and Coca-Cola were a few of the large, vertically integrated enterprises established by the time of the Pure Food and Drugs Act of 1906. These firms competed with smaller regional and local firms. Chain stores like the Great Atlantic and Pacific Tea Company challenged traditional, local grocery stores. H. J. Heinz bypassed wholesalers and jobbers entirely by distributing its own products.[2]

It was in this atmosphere of change that the call for federal food regulation occurred. Although most of the rhetoric of regulation addressed itself to issues of nutrition and health, most of the actual regulation addressed itself to competition. Like the regulation of railroads, trusts, banks, and utilities, the regulation of food was aimed at the economics of the industry.

Bread, a staple for many Americans at the turn of the century, was one of the earliest foods to move from home to market. Although baking a good loaf of bread was considered a necessary accomplishment by middle-class housekeepers, its preparation demanded a considerable amount of time and large amounts of fuel. Given this, it is not surprising that bread making moved from the home to the local bakery. In doing so, it reflected America's European heritage. In Europe, the color of the bread had indicated the social class of the consumer: the darker the bread, the lower the class. As a result, American consumers desired white bread, but until the latter half of the nineteenth century their bread was not very white. Soft wheat was stone ground and then sifted, which removed the bran but little else. Thus, the flour used in bread making was sprinkled with bits of brown. It was wholesome but regarded as inferior to pure white flour. In the late nineteenth century, the opening of new wheat lands in the West, where hard spring wheat could be grown, and the adoption of porcelain and chilled steel rollers by flour mills made the production of a totally white flour the American standard. Milling now separated the bran and the germ from the starchy white part of the wheat berry. Because the germ contained the oils that caused rapid spoilage, its removal markedly increased the storage life and produced the white flour that American consumers preferred. At the same time, the removal of the germ made the flour less nutritious.[3]

The market for canned foods also grew large at this time. The idea of canning food had originated in France. Searching for a way to feed his armies, Napoleon had offered a prize of 12,000 francs to anyone who could develop a way of preserving food. The winner of the prize was Nicholas Appert, who invented a way of vacuum packing food in hermetically sealed jars. The French attempted to keep his method a military secret but failed, and canning eventually became one of the most popular methods of preserving foods. When the Civil War began, the American canning industry was in its infancy. The war, however, created a vast demand for canned products, with the government frequently contracting for the entire output of a canning plant. While canned meats, fish, fruits, and vegetables were all used by the Union army, one of the more popular products with the troops was canned milk, which was also condensed. Its inventor was Gail Borden, an inveterate tinker and promoter.

Borden was a great believer in condensing things, including sermons and milk. According to legend, he had been shocked by the Donner Party disaster and believed that if the members of the party had had some way to carry condensed food, they would not have starved. He dropped his work on a sail-driven prairie wagon and began work on a meat biscuit. After several years he developed a product that was used on some Arctic expeditions. Apparently, however, it was not very palatable; it did not become a commercial success.[4]

From the meat biscuit, Borden turned his attention to milk. He had observed during a transatlantic voyage that the rigors of the trip frequently caused cows to stop giving milk, and he began to look for a way to process milk so it would keep for the duration of a voyage. Ignoring the advice of friends and experts to forget it, he finally discovered a way to condense milk using a vacuum pan. He patented the process and opened a plant near New York City. At the time the plant opened, the milk sold in New York markets was uneven in quality and often blamed for the spread of disease. In order to succeed, Borden had to overcome any suspicion that his milk was contaminated. He developed a strict set of sanitary rules for the farmers who supplied milk for his company and even sent inspectors around to ensure that his standards were met. In fact, he went out of his way to make sure his product was sanitary, and he said so in his advertisements.[5]

From the beginning, Borden's product was successful locally; the Civil War made it successful nationally. When the army bought all his existing supply, Borden opened additional plants and licensed the process to other companies. Returning home from the war, soldiers who were familiar with the product created a demand for it in all parts of the country. Borden's condensed milk became one of the first canned products to develop a national market. Crucial to its success was Borden's reputation for wholesomeness and purity.[6]

The canned fish, meat, vegetables, and fruits supplied to Union troops during the war also became familiar products. Originating with the Civil War, the market for canned foods grew throughout the rest of the nineteenth century and into the twentieth. With the development of steam retorts for cooking and automatic canning machines, industrial output took a quantum leap. Because of the high temperatures at which foods were canned, most canned products were sterile and largely free from contamination. Although preservatives usually were not used, many canners, particularly canners of fruits, did use large amounts of sugar as well as dyes, which made their products look fresh.[7]

Canned goods changed the American diet. They seldom spoiled and they were convenient to use. They made available year-round a variety of foods that previously had been eaten only in season. Because canned goods were quick to prepare and required little or no cooking, they saved time and fuel in the home. By the turn of the century, an entire meal could be served using only canned goods. Rusted cans began to litter the American country-side, evidence not only of the urban use of canned goods but of rural consumption as well. Because of their advantages and reputation, canned foods did not greatly concern food regulators. Nevertheless, many canners, particularly those with brand names, supported national food regulation. A national law that required purity would, they believed, benefit the image of their products.[8]

The late nineteenth century also saw the introduction of creamery butter and margarine. In 1869, in an article for the *American Woman's Home*, Catherine Beecher and her sister, Harriet Beecher Stowe, wrote that rancid butter was one of the worst problems with American food. Only one out of every twenty firkins they tried, the sisters said, was edible. The butter they tested was usually produced by women on the farm. Its quality varied widely because it depended upon the care the farm women took in its production. These women would exchange butter they made at home for cash or goods at their local grocery. The grocer would then pack all the butter purchased in a barrel and sell it to a merchant in the city. Apparently, the grocer made no effort to control quality and paid the same for good and bad butter. Thus, the woman who took care in preparing her butter was paid as much as the woman who did not. By the 1870s, this butter, which was called farm butter, was in competition with margarine in working-class markets.[9]

Margarine was invented in France in 1869, the same year the Beecher sisters complained about American butter. Its inventor was Hippolyte Mege-Mouries, a food chemist who hoped to win the prize Napoleon III offered for an inexpensive substitute for butter. While neither Napoleon III nor his army benefited from its invention, margarine was soon widely used in Europe. In 1873, the United States Dairy Company of New York acquired the Mege patent and began production. However, other companies, using different processes, had already begun to produce similar products. Would-be margarine makers applied for 180 different patents, of which thirty-four were granted, before the turn of the century. While the new product was welcomed by the working class, it was detested by dairy farmers, who were suffering from the economic woes of the post–Civil War era. Almost at once state governments began passing laws against margarine. By 1877, New York and Pennsylvania had outlawed it. Ultimately, despite the fact that it never posed a health problem, margarine had more laws passed against it than any other food product in American history.[10]

Creamery butter arrived at U.S. stores beginning in the late 1880s. Unlike farm butter, creamery butter was produced under controlled conditions. It was accordingly more expensive and therefore usually purchased by the middle and upper classes.

As the American food industry grew, competition between food companies also grew. Indeed, competition between national brands and local brands intensified throughout the Progressive Era. Local brands were produced by manufacturers who filled contracts for wholesalers and jobbers. The manufacturers affixed whatever label was required by their contracts. Sometimes they left it to the wholesaler to label the product. Because they usually produced for small regions that covered only a few states, these local distributors easily met state labeling requirements and other food laws. This gave them a competitive advantage over national brand manufacturers, who had to make special labels for each jurisdiction they covered. Local distributors relied on name recognition and retailer recommendations to promote their products, which were manufactured to suit local tastes and pocketbooks. Local grocers, who filled orders and offered advice, often recommended these products because profit margins were higher for them than they were for national brand products. As competition increased, national brands found it useful to accuse local brands of adulteration. If a firm could convince consumers that a competitor's product was unwholesome, it might very well increase sales. It was this strategy that erupted into the spectacular baking powder trade war.

The first American cookbook to call for chemical leavening was Amelia Simmons's *American Cookery*, which was published in 1796. Because it was simpler, quicker, and cheaper than using yeast or eggs, chemical leavening quickly became popular and was in common use by the latter half of the nineteenth century.[11] At first, the soda and acid were added to food separately, but it was difficult to get the measurements exact enough to produce the proper chemical reaction. A druggist in Indiana remedied the difficulty by offering premixed packages of cream of tartar, soda, and starch. By 1875, the baking powder business was on its way.[12]

Two companies, both named Royal, dominated the market. One firm was owned by William Ziegler, the other by the Hoagland family. When a lawsuit was unable to determine which company was entitled to the name, the companies merged, becoming the Royal Baking Powder Company. The firm soon faced competition from new companies that used tartaric acid, calcium acid phosphate, aluminum phosphate, and sodium aluminum sulfate as the acids in their preparations. These products were called alum powders, even though they did not actually contain alum. They were cheaper to make and frequently sold for one-fifth the price of Royal's cream of tartar powders.[13]

Royal dominated the cream of tartar industry but was facing over 500 competitors that made alum powders. Under competitive pressure, Royal fired the first shot in the trade war. The company began to sponsor advertisements that claimed the ingredients in alum powders were poisonous. It set up phony pure food organizations that released findings stating that the lives of women and children were threatened by alum powders. The company also hired women who went from door to door posing as pure food inspectors. Whenever they found an alum powder in a home, they would warn the user that it might endanger her family's health.[14]

Royal went even further and tried to have alum powders outlawed altogether. It was not averse to paying off politicians to accomplish this goal. State legislators in Missouri were caught taking bribes to support the outlawing of alum baking powders. At the same time, apparently diversifying its risks against its own questionable practices, Royal bought shares in companies, particularly in the South, that made alum baking powders.[15]

The makers of alum powders fought back in the courts and legislatures. They formed a trade group called the American Baking Powder Association. The group had its own scientists, who tried to allay the fears instilled by Royal by pointing out that there were no poisons in alum powders and that consumers did not actually eat the powders but rather the salts that remained after leavening. The association also claimed that cream of tartar powders left behind Rochelle salts, a known irritant and purgative. This claim was dropped, however, when it was discovered that alum salts were also an irritant. The baking powder wars continued through the passage of the Pure Food and Drugs Act, albeit with much less fury after 1904.[16]

A Revolution at the Table

Americans of the period were affected by the growing food industry and competition within it in different ways. Prior to the changes brought about by industrialization, Americans had eaten much, at least by the standards of the day, but they had not eaten particularly well. Their diet for most of the year had consisted mainly of cornbread and salt pork dipped in molasses (when molasses was available). Commentators on American food in the early nineteenth century praised its abundance but not its quality: at least one commentator described the American diet as a "monotonous round of badly cooked food."[17] Only occasionally was heard a kind word about American food. Arthur M. Schlesinger tells of a Captain Basil Hall who visited New York in 1827 and reported on the abundance and variety of the diet. According to Schlesinger, corn and pork were served in various guises, but fruits and vegetables were conspicuous by their absence. Food was usually fried and served quickly; breads and pastries were heavy. Critics charged that fast greasy food caused the frequent indigestion that plagued

Americans. Some claimed that a poorly balanced diet of ill-prepared food quickly eaten resulted in impaired physical fitness, a claim that has a familiar ring in our own time.[18]

Prejudice and myth kept many healthful foods from being eaten. There was a widespread belief, for example, that fresh fruits and vegetables caused cholera. Dyspepsia and other gastrointestinal complaints were common and may have been the result of overeating or contaminated food and water. Whatever the causes of distress, the result was the emergence of the American food reformer.[19]

Perhaps the most famous of the mid-nineteenth-century reformers was Sylvester Graham, architect of the Graham cracker. Graham toured the country, giving lectures and promoting his special diet. He even established Graham boardinghouses for his followers. While his views were criticized as extreme—his lectures sometimes drew agitated hecklers who caused near riots—Graham's followers believed in him wholeheartedly.

Graham advocated a strict vegetarian diet, the heart of which was bread made from unbolted flour. Bread was a staple of the working-class diet at this time, and bread made from bolted flour (flour from which the bran had been removed) was popular. While bread made from this flour lacked the nutrients of bran, Graham's dislike of bolted flour was not based on nutritional knowledge. Like other early reformers, he attached a moral and spiritual quality to diet.

> Could wives and mothers fully comprehend the importance of good bread, in relation to all the intellectual and moral interests of their husbands and children, and in relation to the domestic and social and civil welfare of man kind, and to their religious prosperity, both for time and eternity, they would estimate the art and duty of bread-making far, very far more highly than they now do.[20]

To Graham, the removal of the bran signified the descent from a natural to an artificial (industrialized) civilization. His lament, which had little do with nutrition but much to do with who made the food, would be repeated again and again by subsequent food reformers.[21]

The upper classes of the late nineteenth and early twentieth centuries were the least affected by what Harvey Levenstein has memorably called the "revolution at the table." Their cuisine was ruled by a French hegemony that did not take kindly to American ideas about diet. Yet even the upper classes experienced some changes in their eating habits. Elaborate hotel dining rooms opened to all who could afford them and were deemed acceptable places for women to dine. The women observed the innovations introduced at the hotels and tried them at home. Thus, foods that could be prepared quickly and cooking methods that saved time (efficiencies require by hotel dining rooms) traveled from the hotel kitchen to the home kitchen of the upper class.[22]

The leading chef of this rationalization of the hotel kitchen was Georges Auguste Escoffier whose influence dominated grand cuisine for decades. Escoffier advocated the simplification of cookery. He emphasized using the juices of ingredients to enhance natural flavors rather than concealing them under heavy sauces. Escoffier's cooking style was what the upper classes understood by the term *natural food*. As his ideas trickled down, more emphasis was place on the purity of each dish.[23]

Working-class immigrants ran little risk of falling under Escoffier's sway in particular or of the French influence in general. Social workers considered diet to be an indicator of Americanization and pressured immigrants to adopt American foods. Elizabeth Ewen describes "constant campaigns to promote the eating of American food in order to transform ethnic culture." Social workers, writes Ewen, would sometimes say of their clients, "Not yet Americanized, still eating Italian food."[24] Irving Howe's *World of Our Fathers* describes the first encounter of a Jewish immigrant with canned foods and bananas. The canned food was eaten but not the banana; it was too mysterious.[25]

Some new food items were quickly accepted. Working-class immigrant breakfasts soon included coffee. Even though it was usually mixed with chicory or cereals, coffee was considered an improvement in diet by many immigrants. There was also a substantial increase in sugar and meat consumption. The increase in meat seemed particularly welcomed by many who had eaten it only on special occasions in their homeland. Sweet rolls, doughnuts, ice cream, and cakes also found ready acceptance. Although there was some criticism of increased sugar consumption, it was widely believe to be a positive addition to the diet.[26]

Despite the pressures for Americanization, many immigrant women fought to maintain their family's traditional diet, but they usually found it was too difficult and too expensive. In time, they found substitutes for old products and accepted new ones.[27] Nevertheless, government food commissioners often grew impatient with their eating habits. R. O. Eaton, the deputy food commissioner for Connecticut, had difficulty enforcing the margarine laws among French Canadian immigrants working in the textile factories. In 1901 he commented:

The operatives in those mills are nearly all of them French-Canadians, French people. They come down there and they want to buy something

cheap. They are over the eastern border of Connecticut and there is a
sentiment there in favor of oleomargarine, and we have great difficulty
in enforcing the law. . . . we are trying to make everybody believe we are
doing them a favor by enforcing the oleomargarine law, and we are
trying to educate them.[28]

Eaton's comments reflect an attitude common among food officials, who
believed that part of their job was to Americanize immigrants. If immigrants
preferred oleomargarine to butter, it was just another indication that they
were not fully Americanized. Studies conducted by W. O. Atwater, an agricultural chemist who was regarded as the leading American expert on nutrition, had concluded that the American working-class diet was superior to its
European counterpart. Atwater had been educated at Yale and in Germany,
where he had learned the German method for determining the nutritive
requirements of man. On his return to the United States, he became a
professor at Wesleyan University and later a special agent for the Department of Agriculture. Using Atwater's standards for caloric intake and consumption of meat and dairy products, C. F. Langworth of the Department of
Agriculture claimed the American working-class diet at the turn of the
century included more food and a greater variety of food than the diets of
European workers.[29]

Despite eating a greater amount and variety of food, working-class
Americans were still poor; they spent between 40 and 50 percent of their
income on food. Consequently, they were highly sensitive to food prices. A
20 percent savings on food could mean a 100 percent increase in the cloth-
ing or heating budget. Given the large percentage of income that they spent
on food, workers often chose the cheaper cut of meat, the less expensive
bread, the lower priced drink. Even goods that were classified as adulterated
found a market if the price was low enough.[30]

It was middle-class women who most felt the impact of the changing
American food industry. The revolution at the table presented them with
new problems of what to serve and how to prepare it. At the same time,
these women were finding it harder to hire competent servants. By the late
nineteenth century, the servant labor force increasingly was made up of
eastern Europeans. From backgrounds of deprivation and poverty, these
persons were unacquainted with the type of housekeeping demanded by the
American middle class. Only in the South was this not a problem.[31]

The seriousness of the servant problem should not be underrated;
between the Civil War and World War I, discussions of this problem occu-
pied more space than any other topic in women's magazines. Up to this
point, the middle-class wife had done more supervising than preparing of

food. As the nineteenth century progressed, the dual problems of a lack of knowledgeable servants and the changing food industry resulted in what middle-class women's magazines called the "tyranny of the kitchen."[32] To the middle-class housewife of the late nineteenth century, science and technology in the form of processed food and cooking shortcuts seemed to offer the most likely solutions to this problem. However, these solutions have also been blamed for the decline in the quality of American cuisine. In her study of the rise and fall of domesticity in America, Glenna Matthews has found two stages in the changing food patterns of the middle class. The first stage was a period of improvement: a greater variety of foods became available to the middle class, and kitchen technologies improved. The second stage, which began in the latter half of the nineteenth century and extended into the twentieth century, was a period of decline. There was a loss of skill in the kitchen and a diminished quality of food that was brought about by industrialization, processing, and "scientific cooking."[33]

Complaints about the quality of food and nostalgia for the good old days seem to be an American tradition when it comes to food. When modern pies or breads or fruits do not live up to the standards of mom's apple pie, we seldom fault memory; rather, we believe that someone has debased the food. Americans, especially their journalists, often point to the food industry as the culprit. Mark Sullivan, an active early supporter of pure food laws, is an example. Sullivan's *Our Times,* published in 1927, paints a loving picture of food on the farm, before the changes wrought by industrialization. He sadly notes that the women of 1927 preferred to spend autumn afternoons "playing bridge, [rather] than picking apples and pears from low-hanging orchard boughs, carrying them in their aprons to the house, peeling them, stewing them; and then enjoying the sense of accomplishment on pouring the completed work into the jar; setting jars and bottles on the window-ledge where their colors [glow] against the autumn sun, distilled essences of the orchard."[34]

With pastoral images of childhood playing in his mind, Sullivan naturally believed that the modern ways of the 1920s were corrupting American food. The coldness of a metal can could not compare to the warmth of home and hearth. But however attractive we find Sullivan's poetic nostalgia, we should not forget what he omitted from his reminiscences. The warmth of the hearth that Sullivan described was usually absent from the urban tenement, the sod house of the prairie, the shack of the sharecropper, and the mining camp of the western mountains. For the American working family, life may not have been nasty, brutish, and short, but it was filled with arduous labor, of which home canning was a part. Despite Sullivan's touching description, home canning was long, tedious, messy, and sometimes dangerous; bottles could explode and broken seals could result in botulism. When given the opportunity, women quickly abandoned home canning for goods produced in the factory.

Food manufacturers, national and local, found themselves responding not only to the move toward urban life, but also to the changes in buyer attitudes. Food reformers, who were regarded as experts on health and purity, often made contradictory claims, as did the food companies themselves. Nearly all parties, government and private, were tied to commercial interests. Rarely did the consumer have access to unbiased judgment. Thus, the turn of the century was a period of widespread contentiousness over proper diet. For nutritional experts, food faddists, and scientists, all of whom supplied opinions about food and its effects on health, it was an age of opportunity, or as Harvey Levenstein has appropriately called it, a golden age of food fads.[35]

Scientific Cooking

Home economists were new professionals in the late nineteenth and early twentieth century. They stressed nutrition over taste and proclaimed that Americans should eat for health, not for pleasure. As one leader of the movement said, food was given to people "primarily for the strengthening of their bodies, not for the gratification of their palates." To enjoy food too much was to favor the sensual over the scientific, which would lead away from the higher forms of life. Scientific cooking, these new professionals claimed, would guarantee nutritious meals.[36]

Despite the home economists' claims to scientific authority, the state of knowledge about nutrition at the turn of the century provided little basis for establishing dietary standards—not that this deterred the experts from proclaiming standards and doing their best to enjoin them on the populace. W. O. Atwater, for example, recommended a daily intake of 3,500 calories. His tables of the nitrogen, fats, and carbohydrates available in various foods became the building blocks of the scientific diet, but his standard of 125 grams of protein, 125 grams of fat, and 450 grams of carbohydrates for a man doing moderate work was double what today's experts recommend. He and his associates believed that vegetables and fruits were largely a waste of money because they contained neither calories nor nitrogen, both of which they considered the essentials of nutrition. Writing for the 1907 *Yearbook* of the Department of Agriculture, C. F. Langworthy noted that the use of celery and oranges in the working-class diet "undoubtedly added to the attractiveness of the diet . . . [but] such foods could be omitted from diet without materially changing its nutritive value."[37]

The increasing number of cookbooks, cooking schools, and scientific cooks reflect the influence of these new professionals who sought to create an efficient and rational American diet, not always with fortunate results. One historian noted that scientific cooking led to the alienation of "trust in one's own taste buds." As Glenna Matthews has pointed out, "personal preferences are inherently anarchic. If the goal was to set standards, then people had to be taught not to trust their own tastes. Further, if people were to follow the advice of experts, they had to be taught to despise tradition and the advice of older women." Thus, anything that did not conform to scientific standards was criticized. Ethnic food was condemned. Recipes no longer called for a pinch of this or a handful of that; measurements became standardized. White sauces, which reduce distinctive flavors, became popular. Forty-five minutes to an hour was the recommended cooking time for all vegetables.[38]

Because the rapid rise of national food companies corresponded with the rise of the home economics movement and cooking schools, the schools and expert scientific cooks are often viewed as agents of the food industry. This is not entirely accurate. It is true that these cooks frequently endorsed brand-name products in advertisements, recipes, and cookbooks. They were also active in the food fairs that toured the country in the 1890s. These fairs glorified new commercial foods and promoted brand-name products. Booths offered cooking demonstrations and samples of dishes made with the products. Locally recognized cooks gave lectures on the wonders of modern food and advised housewives to use brand names to avoid adulteration. Reputation, they said, was protection against fraudulent and adulterated products. Occasionally, the new scientific cooks even attached their names to a product, as Miss Lincoln of the Boston Cooking School did. Still, most of them viewed these actions as a part of educating the housewife. They claimed to endorse only the best and purest products. In the eyes of the scientific cooking movement, *pure* meant uniform in taste and texture. An adulterated product was one in which a less expensive ingredient was substituted for a more expensive ingredient, which they viewed as cheating the customer. They believed that most food was healthful and most food producers were honest. The occasional unscrupulous business seeking quick profits through adulteration, they said, would be put out of business with a little education, which included their endorsement of certain products. The dietary recommendations of these cooks were much the same whether or not they worked for a food company.[39]

The Pure Food Movement

While scientific cooking attempted to cope with the rapidly changing food industry by standardizing diet, the pure food movement offered a different solution. Regulation by federal officials, its advocates argued, would simplify the myriad requirements of state regulations and provide trustworthy information about the purity of food. The term *pure* remained vague, of course. Food manufacturers called almost every product made in the late nineteenth century *pure*. Nor was there any definite meaning of *impure* or *adulterated*. For example, because canned goods were quickly consumed after opening, few canners used chemical preservatives. Catsup, however, which was used over an extended period of time, required preservatives. As late as 1905, the H. J. Heinz company, which maintained its own research staff and which would later pride itself on making catsup without additives, used a preservative in its catsup. Was the product pure if a preservative was necessary to prevent spoilage? Honey mixed with sugar was considered adulterated, but there was no well-defined chemical formula for honey that made it possible to tell if a particular honey had too much sugar in it. Honey was not consistent from hive to hive; moreover, honey contained many of the same ingredients as commercial glucose (corn syrup). A detailed chemical analysis was necessary to determine if glucose had been added to honey, and even then a clear judgment could not always be made.[40]

Amid the growing number of food experts and the ambiguity about nutrition, health, and purity, Harvey Washington Wiley stepped forward as a champion of pure food. Chief of the division on chemistry in the Department of Agriculture, Wiley opposed the studies of Atwater and criticized the department's allocation of funds to Atwater. The purity of food, Wiley argued, could be determined by chemical analysis. However, chemical analysis implied nothing about nutritional quality or palatability. Wiley and the pure food movement did not overtly claim that adulterated products provided inferior nutrition. Instead, like the scientific cooks of the period, they argued that the consumer was cheated when a cheap ingredient was added to a product.

Suppliers of food for the working class looked for ways to keep their costs and prices low, and adulterants were one way they accomplished this. Even so, adulteration does not appear to have been widespread. Studies have shown that only 5 to 15 percent of the food was adulterated. Furthermore, most of these products were not adulterated with substances that were harmful to health or even to nutritional value.[41] The substitution of glucose for sucrose, for example, was considered an adulteration, but there is little if any nutritional difference between the two kinds of sugar. At the time, the primary difference between products with sucrose and products with glucose was the difference in price. Sucrose was expensive compared to glucose because U.S. sugar producers were protected by a tariff. Similarly, mixing chicory with coffee adulterated the product and lowered its price, but did not significantly affect the nutritional value of coffee. Products like alum baking powders and rectified whiskey found ready markets among the working class simply because the alternatives were more expensive. The nutritional differences between straight and rectified whiskey or between tartar and alum baking powders were insignificant, yet these were the products that were classified as adulterated or fraudulent by food regulators.

A striking fact about the Pure Food and Drugs Act of 1906, a fact with which every interpretation of the act must come to terms, is that urban workers and families did not agitate for its passage or enforcement. No general outbreak of disease or death from food in the cities was recorded. No epidemic of malnutrition swept through the urban populace. No public outcry over food was ever heard from the working classes. The movement for a national food law came from food commissioners, agricultural chemists, manufacturers of expensive foods, representatives from rural agricultural states, and a small number of middle-class women. The rhetoric of regulation was "pure food for the mass consumer," but its impetus came from the professional classes.

The controversy over butter and margarine exemplifies this as well as other common features of the passage of food regulation. Margarine was popular in the lower income areas of urban America. Many new immigrants were not from the dairy-producing regions of northern Europe. They were not familiar with butter and frequently preferred olive oil. For them, butter was not, as some Americans believed, a sign of higher civilization. They welcomed margarine as a low cost ingredient for cooking or for eating with bread. The call for its ban came from rural areas, which produced butter and which wielded considerable political power.

The testimony of margarine's defenders and opponents contained wild exaggeration. Opponents claimed it was made from unhealthy, diseased, and dead animals—dogs, rats, and anything else an unscrupulous margarine manufacturer could find. They asserted that it caused cholera, tuberculosis, and trichinosis. They even claimed that margarine was so full of living worms, germs, and spores that you could feel them move a knife blade. Defenders claimed their product was purer than butter. Some even claimed that it *was* butter, and some denied ever having sold it as butter. They accused the nation of worshiping a false idol, the dairy cow. They invoked the holy name of science, claiming that margarine was a scientific breakthrough and that butter was merely a victim of progress.[42]

In 1886, Congress passed a law placing a tax of two cents per pound on margarine and requiring license fees from manufacturers, wholesalers, and retailers of the product. Although burdensome, the legislation did give margarine official recognition as a food product.[43] The following year, Wiley's chemistry division published part 1 of Bulletin 13, which dealt with dairy products. Citing some of the various statements made in Congress the year before, the bulletin acknowledged there was a wide difference of opinion on the wholesomeness of margarine. It concluded that margarine, if carefully made from bullock or swine, did not injure health but that carelessly made margarine could affect health. While avoiding excessive claims, the report was nevertheless biased in favor of butter.

> While it is true that chemical analysis and certain digestive experiments have not hither to shown that pure butter possesses any marked superiority over butter surrogates as a food, yet it must not be forgotten that butter has a much more complex composition than lard or tallow or cotton seed oil, that it is a natural food, and doubtless possesses many digestive advantages which science has not yet been able to demonstrate.[44]

This passage demonstrates two kinds of arguments that Wiley would make in the years ahead. First, even if science could not demonstrate the superiority of a product at present, it might do so in the future. While this argument is indisputable, it is equally true that science might demonstrate the inferiority of a product in the future. Certainly, in the case of butter, science has demonstrated that butter contains important vitamins, but it also contains saturated fats that can damage health. Second, Wiley's argument speaks of "natural" products, but there is no firm basis for the use of this term. By calling butter a "natural food," Wiley implied that lard or margarine was not. Butter, however, does not occur naturally; it does not exist without a manufacturing process devised and carried out by human intervention. By the 1880s, this intervention was very sophisticated. The creameries that produced the highest quality butter used modern machinery and technology; they used preservatives, and they dyed butter to achieve the golden color that consumers associated with the product. Wiley used the term *natural* not as a scientific term, but as an emotional term that commended products of which he approved. Based on samples obtained by Wiley's chemistry division, the most common adulterations occurred in butter, not margarine. Not only were dyes added to the product, manufacturers would sometimes blend cottonseed or other oils into it.[45]

Opponents of margarine continued to agitate for strict regulation of the product. In 1902, they succeeded in getting a law passed that placed a tax of ten cents per pound on artificially colored margarine. Dairymen argued that white margarine could not pass itself off as butter and thus the law would prevent fraud. This was not the real issue. The advantage of margarine lay in its lower price. The Internal Revenue Service recommended placing a tax stamp on all individual containers of margarine that would show consumers that they were buying margarine, which was taxed, rather than butter, which was not. The dairy interests opposed the use of a stamp. They did not want to help the consumer differentiate between butter and margarine; they wanted, in the words of Henry C. Adams, pure food commissioner of Wisconsin, "to pass this [tax] law and drive the oleomargarine manufacturers out of business."[46]

Conclusion

The wave of creative destruction that swept through the U.S. economy after the Civil War had its effects on American food. On the production side, large national chains rose to compete against local distributors and retailers. New products, such as oleomargarine and alum baking powder, were introduced to compete against traditional products. Old products made by new technologies—such as bread and canned milk—brought foods increasingly into the market nexus. On the consumer side, the change from growing food on the farm to buying it in the market created doubts about purity and healthfulness. These doubts were the origin of demand for food experts. Reformers such as Sylvester Graham and the scientific cooks offered advice and opinions about what to eat and how to prepare it. Government experts, such as W. O. Atwater and Harvey Wiley, conducted their own studies on health, nutrition, and purity. They also sought federal funds with which they could carry out this research and offer the public advice about food and diet.

The regulation of margarine illustrates a pattern that recurred, albeit with lively variation, throughout the passage and enforcement of the Pure Food and Drugs Act of 1906. Advances in technology created a new good (margarine) that could be substituted for an older, more established one (butter). The new good cost less to produce, sold for a lower price, and attracted many buyers from lower-income families. As the new good gained acceptance, the manufacturers of the established good responded by denigrating the new good and by attempting to secure governmental regulation that would favor the established industry. Meanwhile, the emerging profession of food experts, in both the public and private spheres, entered the debate with pronouncements on the nutritional value or purity of the contesting products. These experts attempted to influence the buyers and sellers of the competing products, as well as the legislation that would regulate the production and especially the marketing of the goods. Among these experts, Harvey Wiley used his division within the Department of Chemistry to conduct chemical analyses of the products. His analyses were competent but not decisive regarding health, nutrition, or economic value. Wiley, however, did not restrict his comments to chemistry. He made other pronouncements regarding the desirability of the contending goods, and his pronouncements favored one of the competing products over the other. Despite the controversies between different segments of the industry and the contentiousness of the experts, no substantial issues of health or purity were at stake. Butter and margarine were two different goods, each with pluses and minuses regarding nutrition, health, and purity. The real issues at stake in regulation were market share, corporate profit, and bureaucratic growth. These issues, however, were hid behind a cloak of rhetoric about the public interest. This is a theme that is played repeatedly in the passage and early enforcement of national food regulation.

Competition and Entrepreneurship in Bureaucracy: Harvey Wiley's Bureau of Chemistry, 1883–1903

The Division of Chemistry was one of the original divisions in the Department of Agriculture; it differed from other bureaus that emerged during the 1890s in both its background and its purpose. It had the department's first scientific laboratory that provided chemical analysis for the entire department as well as for other government agencies. If it had any particular assignment at the time Wiley became its leader, it was to aid in the development of an indigenous sugar industry. Its narrow concentration on an industry that could only exist behind a protective tariff made the division vulnerable to changing political attitudes and administrations.

The Department of Agriculture had begun its quest to establish a sugar industry in the United States as early as the Civil War. Given time and development, politicians and sugar producers believed the country could become self-sufficient in sugar production. Under the leadership of William G. LeDuc, the commissioner of the Department of Agriculture, the Division of Chemistry began research into sugar beets and sorghum production in the 1870s, but efforts to promote the sugar beet had little success. LeDuc rather bitterly claimed this was because U.S. farmers were not willing to grow crops that required them to work on their hands and knees when they could sit in comfort on their double sulky cultivators. In any case, LeDuc in 1878 switched his attention to sorghum in 1878. The crop, a sweet grass originally cultivated in the Middle East, had been introduced in the United States before the Civil War. It was resistant to drought and would grow anywhere corn would grow. Its drawback for sugar manufacturing was the difficulty of crystallizing the sugar. For twenty years following the Civil War, efforts to find economical ways to make sugar from sorghum and to increase the efficiency of cane sugar manufacturing would dominate the activities of the Division of Chemistry.[1]

LeDuc's enthusiasm for sorghum was encouraged by Peter Collier, who was head of the Division of Chemistry from 1877 to 1883. A Yale-trained chemist, Collier vocally promoted the production of sugar from sorghum. He claimed that sorghum would soon supply all the nation's sugar needs and perhaps even become an export crop. When George Loring replaced LeDuc as the commissioner of the Department of Agriculture in 1882, Collier ran into trouble. Loring thought Collier's claims were excessive and in 1883 replaced him with Harvey Washington Wiley.[2]

Wiley, who was a chemist at Purdue University at the time of his appointment, had already achieved some national recognition for his work on sugar. Like others of the period, he believed that sugar consumption marked the degree to which a country was civilized. Thus, he thought it was an appropriate part of all American diets, particularly the diets of children. "Childhood without candy," he said, "would be Heaven without harps." He believed the United States should be self-sufficient in sugar but did not share Collier's enthusiasm for sorghum; Wiley advocated a broader base of production that included cane and beets as well. He also favored a tariff to protect the U.S. farmer from the cheap sugar produced in tropical areas. According to Wiley, tropical farmers could lie on the beaches and eat coconuts and bananas and still survive if their sugar crops failed, but the American farmer would freeze and starve if his crop failed. A tariff could serve as a kind of equalizer.[3]

To Loring, who shared many of these views, Wiley seemed an ideal replacement for Collier. Loring hoped Wiley's appointment would diminish the opposition of the sorghum advocates who supported Collier, but his hope was short-lived. Farm journals used Collier's dismissal as a reason to attack Loring, whom they opposed anyway. Meanwhile, Collier organized a campaign against Loring and Wiley. Attacking Wiley's professional competence, Collier started a feud that lasted for ten years and kept Wiley from becoming securely ensconced as chief of the chemistry division. Between the Collier feud and the uncertainty created by changing political administrations, Wiley's position as chief of the chemistry division required continuous political vigilance.[4]

Government help in developing the sugar industry involved more than just scientific research; it involved a political astuteness as well. Wiley honed his skills at both. Upon taking office, he cultivated the political support of the Louisiana Sugar Producers Association. He involved the Louisiana sugar producers in decision making and used his appointive powers for jobs in his division to build alliances. He also changed the direction of the division's research. The sugar beet industry had developed successfully in Europe, and Wiley turned there to learn new methods of manufacturing sugar from beets. He also conducted a series of experiments to remove sugar from both

sorghum and sugarcane by osmosis. The experiments, which were conducted in Kansas and Louisiana, also tried various methods for more economically refining the syrup. Wiley employed a number of chemists to assist
him in his experiments. Among them was M. A. Scovell, who had failed at a
sugar-making venture and was looking for work. Scovell, who would later
play an important role in Wiley's campaign for a national pure food law,
proved to be a valuable employee, and Wiley helped him to become the
director of the Kentucky Agricultural Experiment Station.[5]

Wiley relied heavily on the Louisiana sugar producers to fend off the
attacks of Peter Collier and to survive the change in administration that
occurred when the Democrats took over in 1885. The Republican Wiley
managed to keep his position by helping Norman Jay Colman in his quest to
become commissioner of agriculture. Colman wrote to Wiley, asking him if
he could help in getting the support of the sugar producers. Wiley evidently
did so and left Colman in his debt. The debt was paid when Colman backed
Wiley after J. Floyd King, a congressman from northern Louisiana, launched
a full-scale assault on Wiley's professional abilities and his honesty. King was
particularly irritated by Wiley's trips to Europe and his attempts to transfer
European technology to American sugar production. Although an anti-
European bias was common in the United States at the time, King's criticisms of Wiley, which could be read in the press and heard from the floor of
Congress, went beyond a general bias and frequently became personal.[6]

King's attacks, many of which were unfounded, were less serious than
the criticisms of W. P. Kirchoff, a sugar chemist who observed the experiments that Wiley conducted at Fort Scott, Kansas, in 1886 for the Louisiana
Sugar Producers Association. Kirchoff was one of three observers sent by the
association to witness the experiments. While the other two observers concurred with Wiley's conclusions, Kirchoff did not. His report, which was at
first suppressed, disputed the accuracy of Wiley's analysis and his yield
calculations. The criticisms may have been well founded; Wiley responded
with a personal attack on Kirchoff and his professional standing in the
American community but did not address his substantive criticisms.[7]

Despite the criticisms of King and Kirchoff, Wiley remained chief of the
chemistry division, and, in the fall and winter of 1887, he discovered a
diffusion process that increased the amount of sugar extracted from cane.
Ultimately the discovery was not commercially significant; the new process
required large amounts of water that had to be evaporated after diffusion,
and the quantity of fuel necessary for evaporation made the process too
costly for commercial use. Wiley eventually abandoned it, but in the short
run he was able to claim victory. He took this moment of success to withdraw his division from further experimentation in large-scale manufacturing

processes, saying, "For my part I do not pretend to be a mechanical engineer and I do not see how I can do any further good in this matter. I propose hereafter to stick strictly to chemistry."[8]

Although Wiley's early political and professional activities revolved around sugar, he did not give his bureau completely over to the sugar industry. Wiley's determination to build his division around the discipline of chemistry was, as we will later see, a political misjudgment that hindered its growth for many years. Nevertheless, the plan was reasonable from an organizational point of view. Wiley had come to Washington from academia, and he looked upon his bureau much as he would an academic department. He saw the Division of Chemistry as a group of professionals with the expertise to conduct all chemical analysis within the Department of Agriculture. He worked to enhance the professional status of chemists, especially agricultural chemists, and repeatedly stressed the need for competent analysis within the department.

In the last decades of the nineteenth century, chemistry was beginning to develop specialties. Although the full impact of specialization was not felt until after the turn of the century, the reasons for specialization can be seen in Wiley's attempts at sugar production. It is one thing to be an analytical chemist working in a laboratory; it is another to build a factory that uses chemical processes. Within private industry at this time, these differences produced two types of chemists—analytical chemists, who worked in laboratories, and production chemists, who designed and built machinery for chemical processes. Production chemists followed the German or the American model. In the German model, chemists worked with engineers and other professionals to build the processing equipment. In the American model, chemists also became engineers, which led to chemical engineering as a discipline. In the American model, analytical chemists were channeled into routine jobs in quality control. Wiley's involvement in experiments with large-scale sugar production required that he either cooperate with a knowledgeable engineer or become one himself. He did neither; instead, he attempted his experiments without an adequate knowledge of engineering. The result was a series of delays, mistakes, and wasted resources. Had he devoted the whole of his department's resources to aiding sugar production, which meant that his bureau would have evolved toward chemical engineering, Wiley might have succeeded with his experiments, developed a constituency, and expanded his bureau.[9]

In the American model, as the work became more standardized and the analyses more routine, less and less actual chemical knowledge was necessary, and the status of analytical chemists declined. The decline was reflected in the wages paid by industry. In 1905 a starting analytical chemist in industry was paid approximately $700 a year, while a skilled artisan might earn $1,200 a year.[10]

In 1884, the Association of Official Agricultural Chemists was founded to advance the professional standing of those analytical chemists working in agriculture. As its first official task, the association undertook to standardize methods for analyzing and classifying fertilizer. Although it succeeded in formulating standards acceptable to the fertilizer industry, it also set in place routine procedures that lowered the skill required to perform analysis. Less skill meant diminished status, even in the eyes of the agricultural chemists themselves.[11]

Wiley was a leading figure in the Agricultural Chemists' Association. He served as its president in 1886–87 and remained the permanent secretary until he left government service in 1912. Although the organization in its original charter was dedicated to establishing uniform fertilizer standards, the association almost immediately expanded its activities to other agricultural products. The Department of Agriculture allowed the association to use its facilities, and the department published the proceedings of the association's annual meetings. As early as 1885 the association expressed interest in chemically analyzing adulterated foods. Commissioner of Agriculture Colman encouraged this interest.[12]

In 1886 W. O. Atwater, a member of the association, suggested they examine the chemistry of human nutrition. He received little response to his suggestion, perhaps because chemists lacked the knowledge and skills to understand nutrition. Although for several years the organization had studied animal feed, the results were not impressive. In an address to the organization, Steven M. Babcock pointed out that, despite their studies, analytical chemists were unable to tell the difference between what an animal ate and what it excreted; chemical analysis showed the same constituent elements.[13]

Analytical chemists, however, could identify many food adulterants. Wiley had been interested in the adulteration of foods when he arrived in Washington in 1883, but the demands of the sugar research kept him from devoting much time to foods. When Commissioner Colman took charge of the department, he encouraged the Chemistry Division to step up the investigation of food adulterations. Colman was concerned about the adverse economic impact that adulteration could have on producers. Wiley welcomed Colman's interest, and after 1886, when the sugar research diminished, Wiley increased his study of food impurities.

In 1887, the first parts of *Bulletin 13*, a detailed study of food adulterations conducted by the Division of Chemistry, were published by the Department of Agriculture. The final part of this study was not published until 1907, a year after the Pure Food and Drugs Act was passed. The first three parts of

Bulletin 13 were on dairy products, spices and condiments, and fermented alcoholic beverages. These were followed in 1889 with parts on lard and its adulterations and on baking powders. In 1889 Congress appropriated $5,000 for further studies of the "adulteration of food, drugs, and liquors."[14]

The association gained a reputation for respectable research into adulteration and used its reputation to endorse the need for pure food legislation. The standards it set for the fertilizer industry served as a model for regulating the food industry.[15] As Alan I. Marcus has written of the association, "basing their claim for distinctiveness on the possession of a technical competence—a dubious contention at best—chemists created for themselves a governmental connection, labored to acquire that technical competence, and finally traded on it to redefine and expand their social role."[16] But in 1887, cashing in on their technical competence was nearly twenty years away. Meanwhile, Wiley was trying to establish his bureau as the sole supplier of chemical analysis to the Department of Agriculture. For fifteen years he would continue his attempts, with little success.

Swimming against the Democratic Tide, 1893–97

In 1889, Colman stepped down as secretary of agriculture. His replacement was Jeremiah Rusk. Although Rusk supported Wiley's work on food adulteration, Wiley did not have the close personal association with "Uncle Jerry" that he had had with Colman. If Wiley missed the personal association under Rusk, he must have felt bereft with the election of Grover Cleveland in 1892 and the appointment of Julius Sterling Morton as secretary of agriculture. Morton believed in limited government, with the emphasis on limited. He disliked government paternalism, thought that most government activity bestowed special favors on particular groups, and believed that most government officials were corrupt. The years under Morton were rough ones for the Department of Agriculture. Not satisfied with his efforts to limit the growth of the department, Morton recommended abolishing it at the end of his term.[17]

The subtle changes in the organization of the Department of Agriculture were even harder on Wiley's efforts to build his division than were the changes in the political environment. The history of the Bureau of Animal Industry exemplifies these organizational changes. Created by Congress in 1884 to check the spread of animal diseases, the bureau brought together experts from a variety of specialized backgrounds, including chemistry. With the power to study a particular and visible problem and to take appropriate regulatory action, this kind of organization brought with it a built-in political constituency. As a consequence, unlike the chemistry division, the Bureau of Animal Industry grew rapidly in the 1880s and 1890s. By the turn of the century, it was the largest bureau in the Department of Agriculture.[18]

Every division and bureau seemed to compete with Wiley's. In 1894, the Division of Soils was created under the supervision of Milton Whitney. Whitney's division was supposed to study the physical characteristics of soil. Wiley's division, however, had begun analyzing the chemistry of soils in 1887. It was not long before an all-out battle for control over the study of soils erupted. Wiley fought hard to retain control of the chemical analysis of soils in his division but eventually lost. He waged an equally futile battle for funds appropriated by Congress in 1895 for the study of nutrition. Instead of placing this work in Wiley's division, which by this time had a long record of studying food adulteration, Secretary Morton gave it to the Office of Experiment Stations. These stations, one in each state, had been created in 1887 by the Hatch Act to aid agricultural research and production.[19]

Wiley attributed his troubles to political differences with Secretary Morton and his assistant secretary in charge of scientific investigation, Charles W. Dabney. Dabney had been the director of the North Carolina Agricultural Experiment Station before becoming president of the University of Tennessee. He was one of the founders of the Association of Official Agricultural Chemists and had known Wiley for years. Wiley initially thought that his association with Dabney would be beneficial, but he was soon disillusioned. In the summer of 1895, he wrote to his former student, employee, and friend G. L. Spencer that he expected to be dismissed any day. He accused Dabney of supporting Morton's attempts to destroy the department and said that Dabney was only interested in increasing his own power. Dabney, Wiley claimed, favored his friends—Galloway, Whitney, and Scribner. In truth, Dabney was interested in reorganizing the scientific sections around specific problems. Because the division of chemistry had no specific problem to study, such a reorganization was bound to diminish it.[20]

Swimming against the Republican Tide, 1897–1903

Wiley was delighted when the Republicans under William McKinley came back into power in 1896. He wrote to his friends that he felt a great burden had been lifted from the country. He also felt sure that a Republican administration would bring back the protective tariff on sugar, which would mean additional appropriations for investigations of sugar. Of course, he still had to survive the final days of Morton and worried that the appropriation for the division of chemistry would be cut even more than it had been. He contacted Senator William B. Allison of Iowa to get appropriations restored to his budget and took the opportunity to tell Allison the damage that had been done to his division.[21]

McKinley appointed James Wilson of Iowa as secretary of agriculture. Wilson had been born in Ayrshire, Scotland, in 1835. In 1851, he and his parents had emigrated to the United States, settling in Iowa in 1855. He was a successful farmer and had served in Congress from 1873 to 1877 then again from 1883 to 1885. From 1891 to 1897, he was professor of agriculture and director of the Iowa Agricultural Experiment Station in Ames. Wilson would serve as secretary of agriculture for sixteen years, during which the department would become a major scientific and regulatory agency.[22]

Because Wiley thought his division's decline was due to partisan politics, he perceived the change in administrations as an opportunity to regain control over all chemical investigations and perhaps even take over the direction of all scientific investigations conducted by the department. Through his political contacts, he passed word along to Wilson that he, Wiley, was the one good Republican among the heads of the scientific sections in the department. He claimed that ten of the thirteen heads had been appointed by the outgoing administration and that he alone was a strong protectionist. Only "the utter uprooting of the last vestige of that hateful period," Wiley wrote to his contacts, could make up for the deprivations his division had suffered under Morton and Dabney.[23] At the same time, in a confidential letter to Dabney, Wiley attacked the work on food and nutrition that W. O. Atwater was doing for the Office of Experiment Stations. The recently published *Bulletin #34*, which dealt with carbohydrates in wheat, was full of "errors of the most dangerous character and statements which are calculated to bring the scientific work of this department into disrepute and ridicule," according to Wiley. He went on to tell Dabney that, by law and custom, this type of work should be supervised by the Division of Chemistry. He did not, he said, understand why it was ever given to the Office of Experiment Stations, whose director did not even pretend to be a chemist. He ended with the comment, "The fact that it is possible for such crude and misleading statements to be published by and with the authority of the Department of Agriculture, is one of the most striking arguments which has come to my attention for the necessity of a directorship of the Scientific Division."[24]

Wiley followed this letter with one to Congressman Long in which he denigrated the chemical analyses done in the soils division and said that *Bulletin #34* would bring disrepute to the department. To make sure that the public would take notice, Wiley sent a copy of the *Bulletin* marked with his own criticisms to his friend G. L. Spencer to use in a review for *Popular Science*. Stepping up his campaign, Wiley sent a long letter directly to Wilson shortly after they met. In it, he detailed his complaints and asked that all chemical work be supervised by his division.[25]

On his arrival, however, Wilson had toured the department and had been impressed with the competency of most of the bureau or division chiefs, particularly Willis Moore of the Weather Bureau, Daniel Salmon of Animal Industry, and Wiley's previous bêtes noires, Whitney and Galloway. Wilson was evidently not impressed by Wiley. Wiley's complaints over the quality of chemical research and his bid to control it got him off on the wrong foot with the new secretary. To make matters worse for Wiley, Wilson, who wanted time to become familiar with his job, decided to keep Charles Dabney as a special agent in charge of scientific and statistical investigations. With its salary of $4,500 per year (the administration's highest salary not requiring Senate approval) the job was a plum. Republicans were angered by the appointment, and Wiley contributed to the ensuing uproar. He wrote numerous letters complaining about the situation. He even resorted to waving the bloody shirt, denouncing Dabney as an "unreconstructed Johnny" who promoted only his friends and had Wilson completely under his influence. He went so far as to lash out at Wilson, complaining that the secretary should be called the minister of foreign affairs because of all the foreign-born persons who worked in the department.[26]

Wilson soon took over supervision of the department's scientific activities and dismissed Dabney, as he had planned. These actions, however, did not benefit Wiley. Wilson then appointed C. F. Saylor, a fellow Iowan, as sugar beet commissioner. Saylor's assignment was to foster the sugar beet industry. He was directed to gather the necessary information on producing sugar from beets, make the information available to any interested party, and prepare for an annual sugar beet report. Wiley was furious. He had been the dominant figure in sugar investigations since his arrival at the department in 1883. He wrote angrily to G. L. Spencer, "The beet sugar work of the department has been taken away from me and given to Dabney and a special agent who has just been appointed and who never saw a beet field or factory and is absolutely ignorant of the whole business."[27]

Wiley continued to complain about the work being done on nutrition in the Office of Experiment Stations and eventually vented his frustration in a letter to Wilson.[28] On Wilson's suggestion, Wiley, W. O. Atwater, the special agent in charge of the nutritional investigations, and A. C. True, the head of the Office of Experiment Stations, met. If Wilson had hoped that the problem could be resolved amicably through such a meeting, he was immediately disappointed. Wiley began by attacking the integrity of the studies done under

Atwater's direction. Again waving the bloody shirt, he suggested that a Southern influence was at work. Why, Wiley wanted to know, was work given to the University of Virginia's Professor Mallett, a British citizen who had made gunpowder for the South during the war? Work on nutrition, Wiley said, had originally been given to his division. In an act of highway robbery, he went on to claim, Morton had removed it and given it to the Office of Experiment Stations. According to Wiley, by right of legislation and seniority, the old divisions of chemistry, entomology, and botany had priority in research. To allow the Office of Experiment Stations "to conduct scientific investigation," he later wrote, "is to sap the life blood of the other divisions." Wiley did not question Wilson's intentions, but warned him that actions like Morton's and Wilson's could lead to a time "when a scientific Samson in the desperate exercise of a futile strength, may gather in his arms the pillars of the agricultural Temple and end his career by its destruction."[29]

Annoyed by the continual friction that Wiley created with others, Wilson wrote, "If anybody here gets too big for his trousers, we shall have to give him the privilege of going where trousers of larger dimensions are furnished." In spite of his annoyance, he encouraged Wiley's investigation of food adulteration, a topic that concerned Wilson because adulteration damaged the reputation of American agricultural products and thus diminished exports. In fact, when the embalmed meat scandal broke after the Spanish-American War, Wilson was more concerned about its effects on American exports than the condition of the soldiers. Because he was worried that the official investigations of embalming were inflaming European opinion against American meats, he began his own investigation with the objective of clearing the good name of American meats. Wiley played a significant role in the investigation. After analyzing canned meats purchased from the open market, he testified that he found no samples in poor condition and no trace of any preservatives, except for a small amount of saltpeter in corned and luncheon meat. These findings met with Wilson's hopes. However, Wilson also wrote to his brother William, who lived in Chicago and was connected to the meat packers, that the report did not contain all of the evidence. The degree to which Wiley knowingly participated in Wilson's desire to make American meats look as good as possible is not known, but there was nothing in Wiley's testimony or in the portion of *Bulletin #13* dealing with preserved meats that contradicted Wilson's public position.[30]

Things improved somewhat for the Division of Chemistry with the turn of the century. After his initial attempts to influence Wilson, Wiley had devoted more of his time to his personal and business affairs, and he had emerged from the investigations of preserved meats on much better terms with Wilson than he had been in 1897. The division was raised to the status of a bureau in 1901 and received new assignments. Even with the improvements, Wiley was dissatisfied. He wrote to Wilson in July, saying, "for reasons not necessary to discuss" the Bureau of Chemistry's appropriation had not been increased since Wilson had taken charge, while "[all] the other bureaus and divisions have grown steadily in their appropriations."[31]

Convinced that Wilson tacitly supported his belief that the bureau should control all the chemical research, Wiley sought outside support. In a letter to N. S. Shaler, dean of the Lawrence Scientific School at Harvard University, he wrote, "there is a tendency in the Department to establish independent chemical and physical laboratories for each of the bureaus and divisions. This tendency is opposed by the secretary who believes that all work should be concentrated under one direction. The influences which are brought to bear upon him, however, for the establishment of the separate laboratories are very strong, and gradually these laboratories are gaining a foothold." He went on to explain that there were now laboratories in the Bureau of Chemistry, the Bureau of Animal Industry, the Office of Experiment Stations, the Bureau of Plant Industry, and the Bureau of Soils. After noting that the Bureau of Animal Industry was expanding beyond its original assignment and recently had taken the analysis of dairy products from the Bureau of Chemistry, Wiley declared that "the avowed object is to break up the Bureau of Chemistry and to distribute it piece by piece in other quarters. The bureau seems to be a veritable Gaul to some of these men and three, at least, are determined to divide it into three parts, if not more, thus out Caesaring Caesar."[32]

Realizing that he needed more than tacit support from Wilson and various members of academia, Wiley sought permission from Wilson to take his case directly to Congressman James Wadsworth, the chairman of the Agricultural Committee. His meeting with Wadsworth brought some success. The committee increased Wiley's salary and passed a resolution that all chemical work in the Department of Agriculture should be under the direction of the Bureau of Chemistry. To preserve peace in the department, however, the resolution was later rescinded.[33]

Other attempts to woo outside support met with similar results. When the Bureau of Soils published *Bulletin #22*, which he believed to be scientifically unsound, Wiley asked Eugene W. Hilgard of the University of California to criticize the bulletin in *Science*. A minor brouhaha resulted but led to no tangible changes in the status of the Bureau of Chemistry. Even criticism by a world-renowned soil scientist in a respected publication could not arouse public opinion or convince those in power to place all chemical work in the Bureau of Chemistry. Nevertheless, Wiley continued his campaign. He presented his position to the Committee on Organization of Government

Scientific Work, which had been formed in March 1903 to improve efficiency. In a memorandum to the committee, B. T. Galloway challenged
Wiley, saying that organization around a discipline had worked in the past,
but was "now antiquated." In response to Wiley's claim that his bureau
would do better scientific work, Galloway wrote: "Now as a matter of fact, the
average analytical chemist knows little about the chemical problems which
confront physiologists and pathologists and could care less, and even then if
work submitted to him were done properly it would be only in the most
perfunctory and unsatisfactory manner . . . When it is a question of ordinary
routine analyses," he went on, "which any chemist can perform, they are
always glad to turn the matter over to the Bureau of Chemistry."[34]

To Galloway, Wiley's battle seemed like a tempest in a teapot. The work
done in the Bureau of Chemistry, Galloway wrote, "should be on problems,
the same as in the other great Bureaus of the Department." He ended his
memorandum with a suggestion for Wiley's bureau.

> There is an imminent field for such a Bureau in the single item of the
> consideration of the multitudinous and constantly increasing adultera-
> tions of food products. There is enough work in this single line to keep
> 100 men employed. This would be putting the Bureau on specific
> problems rather than confining it to one narrow method and would do
> much to increase its usefulness.[35]

Galloway's comments on organization carried the day. In its report to Presi-
dent Roosevelt, the committee recommended transferring the Bureau of
Chemistry's road material laboratory to a new Division of Roads in the
Geological Survey Bureau, its dendrochemistry laboratory to the Forest
Service, and the soil analysis laboratory to the Bureau of Soils.[36]

The one area in which the Bureau of Chemistry went unchallenged by
others in the Department of Agriculture was the examination of foods for
adulteration. The publication of the first three parts of *Bulletin #13* in 1887
had established the bureau as an expert in the area and a leader in the efforts
to stop adulteration. As interest in national legislation grew, Wiley's primary
problem, as always, was to ensure that the enforcement of a food law would
not be taken over by an agency outside the Bureau of Chemistry.

Charting a Successful Strategy

The National Food and Drug Congress met in 1898, thanks to the efforts of
a Virginia farm journal editor, Alexander J. Wedderburn, who called to-

gether a group of citizens, grocers, newspaper men, farmers, state officials, and chemists to discuss the need for national regulation of food and drugs. While all those who attended agreed that legislation was necessary, they disagreed over how such legislation should be administered. Wiley and his supporters wanted the administration to be in the Bureau of Chemistry. Wedderburn and others wanted the creation of a new organization under the control of an appointed food commissioner.[37]

Working with William Frear of Pennsylvania, Wiley moved to isolate Wedderburn and ensure that the administration of any bill would be in his hands. Over the next several years, he worked on two fronts simultaneously—one to promote the passage of legislation and another to ensure that the administration of the legislation would reside in the Bureau of Chemistry. There were a number of disputes over who should administer the law. Some involved personal attacks on Wiley, some involved special interest groups that hoped to benefit from a new organization, and some originated from the legitimate belief that a new organization would be the best way to administer the law.[38]

By 1902 it seemed likely to Wiley that Congress would pass some form of legislation. Under these circumstances, he was extremely concerned about the position of the National Association of State Food and Dairy Officials, an organization of state officials who hoped to obtain uniformity among state laws. From their experience in enforcing food laws, these officials were well aware of the shortcomings of various state statutes, many of which they knew were the instruments of special interests rather than protection for the public. Many in the association thought that the Department of Agriculture represented only the interests of agriculture, and therefore they advocated an independent agency that would represent the consumer, manufacturer, and distributor as well as the farmer.[39]

In January 1903, delegates from the association testified before Senator Porter J. McCumber of South Dakota, one of the sponsors of a pure food bill then under consideration. Wiley favored the McCumber bill, which would place the authority for its administration in the Bureau of Chemistry. The delegation, however, was divided. R. M. Allen of Kentucky spoke for the bill and Professor Hamilton of Pennsylvania against it. Although, according to Wiley, Hamilton made a poor impression and Allen made a good one, the bill did not pass. Wiley was puzzled. He did not think the association's opposition was the reason, but it remained the only group that favored a national law yet opposed the Hepburn–McCumber bill. Wiley hoped to change its position.[40]

R. M. Allen of Kentucky, who had spoken in favor of the bill, was the association's secretary and an employee of M. A. Scovell, Wiley's friend and associate. Looking for support to publish the annual proceedings of the association's convention, Allen asked Wiley about possible support from the Department of Agriculture. Wiley told him that any such support would require more cooperation from the association: "Cooperation in regard to food legislation has never yet been secured. If your officials would come into harness and work for the pure food law without insisting on another particular form of legislation the way would be clear." He went on to explain his position. "There is a great danger in organizing a separate bureau of a political or semi-political nature where the incumbent would be tempted, as is the case in some states, to magnify the importance of his office by unnecessary prosecutions ... I believe that if your organization could be brought to the patronage of the secretary much could be done to unify those who are in favor of a pure food bill." It is not clear if Wilson had approved this offer of patronage, but Wiley was confident enough to make a similar offer to the president of the National Association of State Food and Dairy Officials.[41]

Allen was sure he could get the backing of his association's executive committee, but suggested that Wiley attend the association's convention in St. Paul, Minnesota, in July with as many supporters as possible. Wiley quickly began to organize a group of supporters and planned to have himself appointed as the official delegate of the Department of Agriculture, which would make him a voting member of the convention. Clearly, Wiley was expecting a fight at the convention, and for good reason. Among the scheduled speakers was Henry C. Adams, a recently elected congressman from Wisconsin, who Wiley knew would oppose him.[42] To counter any opposition at the convention, he wrote detailed letters to his supporters, outlining the arguments that they could offer to support the McCumber bill. Among other things, Wiley pointed out that the Department of Agriculture was already organized and equipped with machinery for enforcing the law; that the establishment of a separate bureau would involve an additional expenditure of public money for official salaries and for the establishment of chemical laboratories; that the secretary of agriculture already had full authority and equipment to execute the food law; that under the Hepburn–McCumber bill the department would cooperate with various state officials; that the bill had the support of all the major interests in the distribution, wholesaling, and retailing of food; and finally, that Congress had already approved the bill's administrative features.[43]

The convention wasted no time getting to the main issue. Congressman Adams spoke eloquently about the need for a national food law, and he did not skirt the issue of administration. He called for a pure food commissioner who would be appointed by the president and serve under the general supervision of the secretary of agriculture. It was, Adams said, "an executive position and the law should not be drawn so that the incumbent of some other office must inherit this office." He went on to say that his stance was not an attack on Wiley; he recognized the great contribution the Bureau of Chemistry under Wiley had made to the cause of pure food. However, he added, "a chemist might be the best man in the world for an executive office, but his scientific training, as a rule, develops him in other directions. The head of the pure food bureau will have under his control chemists, detectives, lawyers, and hundreds of agents all over the United States. It is a position for an active man of affairs rather than a scientist."[44]

Wiley and his supporters were prepared. R. M. Allen spoke about the need for the law and the success of the Hepburn–McCumber bill in passing the House of Representatives in the last session. He claimed that Congress would oppose the establishment of a new bureau and that to insist on one would cause the failure of any pure food bill. Wiley spoke next, saying that he would support any pure food bill that came before Congress but that he favored the Hepburn–McCumber bill. He cautioned against changing the bill in any form, saying that it was a compromise of many interests and that to change it could result in opposition from groups now supporting it. Carefully playing the role of a public servant who is above the political squabbles, he went on to say that he did not care about the administrative features of the bill but that the secretary of agriculture did, and there would be no chance of passing the bill without Wilson's support.[45]

Following Wiley were William Frear and M. A. Scovell, both of whom spoke in support of the Hepburn–McCumber bill but did not address the administrative features. L. M. Frailey, who represented Campbell Preserve Company and the Association of Manufacturers and Distributors of Food Products, also spoke in favor of the Hepburn–McCumber bill. However, his remarks caused an uproar among the state food officials when he misstated one of the arguments Wiley had sent to him: "those who are called upon to enforce the law should have the least to say in regard to its making," said Frailey. Believing their expertise should be central to the framing of any food law, state food officials were outraged. Wiley came to Frailey's defense, saying he believed the words were meant to apply to the national law and particularly to himself, and he agreed with Frailey that it was not his job to tell Congress what bill to pass. Wiley's remarks soothed ruffled feathers, but his actions reveal that he had every intention of using his influence to secure the bill he wanted.[46]

Many who attended the convention were unaware of the significance of the debate and wondered why so much time was being spent on how a food law would be administered. R. J. Mauck, a state chemist from Ohio, said: "So far as the [administrative] details are concerned I know nothing of them and am not interested. If the Department of Agriculture wants the work, let them have it, if the Department of Commerce wants it, let them have it, but for God's sake, rather give it to the Department of Navy than not get it at all."[47]

In the end, the convention did not unanimously support the Hepburn–McCumber bill. Instead a resolution was passed that left it to the executive committee to do what it thought advisable. As Wiley's supporters now dominated the executive committee, thanks to R. M. Allen, his position was assured. Thus, Wiley emerged from the St. Paul Convention triumphant. With no organized group now opposing his version of a national food bill, Wiley believed the way was now clear for the passage of a national food law that would be administered by his bureau in the Department of Agriculture.

CHAPTER 4

The Struggle for Legislative Dominance, 1903–4

Administrative control of a national food law was not the only controversial issue discussed at the St. Paul convention of the National Association of State Food and Dairy Departments. Members also debated food standards, which had been an item of contention at annual meetings since the organization's inception. State food officials had long hoped to establish uniform laws among the states, but they believed that it was first necessary to establish standards for foods. Since many state food officials were also state chemists, they had asked the Association of Official Agricultural Chemists to perform this task. The association had established a standards committee in 1896 and had chosen Wiley to head the committee, but without funding, the process of investigating foods was slow. In 1902, when Congress authorized the secretary of agriculture to appoint a committee to establish food standards, Wilson had selected the association's food standard committee and authorized it to receive funds from the Department of Agriculture. To avoid the appearance of an improper partiality, Wiley resigned as chairman. He was replaced by his friend William Frear. Under the terms of the appropriation bill, food standards would establish uniform analytical methods that would help state food officials and courts to determine which foods were adulterated or misbranded. Although the food standards committee planned to consult all interested parties—consumers, manufacturers, dealers—as part of the process, it soon became evident that the standards set by the committee closely conformed to Wiley's.[1]

There was little difficulty in establishing standards for products derived from a single source. Maple syrup had to come from the maple tree; dairy products had to contain a certain level of butter fat. However, compounded and prepared foods were more complex issues. Ice cream, for example, could be sweetened with sugar (sucrose) or with corn syrup (glucose). On what basis should it be decided that the one ice cream was pure but the other adulterated, or should both products be declared pure or both adulterated? This was the kind of issue posed by foods composed of many ingredients.[2]

Addressing the St. Paul convention, M. A. Scovell and William Frear explained the committee's methods of establishing standards and the difficulties committee members had encountered. These difficulties arose from the limits of scientific knowledge. Committee members were attempting to classify foods into a taxonomical scheme similar to that used by paleontologists to classify fossils. Scovell explained how different species of bees using different pollens produced different honeys at different times of the year. The variations in honey, he said, made it impossible to define one standard of purity, and yet multiple standards would make it impossible to establish a scientific taxonomy that could be used to regulate commercial food products.[3]

E. N. Eaton, a food chemist and delegate from Illinois, and E. O. Grosvenor, a former dairy official from Michigan, also emphasized the arbitrary nature of official food standards. Grosvenor expressed doubts about establishing standards for compounded products and warned of the potential for abuse. Eaton pointed to the extrascientific in classifying human foods, saying, "their value depends more on flavor and taste, as well as all sorts of human idiosyncrasies, than on nutritive properties." It is clear from the statements made by food officials that food standards involved issues that lay beyond the domain of scientific classification. The inability to rely on science to set food standards would tear apart the congenial atmosphere of the food officials' conventions in future years. The association would split into contending factions, each of which would denounce the honesty and integrity of the other. In the end, the association would adopt food standards based on commercial and political interests rather than on science.[4]

The Strategy Matures

The infusion of commercial self-interest into food standards began when Wiley asked Old Taylor, a manufacturer of straight whiskey, to send a representative to the St. Paul convention. Straight whiskey competed with rectified and blended whiskeys for the consumer's dollar. The chemical composition of these types of whiskeys was nearly identical, but each type differed in the way it was manufactured and in its color, taste, smoothness, or other qualities that were important to consumers.

Both straight whiskey and rectified whiskey were produced by fermenting rye, corn, wheat, or barley. After fermentation, the product was distilled once to produce what were called "low wines." These were then distilled again at a different temperature to produce what were called "high wines." Rectified whiskey was produced by running the high wines through charcoal or by distilling them yet again. Originally, a pot still was used in the distillation process, but around 1880 the continuous still came into use. It produced a more palatable product that did not have to be run through charcoal. Whether run through charcoal or not, the distillate was then reduced to drinking strength, or "proof," by adding water. Usually the product was colored by adding caramel or burnt sugar. This was done because consumers liked an amber-colored drink, similar to the Irish and Scotch whiskeys. Sometimes, small amounts of peach or prune juice were added for flavor.

The advent of straight whiskey occurred shortly after the Civil War, when some distillers began to store the high wines in a barrel for several years. It was believed that barrel aging had the same effect as running high wines through charcoal because aging removed the odor of the fusel oil (the amyl, butyl, and propyl alcohol) produced during fermentation. Fusel oil was universally regarded as objectionable not only because of its odor but also because it was more harmful to the body than ethyl alcohol, which was the main constituent of high wines. If the barrel in which the high wines were stored was charred on the inside, the product absorbed a color similar to that of caramel. Straight whiskey usually had a stronger flavor than rectified whiskey and, like the single-malt scotch whiskeys of today, was more expensive than rectified or blended whiskeys. Blended whiskey was a mix of straight and rectified whiskey. Because it was a mix, only a part of a blended whiskey was aged, although some blends, for example, Canadian Club, also aged the rectified portion of their blend.

As it was cheaper to produce than straight whiskey, rectified whiskey was sold at a lower price and thus constituted about 85 percent of the whiskey consumed in the United States. Rectified whiskey manufacturers often stressed the purity of their brands, primarily because they had less fusel oil than straight whiskey. Straight whiskey manufacturers, on the other hand, emphasized the age and character of their products. Because straight whiskey was stored in warehouses monitored by government revenue agents who stamped each bottle when the taxes that were due were paid, straight whiskey manufacturers often claimed that the green government stamp, known as a bond, was a symbol of government approval. They often referred to their products as bottled-in-bond.[5]

Setting Standards for Whiskey

It was R. M. Allen who first saw the potential benefit of the Kentucky straight whiskey producers to Wiley's campaign for the Hepburn–McCumber bill. Their support could help to sway the convention. Furthermore, endorsement of the bill by commercial interests and the convention would help to persuade Congress to pass the bill. Certainly, there was plenty of potential commercial support for some kind of pure food bill. Many firms wanted national legislation because of the inconvenience caused by differing state laws. There were also firms that hoped to use national legislation to gain a competitive advantage. Few of these firms, however, were committed to Wiley's bureau as administrator of the law. Wiley's solution to this problem was to offer firms a competitive advantage if they would support his bid for administrative control.[6]

At the urging of Allen, who was a personal friend of Edmund W. Taylor, the son of Edmund H. Taylor Jr., the founder of the firm, Wiley began a correspondence with the elder Taylor and persuaded him to send a representative to the St. Paul convention. "I trust that this representative will strongly endorse the principles of the Hepburn and McCumber pure food bill," Wiley wrote. "If the manufacturers who attend the St. Paul convention stand firmly for the administrative features of the Hepburn bill I believe it will secure the endorsement of the convention." Wiley went on to say that Taylor should talk with Professor Scovell on these matters. Taylor sent his son as the representative, and Allen, who was secretary of the association, arranged for him to speak before the convention.[7]

The younger Taylor generously entertained the food officials, passing out the products of his father's business and building goodwill among the officials. In his speech to the convention, he quoted Wiley's praise of straight whiskey: "While you can imitate nature you cannot substitute the artificial for natural products without impairing the quality of the product. There is something almost indescribable which makes a difference between the compounded and the natural product."[8] Taylor made it clear that he favored Wiley's definition of whiskey. The food standards committee then persuaded the convention to pass a resolution endorsing the bottling-in-bond law and urging its extension: "That we approve of the bottling in bond law as it stands, and recommend that it be modified and extended in any way that would still further facilitate the distribution of pure whiskey from the distiller to the consumer." This official standard corresponded to Wiley's own tastes in whiskey.[9]

Wiley's preference for straight whiskey was based on his family background and the acquired sophistication of a middle-class gentleman. Raised in southern Indiana near Kentucky whiskey country (his relatives at one time produced straight whiskey), he was personally acquainted with the product. He often served as a judge of whiskeys and had rated straight whiskeys above blends at the Paris Exposition in 1900. Not only did he correspond with straight whiskey makers, he also accepted their products as gifts. As a member of the elite Cosmos Club in Washington, D.C., he oversaw the purchasing of the club's whiskey stock for many years. He made a sharp distinction between the expensive whiskey served to gentlemen and the cheap alcoholic drinks served in working-class saloons.[10]

The Poison Squad

Increased commercial support was not the only thing Wiley needed to induce Congress to act in a way that would favor his version of a pure food law. He needed public support, and he proved adept at gaining it. In 1902 Congress had appropriated funds that authorized the Department of Agriculture to investigate food preservatives. Wiley took charge of the investigations and, in November of that year, began a series of studies using human subjects. After establishing a kitchen and eating area in the Bureau of Chemistry, he solicited volunteers for a series of experiments to measure the effects of preservatives on health. Wiley referred to the experiments, which continued for the next five years, as the hygienic table, but the press, led by George Rothwell Brown of the *Washington Post*, soon named the group of young men "the poison squad."[11]

The first experiment tested borax and boric acid. The food and drink consumed by the young men were carefully measured, and the amounts of borax and boric acid used as preservatives were administered in capsules. Feces and urine were analyzed, and the physical condition of the subjects was monitored and recorded, in an attempt to discover the effects of preservatives on health. Sensational press reporting alerted the public to the presence of additives in food and drew Wiley into public prominence.

Two aspects of the experiments diminished their scientific value. First, there was no control group. Although fluctuations in health, weight, and appetite were recorded, there was no norm with which to compare them. Second, Wiley began his experiments with some firmly entrenched but unusual ideas about digestion and preservatives. Spoilage and digestion, in his view, were the same process, and so preservatives, which interfere with the normal decay of a substance, necessarily interfered with digestion. He also believed that some preservatives, those proven safe by long usage, were less harmful than others. According to him, traditional preservatives—salt, vinegar, spices, wood smoke, sugar, peppers—compensated for their preserving action in the stomach by causing "the secretion of ferments in the intestinal canal."[12] As he cited no chemical analysis or laboratory experiment for his beliefs, they were apparently just that—beliefs without scientific foundation even by the scientific standards of the day.

Wiley welcomed the publicity his experiments brought but worried about the effects that sensationalism would have on the scientific community's acceptance of them. Although he objected to the name "poison squad," he continued to give press interviews until Wilson cautioned him against seeking further publicity. Wilson did not think it proper for an employee of the government to promote legislation publicly. Still, the publicity spawned by the experiments increased Wiley's demand as a speaker and gave him additional opportunities to argue for a pure food law while providing the public with information. The effect of the information was not always what Wiley hoped for. When the press reported that borax produced a pink and white complexion in the subjects, women wrote asking for more information about this wonderful discovery.[13]

Opposition

Wiley's use of the National Association of State Food and Dairy Officials to endorse straight whiskey marked a new phase in the campaign for a national pure food law. Although historians of the pure food law have noted a qualitative change in the campaign after 1903 and have attributed the change to the emerging Progressive movement, the politicians who sponsored pure food legislation, Porter J. McCumber, William P. Hepburn, and Weldon B. Heyburn, were not Progressives. Wiley himself was a high-tariff Republican. Only after years of political infighting would he abandon the Republican Party and support the presidential aspirations of Woodrow Wilson. Given these facts, it seems unlikely that it was the emerging Progressive movement that effected food regulation, although the movement did make it easier for Wiley, Hepburn, McCumber, and others to bring about change.[14] What did change in 1903 was Wiley's strategy. He concentrated on making alliances with commercial interests that could benefit from his administration of a national food law. As a consequence, the conflict increasingly centered around Wiley's opinions and his administration of the law, rather than the law itself. Although Wiley would claim that his opponents were against a pure food law because they wanted to cheat and poison the public, this claim was largely unfounded. Wiley's opponents did not oppose a law per se; they simply opposed a law that, under Wiley's influence, would discriminate against their products.

The Whiskey Rectifiers

By the fall of 1903, the publicity Wiley had garnered from his experiments and his successes at the St. Paul convention led him to believe that he could secure the passage of the Hepburn–McCumber law in the upcoming session of Congress. He was mistaken; he underestimated the amount of opposition that he had created.

The manufacturers of rectified whiskey had begun to view Wiley with some concern when the Bureau of Chemistry, under additional authority granted to it by Congress, began to inspect imports early in 1903. In retaliation for the discriminatory trade practices of European countries, the bureau was given the authority to deny entry to any product that was falsely labeled or the sale of which was prohibited by the exporting country.[15] The bureau had quickly established inspection facilities at large ports of entry, and Wiley had made clear to importers that fraudulent labeling would no longer be tolerated. This in itself did not create opposition, but manufacturers of rectified whiskey were alarmed at Wiley's claim that whiskey made by a stack still or filtering through charcoal, that is, rectified whiskey, was falsely labeled.[16] The endorsement of straight whiskey by the St. Paul convention in July had increased their concerns. Prior to this time, the industry as a whole had paid little attention to a national pure food law; it was more concerned with the growing prohibitionist movement. After the St. Paul convention, however, it had become apparent to the makers of rectified whiskey that straight whiskey manufacturers were attempting to use pure food laws for commercial advantage.

The potential advantage to straight whiskey makers is seen in Wiley's private correspondence. That October, after receiving a case of rye whiskey "with that little green stamp" from the Overholt Company, a straight whiskey manufacturer, Wiley wrote a note saying, "I thank you very much for your courtesy and will take pleasure in bringing the matter of bottling in bond as a guarantee of purity before the Food Standards Committee officially authorized to advise the Secretary of Agriculture in these matters."[17]

In November 1903 Congress was again in session, and pure food bills were introduced in both the House and the Senate. Wiley, working with Congressman William P. Hepburn of Ohio, changed the provision of the House bill dealing with food standards. The original bill had proposed the appointment of a special committee to establish standards. In its place, Wiley substituted a provision similar to the provision in the appropriation bill for the Department of Agriculture, which allowed the secretary of agriculture to use the Association of Official Agricultural Chemists to recommend standards. This provision would empower Wiley to control food standards on a national scale.[18] Alerted to possible problems for the industry from pure food legislation, Warwick M. Hough, the attorney for the National Wholesale Liquor Dealers Association, contacted Wiley to determine the status of whiskey in the proposed legislation.[19]

On 2 January 1904, Wiley gave Hough an encouraging answer. "I do not think that distilled spirits are mentioned in any of the food bills now pending and the only inspection they would undergo, under the law, if it should become one, would be that of determining the extent of their adulteration." He assured Hough that such a provision would benefit whiskey

rectifiers and that nothing in the bill discriminated between different kinds
of whiskeys. Wiley also denied any influence in shaping the bill, saying, "I
reply that I had nothing to do with the framing of the bill; I was chairman of
the committee of the Pure Food Congress which drafted the bill but took no
part in the discussion and acted only as a presiding officer."[20] Given his
earlier correspondence with Edmund Taylor, Wiley was less than candid
with Hough.

While he was assuring Hough that there was nothing to worry about,
Wiley was opposing an amendment offered by Congressman William Lorimer of Illinois that would have exempted whiskey and other spirits from
the purview of the pure food law. When Lorimer argued that items already
inspected under internal revenue laws should not be covered by a pure
food law, Wiley responded that internal revenue laws were intended only
for the collection of revenues, not for the determination of adulteration.
"No one denies," wrote Wiley, "the extended adulterations of distilled
spirits; in fact, it is well known that probably more than half of the distilled
spirits consumed in the United States are purely artificial and are not made
by the old fashioned process which was considered so necessary to health,
purity and flavor."[21]

Shortly after writing Hough, Wiley met with him and agreed to help
remove any provisions from the pure food bill that would require blended
whiskey firms to list their ingredients. Wiley also agreed to support a modification of the Lorimer amendment, which now officially recognized the bond
used by the Treasury Department on straight whiskey. This compromise was
not a significant concession for Wiley because the standard setting and
labeling provisions of the bill remained intact, which gave Wiley enough
discretion to enforce his views on whiskey. He was convinced, however, that
this modification of the Lorimer amendment would end the opposition of
the National Wholesale Liquor Dealers Association to pure food legislation.[22] On 5 January, he wrote L. M. Frailey that opposition to the bill was
feeble and that the whiskey men were divided into two camps, the straight
men who supported the bill and the "artificial" men who desired only one
amendment, which could be inserted without injury to the bill.[23]

In his correspondence, Wiley continued to assure Hough that the whiskey rectifiers had nothing to fear from the Hepburn–McCumber bill but
warned him that opposition to the bill would put the whiskey rectifiers in a
bad public light. At the same time, however, he wrote to F. F. Gilmore, a
Kentucky distiller, "There is no question here concerning the comparative
wholesomeness of the two products [straight and rectified whiskeys]. We
may assume, for the sake of argument, that they are equally wholesome, or
equally deleterious as the case may be . . . yet they stand in a different atti-

tude toward the pending Pure Food Bill, because one is a natural product and the other an artificial mixture."[24]

R. M. Allen continued to criticize rectified whiskey manufacturers, telling Wiley that they were out to defeat the bill while the straight whiskey manufacturers were doing all they could to support it. Allen noted that straight whiskey firms had raised over $80,000 to educate people about the bottled-in-bond act, and that he could use as much of the money as he needed for the International Pure Food Congress, which the National Association of State Dairy and Food Officials was sponsoring at the Louisiana Purchase Centennial Exposition in the coming summer.[25] At Wiley's suggestion, other money to support the passage of pure food legislation was sent to William Frear. Hoping to build goodwill among the potential regulators of food, Gallus Thomann of the United States Brewing Association was active in obtaining funds to assist the pure food cause. Because brewers were frequently under attack for adulterating their products, they hoped that a close relationship with Wiley, who had defended them in the past, would prove fruitful.[26]

The Hepburn–McCumber bill passed the House on 20 January 1904, and success seemed at hand for Wiley. The Senate, however, soon showed signs of resistance. McCumber was replaced as chairman of the Committee on Manufacturing by Weldon B. Heyburn of Idaho. Heyburn, although he worked enthusiastically for the bill, was new to the Senate and did not have the influence of McCumber.[27]

The Drug Industry

Opposition from rectified whiskey manufacturers was not the only challenge Wiley faced in 1904. For the first time in the campaign for a pure food bill, drugs and patent medicines became a major issue. Under the terms of previous bills, only those drugs recognized by the United States Pharmacopoeia—and most patent medicines were not—would have been regulated. McCumber, however, added a provision that expanded coverage to "any substance intended to be used for the cure, mitigation, or prevention of disease." He did so at the urging of the representatives of a few proprietary medicine firms, who claimed that they would gain protection from imitations and substitutes. The industry as a whole was opposed. The National Association of Wholesale Druggists, the National Association of Retail Druggists, and the Proprietary Association of America all descended on Washington to oppose the inclusion of proprietary medicines in the bill.[28]

Patent medicines provided revenues not only for their manufacturers but also for those who supplied manufacturers with ingredients, for retail

druggists and physicians who sold such nostrums, and for magazines in
which the manufacturers advertised. Combined, these commercial elements
constituted a large and potentially powerful interest group that acted more
or less in concert. Wiley had aroused some concern among the group in
1903, when he recommended printing the formula of any patent medicine
on the medicine's label. He had also advocated requiring a physician's
prescription for any remedy containing alcohol and cocaine.[29] However, as
soon as the patent drug industry threatened to oppose the bill, Wiley contacted Senator McCumber and urged the deletion of the offending passages,
saying that although he (Wiley) personally approved the broader definition
of drugs, he feared the definition "if left in will invite the active opposition of
many of the powerful drug interests." He added, "out of regard for our
druggist friends who have stood by the bill all along, it seems to me advisable that it be omitted." McCumber agreed but was unable to get Heyburn
and the rest of the committee to go along. Even if the provision were
changed, McCumber informed Wiley, opposition to the bill was far greater
than he had anticipated. In fact, it seemed unlikely the bill would have a
majority if it came to a vote in the Senate.[30]

Wiley then wrote to M. N. Kline, who represented the National Wholesale Druggists, saying that McCumber had been unable to have the bill
changed in committee but that it could be changed on the Senate floor, or if
not there, certainly in the Conference Committee. He went on to suggest
that opposition should "be confined solely to secure the desired change in
the definition and not be exerted against the bill as a whole." He added, "I
myself feel as you do that it was unfortunate the committee did not make
the change, and I must still be allowed to believe that it is because they did
not fully understand the argument made by you and myself."[31]

Wiley's concern about the opposition of a powerful interest group was
well placed. Senator Heyburn later told Wiley that he had been contacted by a
representative of a group of publishers who wanted the expanded coverage of
drugs removed from the bill because they feared the regulation of medicines
would adversely affect their advertising revenues. Wiley was quite willing to
accommodate these commercial interests; throughout his campaign to obtain
and enforce legislation, he paid scant attention to patent medicines.[32]

Reassessment and a New Plan

Much to Wiley's disappointment, the Senate adjourned in 1904 without
considering the Hepburn–McCumber bill. While Wiley suspected there
were well-organized interests opposing the bill, he was not sure who these

interests were beyond the patent medicine and publishing industries. He wrote to Allen, saying, "there is a deep and secret opposition to it [the pure food bill] which it is very difficult to explain." He repeated this belief in a letter to William Frear: "There is a deep undercurrent of opposition among the Senators which it is hard to explain. It did not exist in the House, but surely does in the Senate."[33]

R. M. Allen had none of Wiley's doubts about the bill's opponents. He bombarded Wiley with letters condemning the manufacturers of rectified whiskey. He claimed that the National Wholesale Liquor Dealers had raised $500,000 from its members and was using this money to pay senators and congressmen to oppose any pure food legislation. He told Wiley that he had warned the manufacturers that their opposition would bring about far more restrictive legislation. At the same time, Allen kept in close contact with the straight whiskey industry. He traveled to Washington with Edmund W. Taylor to meet with Wiley and to testify before the Senate on behalf of the purity of straight whiskey.[34]

Wiley may not have believed that rectified whiskey manufacturers were responsible for much of the opposition. He wrote to F. N. Barrett, publisher of *American Grocer,* that there was a large group of impressive men from the whiskey industry in Washington to oppose pure food legislation and that these men "had a large barrel to draw from." During this same period, however, he wrote to his friends that there was no evidence of rectified whiskey interests opposing the bill.[35]

The failure of the Hepburn–McCumber bill caused Wiley to reassess what was needed to secure legislation. Although John F. Queeny, founder of Monsanto Chemical Company, which had been formed two years earlier to manufacture saccharin, had testified that the bill gave too much power to a few men, the administrative features of the bill had not been challenged by any organized group.[36] Removal of the expanded definition of drugs from the bill during the fall session, Wiley thought, would reduce Senate opposition. He wrote to Senator Heyburn:

> I am to say also, that the great drug organizations will oppose that feature of the bill which includes patent and proprietary medicines. If the definition for drugs was left in the bill as it passed the House this interest would support it. I would like to suggest, for your consideration, if you do not think it would be better to restore that part of the bill to the form in which it passed the House and then after the bill becomes a law, secure an amendment including these remedies. The interests at stake are so great that it appears to me that it would be advisable to make a concession of this kind.[37]

At the same time, Wiley had come to believe that simply quieting the opposition of the drug industry would not be enough. Passage would require, he felt, widespread public pressure to force the Senate to act. Realizing that the Steering Committee, which was made up of Senators William B. Allison, Henry Cabot Lodge, and Nelson Aldrich, would have to give its consent for the bill to make it to the Senate floor and having heard that Henry K. Frick, the steel magnate, was also one of the owners of Old Overholt, Wiley wrote Allen, saying, "I wish Mr. Frick would organize a campaign to pass the pure food bill. Do you think he could be induced to do something to secure an overwhelming attack on the Senate at the beginning of the December session?"[38]

While these actions were a start, Wiley was not one to wait for someone else to do his organizing. He contacted Alice Lakey, a young woman whose career as a concert singer had been cut short by poor health and who now lived with her father in Cranford, New Jersey. Lakey had met Wiley when he had addressed Cranford's Village Improvement Association. She immediately became his devoted follower, proclaiming that Wiley was "a Moses given to the people by God." She became a tireless worker for Wiley and his campaign. After Wiley noted in a letter to her, "it is not considered quite good taste for one in my position to make a public canvas in favor of any pending measure [because] some opponents of the bill may say that it was prompted by me for the sake of increasing my duties and possibly emoluments," she willingly served as his surrogate spokesperson. She contacted women's groups favoring pure food regulation and argued that Wiley was the only one who could enforce the law honestly.[39]

As part of his plan to bring pressure on the Senate, Wiley instructed Lakey to obtain resolutions demanding the passage of a pure food bill from these groups and to send the resolutions to the Senate. He wanted her particularly to bring pressure to bear on Senator Kean of New Jersey, whom Wiley believed to be obstructing passage of the bill.[40]

Plans were made for meeting in the Shoreham Hotel in Washington, D.C., on 15 June 1904, where Wiley planned to initiate his new plan to attack the major opponents of the food bill, except for the patent medicine industry, which he still hoped to exclude from legislation. He already had organized support from women's groups and the American Medical Association, but he felt this would not be enough. After considering the possibilities, Wiley and his allies chose the rectified whiskey industry as their main target. The industry was held in disfavor by public opinion, and a vigorous attack would gain the support of the powerful temperance movement. Reluctant senators, thought Wiley, could be pressured if the public associated them with the rectified whiskey industry.[41]

Wiley and his group launched their attack at the Inten Food Congress in St. Louis in September 1904. Sponsored by Association of State Food and Dairy Officials, the congress, whi of the Louisiana Purchase Centennial Exposition, proved to b platform, giving the attack an official and scientific countenanc Exposition proved to be a turning point in Wiley's campaign to secure a federal food law.[42]

CHAPTER 5

The Struggle for Legislative Dominance, 1904–6

The Louisiana Purchase Centennial Exposition held in St. Louis, Missouri, in the summer of 1904 was one of the great events of its time. The cost of staging the event exceeded the $15 million originally paid for Louisiana. Over 19 million people passed through the exposition's gates to see its wonders. Seventy-five miles of walks and paths led visitors through the various exhibits and demonstrations. A huge Ferris wheel, 250 feet high, loomed over all, thrilling those who tried it. In addition to the exhibits, demonstrations, and Olympic games, a series of international congresses brought the world's leading scientists and men of letters to the exposition that summer. So much was there to see and do that some visitors collapsed from exhaustion, and others complained of the enormous mental toll exacted by their visit.[1]

Henry Adams strolled the exposition's great white way, lit by thousands of electric lights, and found among the wasted power, indifferent art, economic failure, and chaos of education, a dim optimism for the future. He returned to Washington and urged President Roosevelt to attend. Roosevelt arrived, stormed through the exhibits, mistook Apollo for Diana, and declared it all wonderful.[2]

It was in the midst of this monument to the progress of white American society that Wiley deployed his forces. The International Pure Food Congress opened at the exposition in September in conjunction with the annual convention of the National Association of State Food and Dairy Officials. Food manufacturers, grocery wholesalers, and editors from grocery trade magazines showed up in force. There were even international experts, thanks to the efforts of R. M. Allen and the straight whiskey manufacturers who had financed his trip to Europe the previous winter. Of course, attendance at the sessions was occasionally spotty as the wonders of the fair distracted even sober men with high purpose from their appointed business.[3]

Nearly everyone at the congress agreed that some kind of pure food legislation would be beneficial. A. T. Holmes, the editor of *Inland Grocer,* for example, thought that pure food legislation was in the best interest of the consumer but suspected that the consumer neither wanted nor would pay attention to a pure food law. Speaking to the congress, he said, "I have sometimes ventured the opinion that the populace as a mass in this regard is better served than it deserves, since with many, perhaps with the majority of food buyers, quality is less a consideration than price. . . . the public cares not a particle for this [pure food legislation]. Food buyers will buy what suits their taste and purse and will abuse the officer who interferes with either. . . . The consuming public, gentleman, will consume anything so long as it is within reach." He went on to point out, however, that pure food legislation could serve the producers of high-quality products by eliminating the production of low-cost goods. He favored this but thought that there would be great opposition because it would inevitably result in higher prices at a time when there was a growing concern over the cost of living.[4]

R. G. Evans, representing the H. J. Heinz Company, showed even less concern for the prices that consumers paid for food. Indeed he chastised the American people for their "bargain counter mania." This mania, he said, "affords the unscrupulous manufacturer a ready market for his products if he could sell them for a very low price. Cheapness thus becomes the goal of his productive ambition, and this ambition was realized and the goal reached by placing on the market products not containing the ingredients they were suppose to contain." Together, Holmes and Evans articulated the reason that many firms, especially those that produced higher priced, nationally advertised brands, supported a pure food law. It was not out of concern for purity or health or the well-being of the working classes; it was for the competitive advantage that such legislation would provide. Pure food legislation would hobble their lower-priced competitors.[5]

Confrontation

The Pure Food Congress attracted widespread news coverage and thus increased public support for food regulation, but disputes over the uses of preservatives, dyes, and saccharin during the convention offered a microcosm of the battles that would loom over regulation. As a result of the publicity that Wiley's poison squad experiments had generated, preservatives were one of the controversial items under discussion. Sebastian Mueller, the brother-in-law of Henry Heinz, explained the difficulties of producing foods that would keep well without the use of preservatives. While preservatives were no longer used in most of its products, he said, the company had not been able to produce a catsup that would keep for more than a few days without the use of benzoate of soda. He argued that it was necessary to permit its use until preservation could be achieved without the use of chemicals. He noted that the company used the smallest possible amount and considered it harmless. What Mueller did not say, and perhaps did not know, was that Heinz was on the verge of producing a catsup that would keep without the use of a preservative. Less than two years later, on discovery of this technology, the company favored outlawing the use of benzoate of soda.[6]

Wiley's address was a full-scale assault on preservatives. He criticized the use of preservatives in all food products except in special cases, such as food carried on expeditions to the North Pole. He argued that it was not the government's job to prove that a preservative was deleterious; it was the user's job to prove that it was beneficial. In his attack on additives, Wiley singled out saccharin, which he claimed was a preservative as well as a sweetener.[7]

John F. Queeny, president of the struggling Monsanto Company, the only domestic producer of saccharin, also spoke. While he favored regulation, he said, he opposed the Hepburn–McCumber bill, which had passed the House in the last session. The bill, according to Queeny, contained obnoxious clauses and narrow-minded ideas, which had led to its failure in the Senate. For a law to pass, Queeny went on, it must have the support of manufacturers and must not hurt honest businessmen. He criticized the provision of the Hepburn–McCumber bill that required saccharin, but not sugar, to be listed on labels and said that this discrimination served to protect the sugar trust from competition. He suggested that it was this type of discrimination that had caused opposition to the Hepburn–McCumber bill.[8]

Wiley quickly disputed the claim that the Hepburn–McCumber bill discriminated against saccharin. Saccharin, he argued, imitated sugar, giving food a sweet taste, but unlike sugar, it lacked food value and lowered the nutritional quality of the food. He also claimed that saccharin was a preservative and therefore interfered with digestion. He made it clear that he would do all that he could to stop the use of saccharin in American food.

Wiley's rebuttal addressed only half of Queeny's argument. It did not explain why sugar should not be listed on a label whenever it was added to food; after all, other products had to be listed. When discussing the addition of molasses to corn syrup for purposes of color and flavoring, for example, Wiley insisted that the product was misbranded if the molasses was not listed on the label. He said repeatedly that any constituents added to foods must be displayed on the label, but he did not apply this edict to sugar. His facility for adamantly insisting on a rule and then ignoring it for products that he favored generated much of the opposition to his version of a pure food law.[9]

The hottest debates of the convention were between the contending whiskey interests. Edmund W. Taylor led the forces of the straight whiskey manufacturers. He argued that straight whiskey was the only pure, legitimate product and thus should be endorsed by the congress as it had been the year before in St. Paul. Following the strategy they had planned in June at the Shoreham hotel in Washington, D.C., Wiley and Allen concurred with his position. When Warwick Hough attempted to explain the position of the rectified and blended whiskey manufacturers, he was interrupted to the point of harassment. Hough was probably not prepared for the confrontation, because Wiley had earlier assured him that rectified whiskey had nothing to fear from a pure food law.[10]

Open confrontation was a new strategy for Wiley and his allies. Previously, he had compromised with those who objected to particular provisions of a pure food bill; he had not sought to harass or punish them. After 1904, however, open confrontation became common except in dealings with the proprietary drug industry, which Wiley went out of his way to mollify and appease. Indeed, patent medicines were conspicuous by their absence from the discussions at the International Pure Food Conference. The only resolution pertaining to drugs was one that called for more efficient drug inspection and asked Congress to pass "such legislation as was needed." The congress specifically endorsed the Hepburn–McCumber bill, which contained a narrow definition of drugs and applied only to those drugs listed in the *United States Pharmacopoeia.*[11]

In the end, the general resolution committee of the congress again endorsed the bottled-in-bond act as a pure food measure. Although the resolution was weaker than the resolution of the previous year, which had declared bottled-in-bond to be the only pure whiskey, Hough now realized that Wiley was behind the tactics to discredit rectified whiskey manufacturers. Although Wiley denied this, he stated his full agreement with the resolution. The fight had begun.[12]

More Whiskey

Shortly after the conference, Wiley was interviewed by the *Chicago American.* In the interview, he claimed that 85 to 95 percent of the whiskey sold in the United States was spurious and that the manufacturers of this imitation whiskey were the power behind opposition to pure food legislation. He branded rectified whiskey manufacturers as the enemies of pure and wholesome food for Americans. In truth, these manufacturers merely opposed legislation that discriminated against them. When the National Wholesale Liquor Dealers Association held its annual meeting in the fall of 1904, it voted to support pure food legislation and objected only to the provisions that discriminated against rectified whiskey. In a series of letters to Wiley in October and November, Hough attempted to explain the association's position. At one point, Hough wrote:

> I agree with you, that it is a deception which should be prohibited, to brand a Bourbon whiskey as a Rye whiskey, or to assert that a whiskey is not a blend when in fact it is a blend, or to say that whiskey is ten years old when in fact it is only five years old, but it is an equal deception for you or any of the distillers interested in the bottled-in-bond goods to attempt to create the impression upon the public, that the stamp on bottled-in-bond goods guarantees either the quality or purity of whiskey, when you know, or should know, that it guarantees neither, and under that stamp can be sold a distillate which is many times worse than any concoction which can be put up by a bartender in the lowest dive in any city.[13]

Wiley, of course, did know that the revenue stamp was not a guarantee quality. He had so testified before Congress in 1904, saying, "The Government's stamp does guarantee purity in respect of the origin of the whiskey and its supervision by the government, but of course it does not guarantee . . . that it is pure in the sense of wholesomeness." However, in singling out the rectified whiskey industry for attack, Wiley displayed a shrewd strategic instinct. The industry was not looked on favorably by much of the public, and Wiley knew that he could exploit its poor image to his own advantage. "As it now stands it is the opinion of the public that if the bill is defeated it will be through the interests which you represent and you know as well as I that such an opinion prevailing in the public mind will not increase the regard in which your organization is held by the public at large," he wrote to E. T. Fleming, secretary of the National Wholesale Liquor Dealers Association.[14]

In the months that followed, Wiley and the rectified whiskey industry battled for public opinion. Using his contacts with muckraking magazines, Wiley attacked what he called "the Whiskey Trust," claiming that it was opposed to pure food and the public interest. The industry countered by criticizing Wiley's opinions on whiskey and publicizing the connections between Wiley, Allen, and the straight whiskey producers. R. M. Allen suffered more from the publicity than Wiley. When Jackson Tinker, a journalist for *Public Opinion*, disclosed the financial support that straight whiskey manufacturers had provided to Allen for the St. Louis congress, Allen was forced to give up any hopes for a Washington job should pure food legislation pass.[15] Still, the publicity made Wiley himself an issue in the passage of legislation. In December 1904, Nelson Aldrich, the most powerful man in the Senate, delivered one of his few speeches on the floor: "Are we going to take up the question as to what a man shall eat and what a man shall drink, and put him under severe penalties if he is eating or drinking something different from what the chemists of the Agriculture Department think is desirable?" This thinly veiled reference to Wiley reflected Aldrich's belief that Wiley was imposing his opinions on the public. Aldrich's opposition effectively killed any hope of a bill passing the Senate in the final session of the 58th Congress.[16]

For the moment, it seemed as if Wiley's strategy had failed. The confrontations at the International Pure Food Congress and the exchanges of accusations in the press had hurt his cause. He appeared opinionated. Hough's threat in January 1905 to sue him for improperly influencing the St. Louis congress did not improve his image. Hough struck again in April after a speech to the Chemistry Club in New York. Following the speech, Hough and several well-known chemists in the audience accused Wiley of practicing "yellow journalism" and, worse yet for a scientist, "yellow chemistry." They charged him with using his influence with straight whiskey producers to manipulate the endorsement of straight whiskey by the St. Louis congress. Reports of the Chemistry Club meeting appeared in newspapers throughout the country.

Indeed, in the early months of 1905, newspaper and magazine articles often criticized Wiley for including whiskey in the provisions of the Hepburn–McCumber bill. Arguing that whiskey drinkers neither needed nor deserved the protection of a national law, *Collier's Weekly* maintained that distilled beverages should be dropped from the legislation. The controversy worried Wiley who, knowing that Secretary Wilson did not like government employees publicly influencing legislation, feared that he might be dismissed from his post.[17]

Wilson was particularly sensitive about negative press reports in 1905. Several scandals, including the sale of inside information on crop reports and corruption within the Bureau of Animal Industry, had brought the Department of Agriculture under intense scrutiny by the press. However, the scandals elsewhere within the Department of Agriculture worked to Wiley's advantage. Wiley had continued his campaign for favorable public opinion. He had supplied Henry Beach Needham, a journalist for *World's Work*, with information for an article entitled "The Senate of Special Interests," which appeared in January 1906. The primary villains of Needham's article, which accused the Senate of obstructing the Hepburn–McCumber bill, were the manufacturers of rectified whiskey. Needham created the image of a heroic Wiley standing alone against dishonest businessmen and

corrupt politicians, including Nelson Aldrich. Other journalists also condemned Aldrich and other senators who opposed pure food legislation. A
few months earlier, Edward Lowery, another *World's Work* journalist, had
accused these senators of representing special interests, especially rectified
whiskey interests, and of working behind the scenes to kill the Hepburn–
McCumber bill. R. M. Allen publicized a letter sent to members of the
National Wholesale Liquor Dealers. The letter said that the association had
defeated discriminatory pure food legislation, which prompted the prohibi-
tionists, especially the Women's Christian Temperance Union, to enter the
fray. The WCTU began to lobby for pure food legislation. With all this
favorable publicity and support, the dismissal of Wiley from the Department
of Agriculture probably would have been viewed by the public as further
proof that Wilson's department was corrupt.[18]

A series of articles on proprietary drugs in the *Ladies' Home Journal* and
Collier's also worked to Wiley's advantage. The articles revealed the contents
of patent medicines and emphasized the harm that these ingredients could
inflict. The publicity the articles engendered increased the involvement of
women's groups across the country in the campaign against drugs. Wiley,
who had earlier worked to exclude patent medicines from the Hepburn–
McCumber bill, now enthusiastically endorsed their inclusion and coordi-
nated his efforts with the American Medical Association, which was opposed
to patent medicines.[19]

Dissenters in the Ranks

The popular press was not the only battlefront. The National Association of
State Food and Dairy Officials continued to reflect in microcosm the struggle that was taking place across the nation. The association's 1903 convention, like the International Pure Food Congress, had been dominated by
Wiley and the straight whiskey interests. By 1905, however, the opposition
was prepared to fight back, and the start of the battle can be seen in the
advertisements contained in the published proceedings of the 1903 and 1904
conferences. The proceedings of the 1903 annual conference were published
in 1904, and advertisements for straight whiskey dominate the publication.
The proceedings of the 1904 annual conference were published in 1905, and
advertisements for blended and rectified whiskeys dominate the publication.
This change in advertisements was effected by Herbert B. Meyers, a former
food official turned publisher, who was charged with finding advertisers to
cover the cost of publication.[20]

At the time of the 1905 convention in Portland, Oregon, Wiley was in

Europe. Because two of his strongest allies, M. A. Scovell and William Frear, did not attend the convention, it was left to R. M. Allen to provide leadership for the Wiley coalition. Allen was handicapped by his well-publicized alliance with the straight whiskey industry. The connection had reflected badly on the national association, and some members thought it had been a mistake to allow the organization to choose sides in a conflict between competing business interests. In an effort to improve the association's image, members decided not to accept advertising to finance publication of the proceedings. They also decided to exclude commercial interests from the convention, because the 1904 conference had left the impression that commercial self-interest was creating the demand for pure food legislation.[21]

The absence of commercial representatives may have eased criticism but it did not eliminate conflict at the convention. The most serious issue concerned the setting of food standards. E. N. Eaton, chairman of the association's food standards committee, addressed the convention at length. He criticized the standards set by the Association of Official Agricultural Chemists for the Department of Agriculture. He pointed out that many of the standards were unrealistic, some were in error, and many others were not practical enough to be used by state food officials. This had happened, according to Eaton, because agricultural chemists did not understand food chemistry. They might be able to judge cattle or analyze fertilizer, but they were not experts on food and they did not have the expertise of state officials, who analyzed food daily. Although the Agriculture Appropriations Act for 1902 called for the secretary of agriculture to consult with the Association of Official Agricultural Chemists and other experts, Eaton noted that no other experts had been called. The reason for this, he alleged, was Wiley. It was Wiley, Eaton pointed out, who oversaw the investigations and dominated the Association of Official Agricultural Chemists. Indeed, over half of the association's members worked for the Department of Agriculture. As permanent secretary for the association, Wiley scheduled the association's meetings in Washington, D.C., and set the agenda for those meetings. The standards set by the association's committee, Eaton said, were nothing more than Wiley's personal opinions.[22]

Having condemned Wiley's dominance as one-man rule by someone with no practical experience in administering food laws, Eaton went on to say it would be a mistake for state officials to accept the association's standards as binding. Congress, he argued, recognized this in the 1905 Agricultural Appropriation Act, when it removed the clause that said the standards were for "the guidance of the officials of the various states and of the courts of justice." Eaton proposed that state officials establish their own

standards rather than accept those promulgated by the secretary of agriculture. Although Allen attempted to stop this effort, he failed, and Eaton was
charged with forming a committee to establish standards for state officials.[23]

The conflict between Wiley and this dissident group of state food
officials would escalate in January 1906 when the first issue of the *American
Food Journal* was published. The editor of the journal was Herbert B. Meyers, the same former food official who had permitted advertisements for
blended and rectified whiskeys in the publication of the 1904 proceedings of
the national association. Meyers announced that the purposes of the journal
were to provide manufacturers with information and guidance on various
food laws and to assist state food officials with the enforcement of these
laws. By publishing the proceedings of the annual convention, the journal
posed as the quasi-official publication of the National Association of State
Food and Dairy Officials. It carried news items concerning the activities of
various state officials and was staunchly anti-Wiley, opposing any law that
would give him additional power. Wiley responded vigorously. He claimed
that the National Wholesale Liquor Dealers Association, the glucose trust,
and other "poisoners and adulterators" were behind the journal.[24]

It was not only among state food and dairy officials that dissension
appeared. By the summer of 1905, those in favor of and those against
national legislation were making hyperbolic accusations and dire prognosti-
cations. Doom, destruction, and death were predicted if no national law
were passed, or if Wiley and his supporters were made dictators of the
American diet. The hyperbole and doomsaying drew the public's attention
to national legislation. Firms that stood to gain or lose from uniform laws or
from a renewed public trust in food products also became more actively
involved.[25]

By and large, women's groups favored legislation but not necessarily
Wiley's version of it. Alice Lakey, Wiley's surrogate voice, and her Consumers League were not representative of women's groups in general. The
home economics movement and the new nutrition movement included far
more members than Lakey's Consumers League. The home economics
movement had been founded by Mary Hinman Abel, who had also co-
founded (with Ellen Richards) the New England Kitchen. Abel was a leader
of the new nutrition movement. In a yearlong series in *The Delineator,* a
leading women's magazine edited by Theodore Dreiser, she presented a
well-reasoned case for pure food legislation. She argued for honest labels
and a better educated consumer. While she believed that some regulation
was needed, she felt that it should only come about after further education
of the consumer, who should ultimately decide which laws were needed.
She had a low opinion of the debate in Congress and an even lower opinion

of the claims of the sensational press. Her thoughtful series of articles, which contained none of the exaggerations of the muckrakers, called for a food bill that did not serve special commercial interests.[26]

The majority of women probably did favor some kind of food legislation. Exhausted by the "tyranny of the kitchen" and probably somewhat bewildered by the variety of foods that were becoming available, they undoubtedly wanted more assurance that the foods they used were healthful and wholesome. It is doubtful, however, that they shared Wiley's opinions regarding sugar, saccharin, corn syrup, preservatives, caffeine, or whiskey. Wiley gained what support he had from women by creating an image of himself as a man standing against giant trusts and corrupt politicians, ever-popular targets of Progressive politicians and the muckraking press. He created this impression by deliberately concealing his own relationships with commercial interests that would benefit from his proposed legislation.

A Law at Last

While R. M. Allen was under attack at the annual convention of state food and dairy officials in Portland, Wiley was in England investigating the production of Scotch and Irish whiskeys. There he discovered, much to his surprise, that the fusel oil (the amyl, butyl, and propyl alcohols) was not oxidized during the aging process. He had testified before Congress that barrel-aged whiskey was purified by the oxidation of fusel oil. He had even proposed an upper limit on the amount of fusel oil that straight whiskey could contain, based on his assumption that the fusel oil was oxidized. But he had never bothered to run experiments to see what happened to fusel oil during the aging process. Now he discovered that straight whiskey contained more impurities than rectified whiskey. At this point, had his main concern been the healthfulness of the product, Wiley should have changed his opinion on the relative merits of straight and rectified whiskeys. It was common knowledge that the alcohols that comprised fusel oil were far more poisonous than ethyl alcohol. Instead, he chose to reformulate his argument in favor of straight whiskey. In testimony before the House Committee on Agriculture to testify on the appropriation bill for the next fiscal year, he said:

> I formerly held—and it is only recently that I have changed my view—
> that I believed in the aging of whiskies it was the so-called fusel oils—
> that is, higher alcohol—that were oxidized. I was altogether mistaken
> in that, and I want to state to this committee that fact. Those elements

which are oxidized are of that form which are known as aldehydes, etc.
Fusel oils are not highly poisonous as has been stated heretofore. The
poisonous properties of freshly distilled liquors are not due to the
alcohols (like amyl alcohol) which are present in very small proportion.
In a pure state they are not injurious. Alcohols are all poisonous. Of
course in one sense even amyl alcohol is poisonous. Straight liquor
contains all these volatile products, some of them changed by aging.
The imitated liquor contains pure spirits, mixed with anything that
they choose to flavor it with, adding prune juice, etc., and some of
those mixtures are not injurious substances, but they make a compound which is totally different, chemically and physiologically, from
the real article."[27]

Besides denying a widely accepted truth—that amyl, butyl, and propyl
alcohols are more poisonous than ethyl alcohol—Wiley's testimony implied
that he preferred a product with a small amount of poison (amyl alcohol) to a
product with a small amount of a healthful additive (prune juice). His attempts to clarify matters did not help. When asked how to tell the difference
between straight and rectified whiskey, Wiley answered, "If it [rectified whis-
key] contained all the elements that nature adds, the chemist would be at sea.
But then the connoisseur comes to your help. You get a product that does not
taste like the natural product; and if you did have one that tasted like the
natural product, then the physiologist comes to your help. It does not have
the same physiological effect." However, he offered no evidence that straight
whiskey differed in its physiological effects from rectified whiskey.[28]
    Warwick Hough, who was fast becoming Wiley's arch-nemesis, testified
before the same appropriations committee. In his testimony, he asked the
committee to withdraw the Department of Agriculture's authority to establish standards for foods, which had been granted in previous appropriations
bills, and recommended the creation of a board of experts from outside the
department to study foods and make recommendations. He criticized Wiley
and Allen for using undue influence in an attempt to have state officials adopt
their standards. He reported that state food officials at the Portland conference had rebelled against Wiley's control, and he told how Allen was promised a job in Washington but had been forced to withdraw because of the
publicity surrounding his involvement with straight whiskey manufacturers.
In an acrimonious exchange with Hough, Wiley denied these accusations, but
the committee withdrew the Department of Agriculture's authority to establish food standards.[29]
    This was a heavy blow to Wiley. If he could not set standards, his ability
to regulate would be substantially diminished. Wiley wrote to William Frear,

"I do not think any more vicious thing ever happened in modern history of American legislation than this and yet no member of Congress was found to raise his voice in opposition thereto." Because the authority to fix standards would remain until the end of the fiscal year, however, he could still exert his influence if he moved quickly.[30]

In the fall of 1905, Wiley had sent Edmund Taylor a copy of the proposed standards for whiskey. "I beg you," he had written, "to consider the enclosed proposed definition and standards for whiskey and see if it meets with your approval." Taylor had been slow to respond, and whiskey standards were not yet set when the standards committee met in Boston in November. Now, Wiley was in a rush to have them adopted before his authority ended. His rush stopped abruptly, however, when a pure food bill was taken up by the Senate.[31]

The Senate Acts

Although things had not gone well for Wiley during the agricultural appropriation hearings, the attention paid to the issue of pure food by the press had made it popular and thus improved the prospects for legislation in 1906. These prospects became even brighter when Roosevelt endorsed the need for it in his State of the Union address that year. Roosevelt had failed to do so the previous year even though Senator Heyburn had requested it. In February of that year, a committee of state food officials, led by R. M. Allen, had called on Roosevelt and had again urged him to press for legislation. Roosevelt had promised to look into the matter and had invited the committee to visit him in the fall. Over the next few months, Roosevelt had made inquiries of Wiley, Ira Remsen (a noted chemist and the president of Johns Hopkins University), and others. When the committee had returned in the fall, Roosevelt had informed it that he would recommend legislation in his next annual address to Congress.[32]

Perhaps more important than Roosevelt's address was the pressure the Senate now faced because of what historian Richard McCormick has called "the discovery that business corrupts politics." Graham Philips's *Treason of the Senate* and Henry Beach Needham's "The Senate of Special Interests" had linked senators with commercial interests, including the rectified whiskey industry. The failure of the Hepburn–McCumber bill was attributed to their corruption. Faced with this kind of pressure and knowing that the majority of the public, and most business firms, wanted pure food legislation, the members of the Senate realized they had to act. They also knew, however, that Wiley attracted both strong support and intense opposition. A reluctance to embody Wiley's one-sided opinions in law led them to pass a

bill that was noncommittal on many of the issues Wiley believed to be vital
and diminished the authority he could wield. Under the bill's provisions, the
regulation of patent medicines was limited to the accurate labeling of their
ingredients, and the definition of whiskey was broadened. The law was to be
jointly administered by the secretaries of commerce, treasury, and agriculture, rather than by the secretary of agriculture alone, and like the House's
appropriation bill, there was no provision for the establishment of standards
by the executive branch.[33]

Senator Aldrich, who had previously opposed the Hepburn–McCumber
bill, let it be known that the bill would be considered if Senator Heyburn
introduced it in the Senate. Historians have never adequately explained Aldrich's change of heart. Twenty years after the bill's passage, Senator Albert J.
Beveridge said that he thought Aldrich wanted to clear the agenda to make
room for bigger battles and to put the responsibility for killing the bill in the
House. Beveridge's proposition seems doubtful. The House, then as now, was
more sensitive to public opinion than the Senate, and Aldrich must have
known that it was likely to pass the bill, as it had done in previous years. It
seems more likely that Aldrich, wanting to get rid of a politically troublesome
bill, decided to pass the problem along to the administration and the courts.[34]

The Senate did not hold committee hearings on the bill, but various
provisions were debated on the floor in mid-February. A substitute bill that
conceded everything to the opponents of Wiley was defeated, and an amendment that allowed the addition of coloring to blended whiskey was adopted.
The bill was finally voted on and passed the Senate 63 to 4, with 22 senators
abstaining. Even in its weakened form, its passage was welcomed by Wiley,
who knew that passage by the Senate meant that legislation had a better
chance than ever.[35]

House Controversies

The key disputes concerning the bill were aired in the hearings held by the
House Committee on Interstate and Foreign Commerce. Because pure food
bills had passed the House in the two previous Congresses, it was anticipated
that the bill would receive favorable consideration. Wiley promptly met with
Congressman Mann, hoping to restore provisions that would strengthen his
hand. However, opposition to Wiley's authority had continued to grow and
was now the major impediment to the bill's passage. Although nearly everyone who testified favored some sort of legislation, many of them opposed
what they saw as discriminatory measures. They distrusted Wiley and resisted
placing enforcement in his hands.[36]

The American Medical Association's Committee on Medical Legislation emerged as an influential lobbyist for Wiley during the final days of debate in the Senate. Wiley had worked with the Association through Dr. Charles A. L. Reed, chairman of the legislation committee and past president of the association, and George Simmons, editor of the *Journal of the American Medical Association*. In the spring of 1905, Simmons and Reed had used the *Journal's* pages to defend Wiley against his critics. Each had attacked *What to Eat* and *Public Opinion* when these publications had criticized Wiley's association with straight whiskey firms. Wiley accepted the association's lobbying support but, at the same time, remained firm in his desire not to antagonize the patent medicine industry. Thus, he worked to temper the association's position on patent medicines. Writing to Simmons in February 1906, he suggested that members of the association should be asked about the efficacy of certain remedies but added, "At the same time, we want to avoid any censure that might obtain to the effect that we are in collusion in a determination to eradicate these products." Although Wiley wanted to avoid antagonizing the patent medicine industry as a whole, he was quite willing to fight firms who were opposed to the food and drugs bill. Responding to Simmons's inquiry about Notobac and Murine, Wiley replied that he would investigate them and wrote, "I think that this ought to be done particularly with 'Murine' because the proprietor of this product appeared before the Interstate and Foreign Commerce Committee giving reasons why the Heyburn bill should not become a law."[37]

Wiley advocated eliminating patent medicines from the House bill entirely, just as he had recommended dropping them from the Senate bill two years earlier. He also wanted lenient labeling provisions that would require producers to list the amounts of alcohol, cocaine, opium, and other drugs on the label, but would not outlaw them. Although Wiley wanted to benefit from the previous year's uproar over patent medicines, he did not want to openly challenge another powerful interest group.[38]

Wiley's attitude toward whiskey differed markedly from his attitude toward patent medicines. He was determined to legally sanction straight whiskey as the only genuine product. In theatrical testimony during the House hearings, Wiley used chemical apparatus to demonstrate how pure ethyl alcohol could be colored and flavored to produce whiskey. The demonstration, which received wide attention in the press, misled both congressmen and the public. Rectified whiskey was not produced by coloring alcohol. In fact, pure ethyl alcohol was more highly refined than any whiskey, straight or rectified, and thus too expensive to use for a whiskey. Moreover, a great deal of whiskey under discussion was produced by mixing straight and rectified whiskeys in varying proportions. The combinations in which these whiskeys could be blended varied widely, and many blends were excellent products. Although Wiley was a connoisseur of whiskey, even he could not always tell a straight from a rectified whiskey. For many years, he had accepted gifts of Green River Whiskey, assuming it was a straight whiskey. On hearing a rumor that it was a blend, he wrote an irate letter to the distiller saying he was "startled to learn that Green River whiskey was not a straight whiskey." As a matter of fact, Green River was a straight whiskey, but Wiley was unable to tell the difference.[39]

As a part of his campaign against rectified whiskey, Wiley asked Reed to testify that only straight whiskey should be used for medical prescriptions and that blended whiskeys should be "marked so that they can be easily known and thus excluded from prescriptions of physicians." Such testimony would make straight whiskey appear to be the more wholesome product. Wiley also contacted Edmund Taylor to propose submitting a bill that would place a tax on rectified whiskey similar to the tax on oleomargarine.[40]

The manufacturers of rectified whiskey resisted Wiley's efforts on behalf of straight whiskey. They objected to the provision in the bill that required them to list added ingredients. Afraid that an administrative ruling by Wiley would require them to label their product "imitation whiskey," they lobbied for an amendment that would allow them to call their product compounded or blended whiskey and that would permit the addition of coloring and flavor. They also tried to limit the power of the Department of Agriculture to make rules and set standards.

They were not the only ones to question Wiley's judgment and fairness. Acting as spokesman for state food officials who felt that Wiley was attempting to build a national organization that would dominate state organizations, the *American Food Journal* vigorously attacked Wiley in cartoons, editorials, and articles. The officials sponsored an alternative bill that was introduced by Congressman William Lorimer of Illinois. Under its provisions, it would be illegal to ship out of state any food that it was illegal to sell within the state. It also banned the shipment of any food into a state that violated the laws of that state. Regulatory authority was placed firmly in the hands of state officials. The bill was never taken seriously, except perhaps by a few backers at the *American Food Journal*. It was a part of an overall attempt to limit the authority given to the Department of Agriculture, and hence to Wiley.[41]

A more serious attempt to curb Wiley's authority occurred when E. N. Eaton, chairman of the association's food standards committee, convened a meeting in Chicago to challenge the Department of Agriculture's standards at the same time that Wiley was testifying before the House Committee on Agriculture. When asked about Eaton's opposition to the Department of Agriculture standards, Wiley replied that the only opposition to the standards came from those "interested in breaking them down for sinister purposes." He attacked Eaton personally and suggested that he should be dismissed from his position in Illinois for the good of the public. The *Chicago Tribune,* a strong supporter of Wiley, launched a campaign to have Eaton dismissed. The success of the campaign added fuel to the accusations of autocratic rule.[42]

The proposed amendment on standards seriously threatened Wiley's authority. The amendment, which was sponsored by manufacturers who used preservatives, would have set up a committee of experts to rule on standards for preservatives. Wiley for some time had wanted to restrict the use of preservatives and, having learned that H. J. Heinz could produce catsup without using preservatives, had recently called for their elimination. During the hearings, he testified that his investigations with the poison squad had convinced him that even small amounts of preservatives were dangerous to human health. This testimony was not entirely accurate. The poison squad experiments had begun in 1902, but his unqualified condemnation of preservatives did not occur until 1906 when he was informed that Heinz could produce a catsup without benzoate of soda, the preservative most frequently used in catsup. Wiley was also not forthright about his connections with Heinz. At the hearings, he said that he did not know anyone from Heinz. He had, however, corresponded with the company and, in all likelihood, had met Heinz's representatives at conventions of the National Association of State Food and Dairy Officials.[43]

In his testimony, Wiley assumed (incorrectly) that Heinz had eliminated the need for preservatives through heat sterilization. He went on to say how all catsup products could be treated this way, but he acknowledged that once opened to the air, they would spoil quickly. He proposed to solve this problem with a special valve that would sterilize the air before it entered the bottle by passing it through treated cotton. Fortunately, this totally impractical idea was never mandated by law, or the American public would still be waiting for its catsup to pour.[44]

The leading proponent of the continued use of preservatives was Walter Williams, a Detroit manufacturer of condiments and pickles. Testifying before the committee, he explained how and why he used benzoate of soda. He argued that it was necessary to keep his products from spoiling and said that he had heard of a catsup free of preservatives but that he doubted its existence. Williams went on to point out that if such a product did exist and the government outlawed the use of benzoate of soda, it would perforce create a monopoly. Williams brought Victor Vaughan, an eminent physician, to the hearings to testify that benzoate of soda was safe. Vaughan also advocated the establishment of a special board with a broad scientific background to judge the wholesomeness of food. "I must say," he testified, "with all due respect to agriculture chemists of this country, many of whom are great men and doing splendid work, that men who are engaged all their lives in assaying soils and estimating the value of fertilizers are not fitted by education to determine the effect of anything on the animal body."[45]

Wiley did not openly confront Vaughan's criticism. Instead, he worked behind the scenes with Secretary Wilson and Charles Reed. In the end, arguing that the board would undermine the authority of the secretary of agriculture, Wiley succeeded, and the provision for the board was eliminated in the conference committee after passing the House.[46] In the interim, however, Reed's opposition to the board brought him into conflict with Vaughan, who also objected to the editorials in the *Journal of the American Medical Association* that opposed the board. The conflict was only temporary, and soon the *Journal*'s editorials were again supporting Wiley.[47]

Beyond what Wiley told them, Reed and Simmons may not have understood the legislation very well. At one point, they supported legislation that contained the weaker definition of drugs. Although they blamed their erroneous position on misleading information put out by the proprietary drug industry, had they been well informed on the provisions in the bill, this would not have happened. In all likelihood, the members of the American Medical Association were even less cognizant of the contents and ramifications of the bills than were Reed and Simmons. Most physicians probably supported the general idea of regulation and relied on the information they were given by Wiley through Reed and Simmons.[48]

Passage

To Wiley's frustration, after the hearings, the pure food bill stalled in the House. He had believed that the forces that were pushing the passage of a meat inspection act would also lead to the passage of a pure food act, but the meat inspection bill was moving smoothly through Congress and the pure food bill was not. Moreover, the agricultural appropriation bill, which eliminated the provision to establish standards, had passed. For a short time, it seemed as if not only would the food bill fail but that the existing activities of his bureau would be eliminated.

All of this changed within a few days. In early June, Wiley wrote Allen that he had just received word that Joseph G. Cannon, the Speaker of the House, was not and never had been opposed to the bill. There was little doubt, Wiley wrote, that the bill would pass. On 23 June, the bill passed the House and was sent to conference, where it was reconciled with the Senate bill. On 27 June, the conference committee reported a bill that, although weaker than

Wiley wanted, gave more power to him than his opponents wished. The bill was signed into law on 30 June.[49]

Historians have devoted considerable attention to why the bill passed in 1906 but not earlier. It has been argued that President Roosevelt intervened with Speaker Cannon to push the bill through. There is no evidence, however, that Cannon was holding the bill back. Indeed, there is reason to believe that Cannon favored bringing the bill forward. Speaking for the public record during an appropriations hearing several years later, Cannon claimed that the bill was essentially nonpartisan. He said that he had always intended to bring the bill forward in 1906 and that it had not come to the floor immediately only because of the normal delays of House procedure. His statements seem credible because a pure food bill had passed the House in the two previous sessions. He also said that he had been criticized by pro-Wiley newspapers, such as the *Chicago Tribune,* when the bill was delayed. Indeed, he claimed that he had received threats of assassination. Although the personal element in these remarks may have been exaggerated, the overall message, that Cannon favored the bill despite the beliefs of Wiley supporters, seems accurate.[50]

Cannon's claims were confirmed by Congressman Mann, who worked with Wiley on the passage of the law. Mann said that the Speaker had assured him he would use all his influence to see that the bill was considered. Writing to Wiley in 1912, six years after the bill was passed, Mann said that President Roosevelt had never brought pressure to bear on a reluctant Speaker of the House. It is true that Roosevelt sent a note to Cannon near the end of May, urging that the bill be passed, but according to Cannon, the letter was unnecessary; there was never any doubt the bill would come up for a vote and pass the House.[51] It was, after all, in the interest of Congress to pass it. Wiley and the muckrakers were portraying its members as corrupt and selfish, pawns in the hands of big business. The passage of the bill would help to dilute that criticism. However, because they were pressured so heavily from various sides, members were not going to pass a law that was conspicuously weighted toward one faction or another. Instead, they passed a rather vague law that was more or less balanced and left it to the courts and the executive branch to contend with the divisive issues.

Historians have commonly believed that the impact of Upton Sinclair's *The Jungle,* which described the filth of the slaughterhouses, helped to push through not only the Meat Inspection Act but also the Pure Food and Drugs Act. However, Sinclair's novel made its impact only after the Senate had already passed a pure food bill, and the Senate had always been the stumbling block to the bill. The reaction to *The Jungle* no doubt helped to create an atmosphere favorable to legislation, but the Pure Food and Drugs Act would have passed anyway. Moreover, the passage of the meat inspection bill would have been enough to quiet the public dissatisfaction resulting from *The Jungle*. Meat was one of the main items in the American diet; but the foods most affected by the Pure Food and Drugs Act were marginal to the diet. Thus, the sentiments and political pressures behind the two bills were largely independent of one another, and so was passage. A pure food bill passed in 1906 because most food manufacturers and distributors wanted a national law. In one way or another, it would be to their benefit. Although some firms, such as Heinz or Royal Baking Powder or Old Taylor, received a competitive advantage from regulation, many firms simply wanted uniform regulations. The variety of state laws was often a nuisance for national producers. Furthermore, the publicity resulting from the hyperbole of pure food propaganda was taking its toll on consumer confidence. The government's stamp of approval on food products would help to restore confidence.[52]

The law passed, too, because of Wiley's indefatigable promotion of it. However, his reasons for promoting the law had less to do with the public interest than with building up his bureau. For twenty years prior to the pure food campaign, he had fought to increase the size and importance of the Bureau of Chemistry. His involvement in the Pure Food and Drugs Act was a continuation of these efforts. His methods of securing passage of the law were scarcely more praiseworthy than the methods of those against whom he fought. In every major conflict in which he was involved, Wiley was tied to commercial interests. He secretly conspired with Edmund Taylor and other manufacturers of straight whiskey; he supported an absolute ban on benzoate of soda only after he learned that Heinz no longer needed it; and he sought to persuade Congress to drop patent medicines from the bill to avoid antagonizing a powerful industry. With methods like these, it is unlikely that the Pure Food and Drugs Act would have as its primary concern the public interest. The law did have some beneficial effects, but these were minor. The main effect of the law was to further Wiley's bureaucratic interests and the commercial interests with which he allied himself.

CHAPTER 6

Setting Food Standards by Government Regulation

The bill signed by President Roosevelt on 30 June 1906 left unresolved the large issues that had stalled it in Congress for several years. In its attempts not to take sides among producers, Congress created an ambiguous law that was vulnerable to wide interpretation. The vagueness of the law set the stage for a six-year battle in which Wiley sought to exercise broad authority and his opponents fought to circumscribe his powers.[1]

The most significant of Wiley's strengths at the time of the bill's signing was his image as the protector of America's health. In the eyes of a significant number of Americans, Wiley stood between the unsuspecting consumer and the unscrupulous businessman. This image had been fashioned by a corps of muckraking journalists and a carefully crafted campaign of publicity financed by the commercial interests that hoped to benefit from Wiley's administration of the pure food act.

Wiley Strengthens His Position

Wiley's ability to exercise his authority in administering the food law was aided by the diminished reputation of his immediate supervisor, Secretary of Agriculture Wilson. Wilson, wanting to protect the reputation of American meat exporters, downplayed the seriousness of charges made in Sinclair's *The Jungle*. Although he supported the federal inspection of meat, he was not as critical of the industry as Senator Beveridge and others. His willingness to compromise with the meat packers left him open to charges that he was lenient toward unsavory business practices.[2]

Scandals in the Department of Agriculture

A series of scandals that erupted in the Department of Agriculture in 1905 had begun the erosion of Wilson's reputation. The most serious of these was the discovery that crop estimates were being leaked prior to their official release date. An investigation prompted by complaints from the Southern Cotton

Growers Association uncovered the scheme. Using his window shades to send signals, Edwin S. Holmes, a statistician in the department, had been leaking advanced information to crop speculators for several years. Holmes and his associates had reaped substantial profits in the commodities markets in this way. Although he suspended Holmes, Wilson did not fire him. Instead, he tried to divert attention away from the Department of Agriculture by pointing to the crop speculators. His clumsy efforts to protect his department and the chief of the Bureau of Statistics, John Hyde, left the impression that he was interfering the investigation. As a result, the Southern Cotton Growers Association accused him of covering up in order to protect himself and Hyde. Although the press also accused Wilson and his son Jasper, who was his personal secretary, of being involved in the scandal, there was never any evidence to support the accusation. The accusations were nevertheless a source of concern to Roosevelt. When Hyde eventually resigned, and Wilson and his son went on a tour of the western forests, thus removing them from involvement in the investigation, Roosevelt expressed his relief.[3]

The crop statistics scandal opened other bureaus in the department to scrutiny. Willis Moore, chief of the weather bureau, was rumored to live well beyond his means and to have accumulated a personal fortune in spite of his small official salary. The press accused him of spending government funds for his own personal use and cited as an example his construction of a lavish summer home at Mount Weather, Virginia. The accusations against Moore were not proven, and he was not dismissed, but Wilson was severely criticized for his lack of control over his subordinates.[4]

A greater blow to Wilson's reputation than the scandals involving Holmes, Hyde, or Moore was the forced resignation of Dr. Daniel E. Salmon, who had been chief of the Bureau of Animal Industry since 1870. The *New York Herald* reported that Salmon was a partner in the George E. Howard Printing Company, which held contract with the Bureau of Animal Industry to print meat inspection labels. Salmon apparently had advanced start-up funds to Howard and had held shares in the company for some time. Although he had sold the shares several years before the *Herald*'s revelations, Roosevelt felt that Salmon's actions were improper and should be punished. Salmon quickly resigned and, with Wilson's help, found a position as head of the veterinary program at the University of Montevideo in Uruguay.

While these scandals created doubts about Wilson's abilities as an administrator and the integrity of his organization, they did not seriously threaten his position. Even when the Keep Commission's report concluded in 1905 that Wilson could not properly control his department, it was not a serious threat to him; he was too popular with farmers.[5] Still, he could not afford a public confrontation with the popular Dr. Wiley, nor could he afford to investigate any conflicts of interest that Wiley as the administrator of the Pure Food and Drugs Act might have because of his close connections with straight whiskey and sugar interests. To have done so would have left Wilson open to still more attacks on his administrative abilities. He had to find other ways to control Wiley's activities.[6]

Business Interests and Family Problems

Wiley himself could have made controls by Wilson unnecessary. By the latter half of 1906, he had obtained pure food regulation and secured the future of his bureau. At this point, he could have severed his connections with business interests to become an impartial administrator of the law. He may have considered this option when he rejected a case of Green River Whiskey from J. W. McCulloch, saying that it was no longer appropriate for him to receive such gifts.[7] However, he soon reverted to his old practice of accepting minor gifts, usually from people whom he had known for some time. As a rule, the gifts created no serious conflict of interest. A gift offered by John Arbuckle, the sugar and coffee entrepreneur, however, was an exception. Wiley had worked for Arbuckle for many years on his own time. When Arbuckle was accused of selling adulterated coffee in an Ohio court case, Wiley had testified on his behalf. He frequently visited Arbuckle when in New York and also entertained Arbuckle in Washington. At one time, Arbuckle had offered to start a pure food company and place Wiley at its head. Although Wiley turned down the offer, he kept discussions open until Arbuckle's death in 1912.[8] In February 1907, while Wiley was out, Arbuckle entered his office and left a package. A note in the package read:

> Doctor,
> As officials are not paid what they deserve please accept the enclosed for helping me . . . I hope you will accept this in the spirit it is given as you do not realize what a help you can be to me in my hobbies."[9]

Wiley responded on 19 March, saying he wanted to see Arbuckle about "a matter concerning which I cannot very well write. It relates to one of the documents you left with me when you were last here." On 11 June, Wiley wrote Arbuckle again, saying that he must return the gift but suggesting another way in which Arbuckle could help and he could benefit in a "pecuniary sense."[10]

Arbuckle had earlier suggested the establishment of a sugar trade laboratory to be headed by a chemist of recognized ability, who would arbitrate the disputes between sellers and buyers of raw sugar over the purity of the sugar they were exchanging. These disputes had been going on for years. Each side would have the sugar examined by its own chemists, who frequently disagreed about the quality of the sugar they were analyzing. Arbuckle had contacted Wiley for assistance in setting up such an organization, and the result was the creation of the New York Sugar Trade Laboratory. Wiley worked as a consultant to the laboratory and was given the authority to choose the laboratory's chemist. He selected Charles A. Browne, who was then the head of the sugar laboratory in the Bureau of Chemistry. It was through these consulting activities that Wiley saw a way to obtain pecuniary benefits. He suggested to Arbuckle that he should be paid $10,000 for heading up this effort. There are no financial records to verify that he received the $10,000, but after 1907 there was a definite improvement in his financial position.[11]

If nothing else, the establishment of the New York Sugar Trade Laboratory offered employment for Wiley's nephew, Maxwell. Max Wiley had been a problem for some time. He had refused Wiley's offer of financial support to attend college but still wanted his uncle to help him find employment. Finding suitable employment for Max was no easy task; he had either quit or performed unsatisfactorily in every position that Wiley had helped him to obtain. Despite his lack of qualifications, Max, who was temporarily employed in the Bureau of Chemistry at the time that the sugar laboratory was established, was one of the laboratory's first employees. Although he apparently performed his work well, Max misappropriated some of the laboratory's funds. When told of the misappropriation by Charles Browne, Wiley repaid the funds and broke off all contact with his nephew. However, Max was not fired and eventually paid back the money and reconciled with his uncle.[12]

Similar relationships, if less obviously beneficial to him financially, existed between Wiley and the straight whiskey industry and between Wiley and the H. J. Heinz Company. These relationships would grow stronger during the early years of Wiley's administration of the pure food law. Although both President Roosevelt and Secretary Wilson were aware of Wiley's close ties to these commercial interests, his reputation and popularity kept them from openly confronting him. Wilson himself was not above reproach in 1906 and 1907, although he had weathered the scandals that had rocked his department in 1905. Wilson openly favored the agricultural business. He disliked anything that cast a bad light on U.S. agricultural products; he feared the loss of export sales. He did not, however, favor one particular segment of the food industry over another. He considered it his job to protect the food industry as a whole, and he did so. Roosevelt did not want to challenge Wiley's popularity, of which he was well aware. He knew that Wiley had established an effective political machine that was capable of bringing pressure to bear on Congress and the executive. He is reported to have told one dissatisfied businessman who wanted Wiley dismissed, "You don't understand, Sir, that Dr. Wiley has the grandest political machine in the country." Indeed, Wiley's popularity forced Secretary Wilson and presidents Roosevelt and Taft to control his activities through the roundabout use of administrative mechanisms. They would succeed only modestly.[13] It was in this atmosphere of control without open confrontation that the battles over the regulation of the food and drug industries took place.

Organizing for the Law

Before the agriculture appropriation bill for fiscal year 1906–7 had withdrawn authority from the secretary of agriculture to set food standards, Wilson had issued standards for nearly three-fourths of the items under consideration, but not for whiskey. Wiley had postponed establishing those standards for fear they would hurt the passage of the bill. Now, however, Wiley want to be sure that any standards that were established were his. Hearings were scheduled to be held in Louisville, Kentucky, later in the year.[14] The appropriation bill included a clause that authorized the secretary of agriculture, "in collaboration with the Association of Official Agriculture Chemists, and other such experts as he may deem necessary, to ascertain the purity of food products and determine what are regarded as adulterations therein." Wiley believed that this wording allowed for further investigations into food standards even if it did not allow the secretary to proclaim standards.[15]

Gaining Control of Food Standards

To continue his investigations, however, Wiley first needed to defeat a dissident group within the National Association of State Food and Dairy Officials (which temporarily had changed its name to the *Interstate* Food Commission) that had challenged the standards of the Association of Official Agricultural Chemists and contributed to the failure of the standard-setting authority in Congress. If he could defeat this group, he could gain control of the national association's standards committee. With Wilson's approval, Wiley attended the annual convention of state food and dairy officials, which convened in Hartford, Connecticut, on 17 July 1906. There, he organized a joint food standards committee made up of agricultural chemists and state food and dairy officials who were his friends and supporters.[16]

In a burning editorial, the anti-Wiley *American Food Journal* denounced the meeting and Wiley's dominance of it. The journal claimed the meeting "was absolutely servile to the will of its master. The Federal forces, led in person by Dr. H. W. Wiley, were early on the scene . . . Federal influence was everywhere dominant." It went on to say, "Dr. Wiley needs all the prestige he can get from the National Association of State Dairy and Food Departments to pull his Standards Committee out of the ditch into which it was tumbled by Congress." Although Wiley may not have had as much control at the meeting as the journal suggested, it did correctly assess the importance of controlling the standards committee.[17]

At the same time that Wiley was working to gain control over food standards, he was also involved in establishing regulations that would govern enforcement. The regulations had to be established under the joint auspices of the secretaries of agriculture, treasury, and commerce. The secretaries set up a committee to do the work. Wilson appointed Wiley and gave him the authority to act in his stead. Although Wiley attempted to influence who was appointed to the other two positions, he did not succeed in doing so. The secretary of commerce appointed S. N. D. North, director of the Bureau of the Census. The Treasury Department appointed James L. Gerry, chief of the Customs Division. In September, the three men held hearings in New York to gather information from commercial interests that wanted to appear before them. The objective of the hearings, Wiley said in his opening statement, was to obtain as much information as possible from the industries on the best methods of enforcing the law. He went on to say that in making rules and regulations it was the intent of the committee to disturb business conditions as little as possible and to create "the least possible annoyance to the manufacturer, the jobber, and the public." He was, he said, entering the hearings with an open mind.[18]

Warwick Hough, who was concerned that Wiley would slip something into the regulations against the interests of the National Wholesale Liquor Dealers Association, had secured the opportunity to speak at the hearing through the secretary of agriculture. Alerted to Hough's appearance, Wiley had written to R. M. Allen and Edmund Taylor to make sure that the straight whiskey manufacturers also appeared at the hearings, which they did. Neither side succeeded in influencing the committee. North and Gerry believed that the whiskey matter should be left to the courts; thus no regulation emerged.[19]

At the hearings, North and Gerry believed that Wiley had agreed with their position, yet a month later Wiley was publicly denouncing rectified whiskey. Angered at what they believed was a breach of good faith, the two men wrote to Wiley about his actions. Wiley responded by denying that he had agreed with their position. He had no intention of waiting for the courts to decide what was whiskey. A meeting of the recently formed joint committee on food standards was scheduled to convene in Lexington, Kentucky, in November. Wiley intended to establish the whiskey standards that he had already drafted and that Edmund Taylor had already approved. Hoping to block Wiley, Hough sent a storm of correspondence, challenging the authority under which the meeting was being held and accusing Wiley of attempting to use his influence for the benefit of the straight whiskey trust. Hough recommended standard setting by a board of college scientists who were independent of the Bureau of Chemistry.[20]

Funding the Machinery of Enforcement

After issuing regulations for the enforcement of the act, the secretaries of the Departments of Commerce and Treasury withdrew as much as possible from enforcement activities. Although they continued to sign food inspection decisions, they took no part in the procedures leading up to the issuance of these rulings, which placed the burden of enforcement on the Department of Agriculture and the Bureau of Chemistry.[21]

The Bureau of Chemistry, however, was in no position to enforce the new law effectively. Wiley had not obtained an appropriation from Congress when the act was passed. In fact, during the hearings on the bill before the Committee on Interstate and Foreign Commerce, there was little discussion on how a law would be administered or what the cost of enforcement would be. When asked what he estimated the costs of administering such a law to be, Wiley had responded that no one could tell exactly but then had said:

> As far as the chemical work is concerned, I can assure you that there will be very little, if any, increase in expenditure. We have a corps of chemists now which can take charge of all this work; and more than that, the law associates four great departments—that is, the Heyburn bill as it passed the Senate; a very good bill, I think—so that they could utilize the machinery of those departments without creating new machinery. That was the object of that. I do not believe it would take one additional inspector. I do not see any place where an inspector could do anything. I see no occasion to use one for any purpose.

> *The Chairman:* In addition to the present machinery?

> *Doctor Wiley:* The present machinery of those four great departments can care for this law. Of course there will be some little expense. I was talking with the Secretary of Agriculture. He asked me what I thought

would be the additional expense of carrying out this law and making it effective, and I told him roughly about $150,000 or $200,000 to pay every expense of every kind; and I think that is a very large estimate of what the cost would be. More than that, it would be the rarest thing in the world that any suit would be brought under the law. Just the moment this law is passed the businessmen of this country, practically all of whom are law-abiding citizens, are not going into the jaws of the law. None of them that knows anything about the law will want to do that. As soon as the law is understood and fully appreciated, they will all conform to it. We have never had a case in court in the execution of the law against foreign foods—never one. People are perfectly willing, as soon as they know the law, to conform to it, and the result is that to-day there is not a package of adulterated olive oil coming into this country, to my knowledge. And so with a great many other things, Moral Suasion does it, and that will be the case with this law.[22]

Wiley's statement turned out to be misleading in every particular. It may be that he misled the committee deliberately to improve the chances of the bill's passage, but it may also be that he was vague about what enforcement would entail; his main focus was promoting passage of the bill. However, he must have known that moral suasion would have little effect on the hotly contested issues. He certainly knew that the states' enforcement had resulted in numerous court cases. He also knew that importers did not take cases to court because it was extremely difficult to get a court hearing for imported goods; foreign producers did not have the same standing in the law as American producers.

Because Wiley had so misjudged the costs of enforcement, he was forced to go before the House Agricultural Appropriation Committee and ask for $250,000 for the remainder of the 1906–7 fiscal year, and $750,000 for the following fiscal year. Wiley planned to place the bulk of the funds in the hands of state officials. They would receive money indirectly in the form of wages paid by the day for the work done under the national law. Wages would run from $8 per day to $20 per day. Wiley estimated that the total needed to pay the state officials would be $460,000. He also planned to increase the salaries of state officials with federal funds. Both methods of funding state officials would allow him to control enforcement by rewarding those local officials who agreed with him and withholding funds from those who did not.[23]

Despite his earlier congressional testimony that enforcement of the act would not take "one additional inspector," he called for the hiring of fifty federal food inspectors. The new inspectors, he said, would track down illegal products and inspect food processing plants. Every state would be assigned one inspector, and the larger states would be assigned more. The cost would be approximately $5,000 per inspector for a total of $250,000. Finally, additional funds of $150,000 were needed, according to Wiley, for new chemists and clerks in the Bureau of Chemistry. His total budget requests were three or four times his earlier "very large estimate" of $150,000 to $200,000.[24]

At the same time that he requested an increase in funding, he asked for the restoration of the secretary of agriculture's authority to set food standards. James Wadsworth, the chairman of the committee, said in response, "There was a great deal of discussion on that [food standards], and there was a good deal in the conference, and I think that the conference was unanimous in wanting to strike them out."[25] Wiley, however, insisted that he needed the authority to set standards, because without the authority he would not be able to enforce the law.

> Suppose you take this out of the bill. Then our only avenue to publicity would be a court trial under the food law. We want to avoid the court trial publicity, as far as possible, under this. . . . I think there is greater reason for this remaining just as it is now than there was before the pure-food law passed. The food law provides for no investigation or publication.[26]

In essence, Wiley was asking for the authority to circumvent the courts. However, his behavior at the hearing did not inspire confidence in granting that authority. Near the end of Wiley's testimony, Congressman Cromer of Indiana said to him, "You have not elaborated on the question of whiskeys yet this morning." The mention of whiskey sent Wiley into a harangue.

> Blended is not the antithesis of straight. "Crooked" is the term you mean. If one is straight, the other is crooked. Crooked whiskey is not whiskey at all, but is made of neutral spirits, flavored and colored. It is an imitation. It has none of those aromatic and flavoring congeneric products which are volatile at the ordinary temperatures of distillation. I think that pure spirits is a poison, pure and simple. It coagulates the protoplasm in the cells.
>
> *The Chairman:* You mean pure spirits?
>
> *Dr. Wiley:* Yes; alcohol. As long as any man can keep his cells limpid and keep his protoplasm limpid he will never grow old. Alcohol absolutely coagulates protoplasm the moment it touches it, but alcohol that

is in whiskey or brandy or rum is so mingled by nature's operations that it is in an entirely different proposition. . . . Nature has a way of combining the elements in food, which man cannot imitate, and therefore when nature produces 20 different substances, as she does every time a whiskey is fermented, and all 20 of them come over in the still, alcohol among them, then you put these natural elements away to become mellow, to marry (as the distiller says), which takes years to accomplish—it is a long, drawn-out ceremony—and you make a beverage which is tonic and wholesome and healthful and non-poisonous; and there is all the difference in the world between a drink of straight alcohol and a drink of whiskey, brandy, or rum.[27]

This outburst shows how emotional the issue had become to Wiley. To call straight whiskey natural, to ascribe longevity to limpid cells, and to accuse rectified whiskey of killing people by coagulating the protoplasm demonstrated a capacity for skewed judgment that was wholly out of place in a man of science, let alone a man who was charged with impartially administering a law to protect the public. This public utterance reveals Wiley's fierce determination to discredit a well-established commercial product. The outburst did not inspire in the members of Congress confidence in Wiley's judgment. Congress did not approve the standard-setting clause. In fact, through points of order that denied that the existing legislation authorized those activities, it almost stripped the Department of Agriculture of any authority to examine, investigate, and report on foods. Wiley blamed Hough for his failure to gain the authority to set standards. He did not seem to realize the extent to which many in Congress distrusted his judgment.[28]

It was perhaps this distrust that led Congressman James Tawney of Minnesota to introduce an amendment to the appropriation bill that forbade the use of federal funds to pay state officials. Had Tawney's provision passed, it would have blocked Wiley's plan for enforcing the new law. The amendment passed the House but was dropped by the Senate. It did, however, serve a warning to Wiley, who promptly abandoned his plan for the extensive use of state officials. As a result, it would be many years before there was widespread cooperation between state and federal food officials.[29]

In place of state food officials, Wiley decided to hire more federal inspectors and to establish more federal food laboratories. Once his program was under way, Wiley showed little concern for it. One inspector of the period later said in an interview, "he was somewhat distant to us. . . . he was an image more than a man." Indeed, in his study of early food inspectors, James Harvey Young has noted, "Wiley, in the six years between the law's enactment and his resignation in 1912, had very little personal association with the new federal inspectors and received only a small amount of enforcement help from state officials." On R. M. Allen's recommendation, Wiley appointed Walter G. Campbell as chief inspector. It was Campbell who managed the inspectors. The Campbell appointment proved to be fortunate as Campbell was trained in law and was an excellent administrator. Eventually, he became the head of the Food and Drug Administration.[30]

The Board of Food and Drug Inspection

Wiley had little time for the routine of administration; he was busy fighting battles for the administrative control of enforcement. To his way of thinking, the new law gave the Bureau of Chemistry the right to examine food and decide whether or not it conformed to the law. He fully expected the secretary of agriculture to routinely approve his findings. Wilson and Roosevelt, however, believed that Wiley had appropriated too much authority to his bureau and moved to constrain him. In April 1907, Wilson, working in concert with Roosevelt to check Wiley's power, informed him that a board of food and drug inspection would be established. The board, not Wiley, would recommend action to the secretary.[31]

The board consisted of three men: Wiley, George McCabe, and Frederick L. Dunlap. McCabe, a Catholic from Ogden, Utah, who had worked as a law clerk in the department while attending law school, was solicitor for the Department of Agriculture. He had become one of Wilson's closest advisers after his appointment as solicitor in 1905. McCabe would be the legal voice on the board. Dunlap, a chemist from the University of Michigan who had received his doctoral degree from Harvard and studied further at Yale before taking a position at Michigan, was appointed after Roosevelt had requested candidates from a number of university presidents. Roosevelt wanted a reputable, scientifically trained chemist who could offer an independent judgment on matters of food adulteration. When Dunlap set back his arrival date in Washington because of duties at the University of Michigan, Roosevelt wrote personally to President Angell of Michigan, asking that Dunlap be released from his duties because of an urgent need in Washington. Wiley would be chairman of the board.[32]

Wilson and Roosevelt, who were receiving many complaints that Wiley was using the food law to impose his opinions on the food industry, no doubt believed that a three-man board would temper Wiley. However, Wiley soon proved that he could not be constrained so easily. When Dunlap was appointed to the board, he became an associate chemist in the Bureau of Chemistry, but his position was difficult. The staff of the bureau was loyal to Wiley and shared his view of Dunlap and McCabe as interlopers. Consequently, workers in the bureau were reluctant to work with Dunlap. Having no authority or cooperation within the bureau, Dunlap restricted himself to working on the Board of Food and Drug Inspection.[33]

Shortly after Dunlap's arrival in Washington, Wiley sailed to Europe to serve as a juror of food at the International Maritime Exposition in Bordeaux, France. During his absence, Dunlap and McCabe moved to strengthen their positions, but resistance from Wiley's loyal staff and the board's lack of clear authority hindered their efforts. They made little headway, and when Wiley returned, he heard about their attempted encroachments on his authority. The result was a strained, adversarial relationship between the three men.[34]

Administering Dr. Wiley's Law

While in France, Wiley missed the annual convention of the state food and dairy officials, which was held in July in Jamestown, Virginia, as part of the tricentennial celebration of Jamestown's founding. That July in the peninsula country of Virginia, the weather was even more humid and hot than usual. The heat took much of the spunk out of the normally feisty convention. The whiskey issue and the acceptance of standards proposed by the joint standards committee provided the convention's only drama.

Prior to his departure, Wiley had urged William Frear, chairman of the joint standards committee, to have the convention endorse the reports of the committee. "While these reports will not have the authority which they would have had, coming from the Department of Agriculture officially," Wiley wrote, "they at least will have great weight with state officials and I believe also with national officials."[35] Due to the oppressive heat and the absence of Wiley's guiding hand, the convention took little action on standards. The convention did endorse the reports, however, so that the Bureau of Chemistry was authorized to use the committee's standards in its examination of foods.[36]

The fight against rectified whiskey was led by R. M. Allen, Edmund Taylor, and Henry Beach Needham, a newcomer to the convention. Needham, who had accused the Senate of obstructing pure food legislation in 1906, had formed a group called the People's Lobby, which had such illustrious names as Samuel Clemens, Louis Brandeis, Frederick C. Howe, and William Allen White on its letterhead. Needham was personally acquainted with Roosevelt and believed that he had influence with the president. Needham's organization seems to have devoted itself primarily to the promotion of straight whiskey. Needham himself was in close touch with Taylor and Allen and presented their positions as those of the People's Lobby. The organization's offices in the Munsey building in Washington, D.C., were probably maintained with funds from the straight whiskey industry. The *American Food Journal* suggested that Needham's group should change its name from the People's Lobby to the Bottled-in-Bond Lobby because of the organization's efforts on behalf of straight whiskey.[37]

In his address to the Jamestown convention, Needham stated the purposes of the People's Lobby and used the whiskey controversy as an example of the group's activities. He had intended to criticize Warwick Hough in his speech, but Hough was in the audience. Needham omitted his criticism of Hough, saying that he was cutting his speech short due to the extreme heat. However, he did not omit the criticism in the copy of the speech he gave to the press. "It would be unwise," Needham said of Hough, "to advertise him further than to say that he is a masquerading lawyer who sells his brains to greedy interests already grown rich through adulteration and deception." The *American Food Journal* accused Needham of cowardice, a judgment with which state food officials agreed. The incident damaged Needham's reputation among these important men and began his decline as an active participant in food issues.[38]

The Guarantee Clause

One of the primary concerns of the Jamestown convention was a clause in the Pure Food and Drugs Act that was known as the guarantee clause. Congress had intended the clause to protect retailers from prosecution if they unwittingly sold products that failed to meet the requirements of the law. To avoid prosecution, retailers needed only to show a guarantee from the wholesaler, jobber, or manufacturer that the product complied with the law. Under the terms of the act, the guarantor would then be held responsible for any violation of the law.[39]

Administrative regulations permitted retail firms to file a general guarantee with the Bureau of Chemistry. Once filed, the firm could display the guarantee on the labels it placed on the goods it had received from the wholesaler, jobber, or manufacturer. The guarantee would read, "Guaranteed by the Food and Drugs Act of 1906, guarantee number _____." The number was issued by the Bureau of Chemistry. The way in which the guarantee was used gave consumers the impression that the government guaranteed the purity of the product, which in reality it did not. As consumers began to use the guarantees as guides to quality, firms found them commercially valuable.

The economic effects of the guarantee could have been avoided by allowing companies to place only the guarantee number on a label. A simple number would not have created the impression that the guarantee applied to the consumer. The Jamestown convention passed a resolution objecting to the way in which firms used the guarantee clause, but Wiley ignored the resolution. He was reluctant to make the change because issuing guarantees increased the power of his bureau, which had the authority to decide whether or not it would grant use of the clause to particular firms and products.[40]

Food Inspection Decision 76, *Dyes, Chemicals, and Preservatives in Foods*, illustrates the power wielded by Wiley through the guarantee clause. In this decision, the right to use the guarantee statement on products containing benzoate of soda, benzoic acid, or sulphur dioxide was denied, even though the use of these additives was legal. This decision gave a competitive advantage to such firms as H. J. Heinz, which did not use benzoate of soda as a preservative in its catsup and thus could use the guarantee.

Because of its discriminatory effects, McCabe and state food inspectors objected to Decision 76. They felt that firms using benzoate of soda should be permitted to use the guarantee clause as the ingredient was not banned by the law. In response, Wiley argued, "it is unfair to the consumer to allow a statement to be made on the label that the food is guaranteed under the food and drugs act, for the consumer may interpret this statement as a guaranty that the food is pure." His statement was inconsistent with his policy of permitting other firms to use the clause. By permitting the use of the guarantee by some and denying its use to others, Wiley was selectively misleading consumers. Even so, the objections of McCabe and state food officials had no effect. Firms continued to use the guarantee clause until two years after Wiley's resignation.[41]

One of the worst abusers of the guarantee clause was the Sunny Brook Distillery, a manufacturer of straight whiskey. The company launched an advertising campaign that claimed that its product had the official approval of government inspectors. Advertisements and billboards displayed bottles of Sunny Brook beside a document entitled "The National Pure Food Law." Above or below the picture, words proclaimed Sunny Brook to be "The Pure Food Whiskey." Other advertisements showed a man in a uniform with "U.S." on the lapels and wearing a cap labeled "Inspector." He held a bottle of Sunny Brook that was stamped "Ok, U.S. Pure Food Inspectors." The label on the bottle read "Sunny Brook Whiskey, Bottled in Bond, Age and Purity—Proof and Measure Guaranteed by U.S. Government." The advertising campaign was an obvious misuse of the guarantee clause and of the Pure Food and Drugs Act; government inspectors did not examine the product's purity or other qualities, and no government official could vouch for its authenticity or quality. Still, Wiley took no action against Sunny Brook until

Secretary Wilson wrote to the firm, telling it to withdraw the advertisements. Only after the company gave the secretary an ambiguous reply did Wiley respond. The firm was neither charged nor threatened with prosecution for mislabeling. Wiley simply wrote the company a letter explaining what was wrong with the label and advertisements. Sunny Brook then offered to correct the problem.[42]

Drugs

Despite its name, the Pure Food and Drugs Act contained few provisions for drugs. Under the law, the names and quantities of specific drugs (alcohol, morphine, opium, cocaine, heroine, alpha or beta eucaine, chloroform, cannabis indica, chloral hydrate, and acetanilide) had to be listed on the labels of patent medicines. The law also prohibited false names and false places of manufacture and declared the *United States Pharmacopoeia* or the *National Formulary* to be the official document for determining the standards and definitions of drugs. If a drug differed from these standards, it had to be plainly stated on the package. There were a few restrictions on patent medicines. Some labels were changed and some claims were toned down, but the same products were available after the passage of the law as before.

Wiley was no more vigorous in pursuing investigations and prosecutions under the law than he had been in seeking legislation against drugs in the first place. Of the first 1,000 cases under the Pure Food and Drugs Act, only 135 pertained to drugs. Historians have explained this by noting that Wiley considered the foods of those days more dangerous than the drugs. This is no doubt true, but Wiley's judgment still seems questionable. He devoted large amounts of resources to his fight over the definition of whiskey, an issue that made no difference to the health of the consumer. He devoted tremendous effort to preventing glucose makers from labeling their product *corn syrup*, but again, there was no important issue of health or nutrition that depended on the outcome of this battle. The small staff that he assigned to drugs devoted much of its time to the prosecution of Coca-Cola, which Wiley claimed was mislabeled because it did *not* contain cocaine. Although he prosecuted the company because it added caffeine to its product, he believed caffeine consumed in tea or coffee to be all right. The few chemists in Wiley's bureau who were assigned to drugs worked mainly on a revision of the *Pharmacopoeia,* an activity that was not part of the official duties of the bureau. This seems a peculiar use of scarce enforcement resources if one's primary goal is the health of the food and drug consumer.[43]

The first case brought under the 1906 act was a drug case. Robert N. Harper, a prominent Washington, D.C., businessman, produced a headache remedy called Cuforhedake Brane-Fude. Early in 1908, Harper was accused of mislabeling his product because (1) it claimed to be harmless but contained acetanilide, which the Bureau of Chemistry considered harmful; (2) it claimed to have 30 percent alcohol but only had 24 percent; (3) it bore the name Brane-Fude when there was no such thing as brain food; and (4) it claimed to cure headaches but pain relief was not a cure. Harper pleaded not guilty to the charges and was brought to trial.

The primary arguments at the trial were over whether or not the principal ingredient, acetanilide, was harmful. Experts testified on both sides. Wiley took the stand only to argue that the product had nothing that could be called brain food and that it was not a cure for headaches even though it might relieve headache pain. The prosecution was not vigorous. In examining these cases, James Harvey Young has written, "There was a simplicity, almost casualness, about the prosecution's case that suggests either inadequate preparation, perhaps from pressure of other work, or, more likely, the feeling that Harper's misbranding was prima facie and needed little more than pointing out."[44] Whatever the reason, it is clear that the case was not pursued with the same vigor that Wiley pursued rectified whiskey, corn syrup, Coca-Cola, or baking soda manufacturers.

The judge's instructions to the jury left the jury little choice but to return a verdict of guilty, which it did. After the verdict but before sentencing, President Roosevelt intervened. Calling the prosecutor to the White House, Roosevelt demanded a maximum sentence, which would have included jail for Harper. Roosevelt's interference created a momentary uproar, but the judge's sentence was for the maximum fine only; no jail sentence was imposed. It is not entirely clear why Roosevelt intervened, but it happened at a time when he had lost confidence in Wiley and rumors of Wiley's conciliatory attitude toward drug interests were circulating in the Department of Agriculture.[45]

Wiley complained of the shortcomings of the law's provisions on drugs to Samuel Hopkins Adams, writing, "While I think the law is good so far as it goes, it really does not meet the case. Notice on the bottle may have secured a deterrent effect on one before the habit is formed, but it is only a guide to one who has formed the habit."[46] He went on to say that what was needed was a law that would allow access to these drugs only through a prescription from a local physician. Still, although he acknowledged the shortcomings of the law and made strong rhetorical statements against patent medicines, he did little to promote additional legislation or to use the full force of the law that existed.

This behavior was in sharp contrast to his behavior toward other products and firms in other industries. These industries against which Wiley would exercise his powers and that would then erupt into regulatory warfare were involved in what James Harvey Young has called "the big, bombastic issues." They were the issues that took up the bulk of Wiley's time and received the press coverage. The controversies over benzoate of soda, whiskey, sugar, baking powder, dried fruit, and Coca-Cola involved Presidents Roosevelt and Taft, Secretary Wilson, and the scientific community. Despite the high stakes and the intensity of the controversies, the majority of the American food industry was not involved. By the Bureau of Chemistry's own estimations, most food producers were in compliance with the 1906 law, even in the first year it was passed. Even the three acrimonious members of the Food Inspection Board agreed on the large majority of cases that came before it. Violations were usually minor and involved products that were marginal to the American diet.[47] By early 1908, rules and regulations that left considerable scope for discretion were in place to enforce the pure food law. Wiley exploited this scope to its fullest. More and more, he came to see the law as his personal fiefdom and to believe that his superiors were taking unwarranted steps to limit his legally granted authority. His superiors, on the other hand, saw him as increasingly opinionated and troublesome. At the same time, however, they recognized his powerful political constituency. To avoid the criticism of Wiley's public, they sought to control him through administrative mechanisms. This situation could only lead to conflict. The more threatened Wiley felt by challenges to his authority, the more he turned to outside interests for support. This required him to interpret the law in a manner favorable to these interests. As he did this, his superiors received more complaints of Wiley's discriminatory activities. From 1907 to 1912, Wiley's administration of the law was marked by bitter disagreements between Wiley, his superiors, and a relatively small number of firms, mainly in the whiskey, sugar, soft drink, baking powder, and catsup industries.

CHAPTER 7

The Whiskey Wars

Shortly after the pure food bill became law, Wiley wrote to W. H. Thomas, "The rectifiers got a shade better of the straight whiskey men in the food bill, but I do not think the victory is very threatening." He was right. The manufacturers of rectified whiskey had persuaded Congress to withdraw from the Department of Agriculture any power to set standards, but the victory was inconsequential. For the next three and a half years Wiley triumphed over Warwick Hough, the attorney for the opposition. Wiley repeatedly defeated the manufacturers of rectified whiskey in judicial proceedings, and in case the whiskey issue reached the Supreme Court, he had Justice Harlan of Kentucky on his side. Wiley also convinced an attorney general and a solicitor general to issue opinions in his favor. Had it not been for the unusual intervention of a judicially minded president from Ohio, the home of whiskey rectifying, Wiley would have changed forever what could be called whiskey in the United States.[1]

Skirmishes

A month after the pure food bill was passed, Hough, recognizing that the controversy over whiskey had been pushed to the executive and judicial branches of government, began to argue his case in a series of letters to Secretary Wilson. Capitalizing on Congress's refusal to allow the Department of Agriculture to set food standards, Hough objected to any government activity that hinted at standards, including Wilson's call for meetings to be held in New York in September to formulate a set of regulations for the law. Wilson had appointed Wiley as his representative, and Hough feared that the meetings would be used to establish standards prejudicial to the manufacturers of rectified whiskey. "As to what is an adulteration or a misbranding under the law, is to be determined by a court, and such issue should not be prejudiced by any action taken by this Commission," he wrote. He made the same objections to the meeting of agricultural chemists and state food officials that was scheduled in Louisville for December 1906.[2]

Hough also questioned the motives and the integrity of Wiley. At one point he accused Wiley of "stockjobbing," of deliberately making public statements that would drive up the price of straight whiskey and depress the price of rectified whiskey, which naturally would affect the stock prices of the firms. In a letter to Wilson, Hough noted that such actions by a public official were "little short of scandalous."[3]

Hough's efforts to prevent the Department of Agriculture from setting food standards came to naught. On 1 December 1906, one month before the law was to take effect, Wilson signed food inspection decision 45. In three paragraphs, the decision declared that straight whiskey was the only genuine product, that rectified whiskey was a "spurious imitation" thereof, and that a mixture of straight and rectified whiskey could not be represented as a blend but had to be called a compound because it was a mixture of unlike substances. Only a mixture of two straight whiskeys could be called a blend. The decision also prohibited any product other than straight whiskey from using the term *whiskey* in its name without qualification.[4]

Wiley timed decision 45 well. By issuing it in December, he ensured that it would be illegal to brand anything as whiskey except straight whiskey when the law went into effect on 1 January. By January 1907, however, Wilson was, according to Wiley, "very much perturbed in regard to F.I.D. 45." On 22 February, he called a meeting of McCabe and Wiley to discuss whiskey. McCabe objected to decision 45, saying, "Dr. Wiley's definition of whiskey is absurd. Whiskey is any alcoholic beverage made from grain, properly colored and flavored, according to the prevailing custom of the trade." Wilson sided with McCabe. Upset with this interference with his authority, Wiley went to President Roosevelt on 25 March. Wiley spent two hours with his distillation apparatus explaining whiskey making to Roosevelt. At the end of the meeting, Roosevelt reportedly said, "Dr. Wiley, I have heard nothing but whisky for the last three weeks, and you are the first person who has ever given me a single idea that I can comprehend." After his meeting with Wiley, Roosevelt sent a whiskey brief, prepared by Wiley, to Attorney General Charles J. Bonaparte and asked for a legal opinion.[5]

The Bonaparte Decisions

Throughout 1906 and 1907, Roosevelt faced a ticklish political situation regarding whiskey. The muckraking press portrayed Wiley as a champion of honesty and purity. To rule against Wiley after his March meeting with him would leave Roosevelt open to charges of cowering before fakers and adulterators or corruption. The recent scandals in the Department of Agriculture would give these charges added force. On the other hand, the press had also reported Wiley's ties with the Kentucky whiskey makers and his various outbursts. In February 1907, Wiley's remarks about "crooked whiskey coagulating the protoplasm" appeared in newspapers. Such a statement must have made Wiley appear something short of impartial. Both Roosevelt and Secretary Wilson had received letters in December from responsible men who charged Wiley with favoritism, calumny, and misuse of his official position. One of the letters came from no less a figure than William H. Taft.

Taft, who was Roosevelt's secretary of war, had received a letter from an old friend of his, J. G. Schmidlapp, president of a Cincinnati bank, complaining of Wiley's leanings toward straight whiskey and the consequent harm done to the manufacturers of rectified whiskey, many of whom were the bank's customers. Schmidlapp acknowledged that his letter "might not be considered the basis of a just complaint if the action complained of was justified by historical and scientific facts, but the truth appears to be that the article [rectified whiskey] which is thus deprived of its name has at least an equal title to it as the article upon which it is to be conferred exclusively." Taft forwarded the letter to Roosevelt with the comment that he had great confidence in Schmidlapp's statement of facts.[6]

Besides the public controversy, Wilson and Roosevelt had disagreed over the meaning of the term *blended whiskey* in early 1907. Wilson had urged Roosevelt to get a ruling from Bonaparte. By placing the controversy with his attorney general, Roosevelt was securing the opinion of a respected legal mind that was free from any suspected connection with the contending parties. Bonaparte received the request 25 March and issued his decision on 10 April. This was not much time, even for a man of exceptional ability, to acquaint himself with the facts of the trade or to judiciously settle a heated controversy. Bonaparte did neither. His decision was a blend of wry humor, acute reasoning, and transparent inconsistency. Using a literary style that might be described as flippant Latin, Bonaparte wrote:

> The following seem to me appropriate specimen brands or labels for (1) "straight" whiskey, (2) a mixture of two or more "straight" whiskeys, (3) a mixture of "straight" whiskey and ethyl alcohol, and (4) ethyl alcohol flavored and colored so as to taste, smell, and look like whiskey:
> (1) Semper Idem Whiskey: A pure, straight whiskey mellowed by age.
> (2) E Pluribus Unum Whiskey: A blend of pure, straight whiskeys with all the merits of each.
> (3) Modern Improved Whiskey: A compound of pure grain distillates, mellow and free from harmful impurities.
> (4) Something Better than Whiskey: An imitation under the pure food law, free from fusel oil and other impurities.[7]

In reaching his decision, Bonaparte noted that "the intention of the law will be best observed by giving to such articles names readily understood and conveying definite and familiar ideas to the general public, although such names may be inaccurate in the view of a chemist or an expert in some particular industrial art, as in the distillation and refining of spirits." After stating this sensible principle, Bonaparte straightaway ignored it. The drinking public did not distinguish between straight, rectified, and blended whiskeys in the way that Bonaparte defined them. For them, whiskey was an alcoholic drink distilled from grain. The rectified product was often advertised as being free from fusel oils; the straight product was often advertised as having the government stamp of purity (the bottled-in-bond stamp). Both products were commonly known as whiskey, and mixed together they were known as blended whiskey. Had Bonaparte adopted the accepted public terminology, all segments of the industry would have been able to call their product whiskey, and each kind—rye, bourbon, straight, blended, rectified—would have been distinguishable from the other.[8]

Ignoring the commonly accepted meaning of whiskey, Bonaparte adopted Wiley's meaning, which Wiley himself had flip-flopped over just two years earlier. Under Wiley's definition, whiskey was a "distillate, at the required alcoholic strength, from the fermented mash of malted cereals, or from malt with unmalted cereals, and containing the congeneric substances formed with ethyl alcohol which are volatile at the ordinary temperatures of distillation, and which give character to the distillate." If the definition sounded as if it came from a chemist or from someone expert in the industrial arts of distilling or refining spirits, Bonaparte seemed unaware of it.[9]

Bonaparte's written decision aroused the righteous ire of the antisaloon league. His use of the national motto, E Pluribus Unum, to classify the devil's own drink was more than the league could tolerate. The secretary of the league shot off an angry letter to Roosevelt. Roosevelt, however, was not only amused by the ruling, he also agreed with it. He instructed Wilson to take appropriate action: "Straight whiskey will be labeled as such. A mixture of two or more straight whiskeys will be labeled blended whiskey or whiskeys. A mixture of straight whiskey and ethyl alcohol, provided that there is a sufficient amount of straight whiskey to make it genuinely a 'mixture,' will be labeled as compound or compounded with pure grain distillate. Imitation whiskey will be labeled as such." Wiley himself could not have written a legal opinion that harmonized more completely with his own views. It was a stunning victory for him.[10]

Following the ruling, Wiley received letters of congratulation from Allen, Scovell, and other friends and supporters. Allen, who was in Louisville when the decision was rendered, wrote that it "was an astounding surprise to the trade" and said that Needham, president of the People's Lobby, had been especially influential with Roosevelt. Wiley was jubilant, even permitting himself a moment to gloat. He wrote to Edward H. Jenkins of Connecticut, "Well, Brer' Hough got it in the neck for once, and I do not think the severed edges of his jugular will ever come together again."[11]

The celebration was cut short by Bonaparte's announcement in early May that he would hear oral testimony in the whiskey case. Believing this to mean that the case would be reopened, Wiley, Allen, and Frear went to work to make sure that the opinion was not reversed. They need not have worried. In a letter to Allen, Bonaparte wrote that "the impression that the question of labels for whiskey is to be reopened by this Department is, so far as I am now advised, erroneous." Apparently, some persons wanted to make statements to him and Bonaparte was prepared to hear them, but he was not going to reopen the case.[12]

The testimony offered on 15 May did not alter Bonaparte's ruling. On 29 May, he issued a defense of his original opinion. "I find no reason to withdraw the said opinion, or to modify it in any respect, and I respectfully report that, in my judgment, this opinion correctly states the law on the subject to which it relates." To the charge that he had adopted a definition of *whiskey* that was sharply at variance with public usage, he replied that the meaning of the term in the pure food statute was a matter of law, not of fact. To the charge that he had not interpreted the term *whiskey* as Congress had intended, he replied that legal custom regarded congressional debates as inappropriate sources of information for construing the meaning of the language in a statute.[13]

Congress had recognized that enforcement of the law would require foods and drugs to be defined. *Adulteration* and *misbranding* lack meaning without a standard of purity or at least acceptability. During the debates prior to the bill's passage, Senator Spooner of Wisconsin had asked Senator Weldon B. Heyburn "whether standards are not absolutely necessary somewhere to understanding and administration of the bill when enacted into law?" Heyburn had replied, "Standards would be necessary if whiskey were a new product which was just being introduced into commerce and into use and we were unfamiliar with it and its effects. But whiskey has obtained, through the long years of its use by individuals and its place in commerce, a recognized standard." A standard of pure whiskey, said Heyburn, "has been reduced to a legal certainty."[14]

By declaring the term to be a matter of law rather than fact, Bonaparte overturned the accepted meaning of *whiskey*. To abruptly change the meaning of a term by legal fiat is bound to produce peculiar results. The term *whiskey* was so commonly applied to the rectified product that the Internal Revenue Service, under a law enacted in 1866, was required to stamp the word *Whiskey* on any package containing a distillate from grain that was reduced to proof (50 percent alcohol and 50 percent water). Wholesale dealers were now transporting and selling something that the IRS had labeled as whiskey but that was, according to Bonaparte's ruling, only an imitation of that product.

The irony of the situation was noted by John G. Capers, commissioner of the Internal Revenue Service, who wrote to Wilson in late 1907, asking:

> Can or should a citizen be prosecuted by one Department of Government and his goods subject to forfeiture, because he ships and sells such goods under a name which is now being placed on them by another Department of the Government and with which name the Government has been so branding such goods for the past forty years pursuant to those provisions of law enacted in 1866, which requires an article to be branded with its true name?[15]

This question eventually worked its way back to the attorney general's desk. On 11 January 1908, Bonaparte acknowledged that the two laws contradicted one another but said, "it seems clear to me that it [the 1866 law] was repealed by the adoption of the pure-food Law." This was the third whiskey ruling Bonaparte had been called upon to issue in less than a year, and he was not done yet. Before his term was out, he would be forced to rule again.[16]

On 12 December 1908, the *Journal of Commerce and Commercial Bulletin* reported:

> Commissioner of Internal Revenue Capers has received from the whiskey interests to-day a complete statement of their side of the current controversy over marking and branding. . . . Mr. Capers expects to study this communication with great care and then to draft a memorandum relating to the recommendations which he will transmit to the Department of Agriculture for examination by Secretary Wilson and Dr. F. L. Dunlap, who are jointly with Mr. Capers members of the new whiskey commission.[17]

The newspaper reports of a whiskey commission took Wiley by surprise. Apparently he did not know that Roosevelt had appointed Capers, Wilson, and Dunlap to look into the labeling of whiskey. He did know, of course, that all three men opposed his stand on whiskey, and he wrote a letter of alarm to Scovell. "Have the Executive Committee [of the National

State Food and Dairy Officials] come here and call on the President and protest upon opening this question again," he urged. Taylor and Allen, he said, were already "doing what they can to circumvent this new scheme and deep conspiracy."[18]

Dunlap wrote the whiskey commission's report and sent it to Roosevelt, who then sent it to Bonaparte. Dunlap's report argued that the term *whiskey* had been applied to various processes of production, including rectification and redistillation, for a long time and that it should not be restricted to the particular process that produced straight whiskey. The report also recommended not forcing the term *imitation whiskey* on the manufacturers of rectified whiskey. It suggested using some term such as *rectified whiskey* or *redistilled whiskey* instead.

Bonaparte reacted angrily to the commission's criticism of his opinion. He replied to Roosevelt "that the assistant chemist of the Department of Agriculture suggests that, on the question of the construction of a statute, a very carefully considered and reconsidered opinion of the Attorney General should be disregarded." Bonaparte repeated his earlier arguments and concluded by saying, "I can only advise you that the conclusions announced in the opinions of April 10 and May 29, 1907, are sound, and that to give effect to Doctor Dunlap's suggestions would be to violate the pure-food law."[19]

Whiskey in Court

In his reply to Dunlap's report, Bonaparte cited several court cases that confirmed his earlier decision. By February 1908, the courts had already ruled in favor of the government's position, but the rulings were rather weak. In *U.S. v. Fifty Barrels of Whiskey*, for example, the court ruled that a distillate made from molasses and sold as whiskey was misbranded. This ruling is not surprising, since whiskey was universally regarded as a distillate made from grain. The decisive case did not occur until August 1908, and its outcome was, if possible, an even more impressive victory for Wiley than the first Bonaparte ruling.[20]

Court action in *The Fleischmann Co. v. Bernard Bettman et al.* was initiated by the manufacturers of rectified whiskey, and they chose their venue and their issues well. The suit was brought in the Circuit Court for the Southern District of Ohio. The court was located in Cincinnati, one of the major centers for the manufacture of rectified whiskey in the United States. The product's manufacturers were highly regarded in the city, as evidenced by Schmidlapp's letter to Taft.[21] The legal issues they selected were ones for which there was precedent on their side.

As Commissioner Capers had noted in his letter to Wilson, the IRS had been marking the casks of rectified whiskey with the label *Spirits,* or, if the spirits had been diluted with water to achieve the proper proof, with the label *Whiskey* on the basis of an 1866 Internal Revenue law that had been amended in 1879. Under the law, casks containing distillates were marked with one of three stamps: "alcohol," "high wines," or "spirits." Spirits was the most highly refined of these distillates. It was sufficiently free of fusel oil that it was often reduced to proof and sold immediately. If the distillate was made from grain, it was sold as whiskey. High wines usually required further treatment before they could be diluted with water and sold as whiskey. Alcohol was the least refined of the distillates and often consisted of the residue left after purifying high wines to make spirits. Alcohol, as the term was used in the trade, was unsuitable for drinking. It was used for industrial purposes.

Based on Bonaparte's decision, the Treasury Department issued Internal Revenue Order Number 723, dated 25 May 1908, which required casks containing spirits to be labeled *alcohol.* To avoid confusion, casks that were previously labeled *alcohol* were to be labeled *commercial alcohol.* It was this change in labeling that the manufacturers of rectified whiskey decided to challenge. On 4 August, the Fleischmann Company, represented by Warwick Hough, filed a motion for a preliminary injunction. The company asked that revenue agents be prevented from marking casks that contained spirits with the label *alcohol.* Hough argued that "the word 'Alcohol' if marked and branded upon the casks or packages containing distilled spirits" would mislead buyers. Alcohol, he went on to say, connoted a different and inferior distillate that was unsuitable for drinking purposes. A misleading label, the company claimed, would inflict considerable financial damage on it. On 5 August, Circuit Court Judge Albert Thompson found that the plaintiff was entitled to a preliminary injunction and ordered revenue agents to continue marking casks with the word *Spirits.*[22]

Having won the first step in their legal battle, the manufacturers of rectified whiskey immediately took the next step. On 10 August, six distilleries, led by the Union Distilling Company, filed another motion for a preliminary injunction in Judge Thompson's court. For forty years prior to the pure food law, neutral spirits that had been reduced to proof had been labeled *Whiskey* by revenue agents. Internal Revenue Order 723, however, stipulated that

Alcohol, commercial alcohol, or high wines, which have been manipulated by the aid of artificial flavors, colors, or extracts, or otherwise, so as to resemble some particular kind of potable spirits, will be marked with the name of such spirits, preceded by the word "imitation"—as, for example, "imitation whiskey."[23]

The bill of complaint submitted by the manufacturers objected to revenue agents labeling casks of rectified whiskey as *Imitation Whiskey*. Pending the outcome of the complaint, they asked the court to issue a preliminary injunction prohibiting revenue agents from using the label *Imitation Whiskey*.[24]

The following day, Sherman McPherson, the U.S. attorney in the case, cabled the Justice Department that he wished "to consult with Dr. H. W. Wiley before injunction case is heard Thursday . . . important that Dr. Wiley should be present at the hearing."[25] McPherson, who had just lost the Fleischmann case, did not want to lose another. Wiley left immediately for Cincinnati and succeeded in getting a one-week postponement of the hearing. During the week, he assembled a collection of expert witnesses, including his friend and supporter Edward H. Jenkins and John Uri Lloyd. Lloyd, according to Wiley, was an expert chemist and a "very personal friend of the Judge himself."[26]

Both sides presented their case the following week, and on 24 August, Judge Thompson ruled in favor of Wiley. In doing so, Thompson quoted Jenkins's testimony at length. Jenkins had testified that rectified whiskey could be made from moldy or otherwise inferior grain and could be consumed immediately after distillation while true whiskey required aging. Jenkins's arguments had clearly impressed Thompson, who said that rectified whiskey was "not a genuine whiskey in the making of which age modifies objectionable elements and develops the flavor which pleases the taste and adds so much to its value." Thompson then ruled that rectified whiskey should be labeled *Imitation Whiskey* and denied the application for a restraining order. Although U.S. manufacturers did not give up, their prospects now looked much more bleak than they had a week earlier.[27]

Foreign Entanglements

Unlike his U.S. counterparts, William Robins, a director of Hiram Walker and Sons, producers of Canadian Club Whiskey, enthusiastically embraced the pure food law. While Hough and U.S. manufacturers of rectified whiskey knew that Wiley's interpretation of the pure food law would produce commercial favoritism, Robins and his firm thought it would help to discourage fraudulent imitations of their product.

Canadian Club Whiskey was made in Walkerville, Ontario, by a process not commonly used in the United States. The company combined straight and rectified spirits as they came from the still. It then stored the mixture in charred oak barrels for four years. The result was a high-quality product that contained little fusel oil. Wiley, who had served as a judge at the 1893 Columbian Exposition in Chicago, had pronounced Canadian Club Whiskey to be "pure and fully up to the examination required." In fact, the whiskey had received an award for "fine aroma, pleasant taste, thorough maturity and an absence of alien matter."[28]

By the turn of the century, Hiram Walker's reputation was sufficiently valuable that other firms began to imitate the Canadian Club bottle, pouring cheap whiskey into bottles and labeling the bottles to look like Canadian Club. It amounted to a trademark infringement and cut into the company's business. During one year, the firm estimated that it lost 30 percent of its sales to fraudulent imitators. To stop the imitation, Hiram Walker instituted a vigorous campaign of publicity. The company hired detectives to track down products imitating the Canadian Club bottle. It then publicized the offending firms to wholesalers, retailers, and the public. Detectives and publicity were expensive, but they were more cost effective than going through the courts, which Hiram Walker believed to be "too slow and too lenient." A firm that had suffered so much at the hands of fraudulent practices would naturally welcome the passage of a law that promised to prohibit such practices and punish the offenders. Consequently, Hiram Walker and Sons "hailed the pure food law as a blessing."[29]

Soon after passage of the law, the firm began correspondence with various officials of the U.S. government, supplying information on imitators. In retrospect, the firm's belief that the food law was meant to curtail fraud against its product seems touchingly naive. It was not until November that the firm got word that Wiley might declare its own product fraudulent, something it found hard to believe. Canadian Club was widely regarded as one of the finest whiskeys in the world.[30]

Concerned that its label might require modification, the company retained the services of two lawyers, Alfred Lucking, a former congressman from Detroit, and Joseph H. Choate, a renowned corporate attorney. Both attorneys issued detailed legal opinions to the company, and both concluded that Canadian Club, as labeled, fell well within the law. "I am therefore of the opinion," wrote Choate, "that when the Act takes effect, there should be no interference with the importation of your whiskey labeled as it always has been because it directly conforms to their law."[31]

As a further precaution, the firm dispatched Robins to Washington to discuss the situation with the Bureau of Chemistry. Robins spoke to Wiley's assistant, Bigelow, who was vague and noncommittal. In a report to the firm, Robins wrote, "the only result of the interview was to give us occasion for very grave uneasiness."[32] During the interview, Bigelow had expressed the opinion that any coloring added to whiskey would make the product a mixture of unlike substances. As such, it would have to be labeled a compound. Robins pointed out that following this principle consistently would force butter to be called a compound product. Bigelow disagreed but produced no contrary argument. By this time, Robins should have realized that Wiley's bureau had no intention of enforcing the law through the application of uniform principles. Instead, he and other company executives naively urged a policy of consistency and restraint upon Wiley. In May, the firm wrote to Wiley, "May we take the liberty of suggesting that this question [of whiskey], which has aroused so much bitter contention and been so warmly discussed for months, might with advantage be laid aside for a time while the nomenclature of other articles is considered. It seems to us that such a step would tend to simplify matters, for we are convinced that if the same line of thought is applied to the whole list of foods, (and they must, of course, all be dealt with upon the same principle), it will very soon become apparent that the theories upon which Decision 65 is based are erroneous."[33] Wiley responded cordially but noncommittally. He had visited Hiram Walker in 1904 and recollected that Canadian Club was produced by mixing straight whiskey with neutral spirits. "The question which presents itself is this," he wrote. "Is this mixture a real whiskey or is it a mixture of real whiskey with silent spirit?" Even after the first Bonaparte decision, Wiley took no firm stand in his replies to the company, perhaps out of respect for the prominence of its attorneys. For its part, the company remained polite but firm and asked that Wiley seize a case of its goods at the border. This seemingly unusual request was motivated by Attorney General Bonaparte's refusal to grant the company a hearing. Since Hiram Walker was a foreign firm, it had no recourse to U.S. courts if its goods were merely stopped at the border; they had to be seized.[34]

Wiley responded to the request for seizure with a vengeance. On 1 April 1908, without warning, he seized 5,898 cases of Canadian Club on the grounds that the product was adulterated. Although the company could now have its day in court, no judicial decision was ever rendered. Instead, the company was among those who took their case before administrative hearings ordered by Taft.

The Final Engagement

Soon after the election of William Howard Taft in 1908, the manufacturers of rectified whiskey petitioned for a hearing. On 8 April 1909, Taft issued an executive order granting the request. He directed Lloyd Bowers, his solicitor general, to take testimony and render an opinion as to "What was the article called 'whiskey' as known (1) to the manufacturers, (2) to the trade, and (3) to the consumers at and prior to the date of the passage of the Pure Food Law." Taft also wanted to know what the term *whiskey* included, if there were a maximum or minimum amount of by-products in whiskey, if there had been any abuse in the application of the term, and if whiskey as a drug was the same as whiskey as a beverage.[35]

The Bowers Hearings

Unlike Bonaparte, Bowers did not rush to judgment. Taft had ordered him to take testimony from "time to time." Bowers took five solid weeks of testimony, which he followed with close attention. The recorded testimony comprises 17 volumes and 2,742 pages, which does not include the mass of documentary evidence submitted. Bowers was thorough, indeed.[36]

The Bowers hearings were the last great confrontation between veteran antagonists. The manufacturers of rectified whiskey were led by Hough. Hough enlisted the aid of Maxwell, who had worked with him on the Union Distilling case, and Armstrong, the attorney for Duffy's Malt Whisky. Alfred M. Lucking and Joseph Choate continued to represent Canadian Club. The straight whiskey interests were represented by Edmund Taylor and John G. Carlisle, who had already enjoyed a distinguished political career. Carlisle had been elected to the Kentucky legislature at the age of twenty-four, had served six terms in the U.S. House of Representatives, three as Speaker, and had been elected to the Senate in 1890. Wiley was also heavily involved. Knowing well the importance of the hearings, he led friendly witnesses through their testimony, cross-examined the opposition, and testified himself. However, he did not want to appear to be the agent of straight whiskey manufacturers. Thus, he told Bowers that he did not wish to be called by either side but would prefer to testify independently. As usual, he testified that only straight whiskey was entitled to the name *whiskey*.

William Frear shared Wiley's desire to appear disinterested. When Edmund Taylor had written to Frear asking him to testify at the hearings, Frear had responded that he was willing but did not "wish to commit a faux pas by seeming to appear as the representative of any trade interest." Bowers never knew that Wiley, Frear, Taylor, and others jointly planned their strategies. He thought of the government witnesses during the hearing as truly disinterested. This is perhaps not surprising as Bowers was new to the dispute and had no ties to either side. Throughout the debates he was committed to carrying out Taft's order. He allowed wide latitude to all parties, and he himself often engaged in penetrating and sustained questioning of the witnesses. He seemed comfortable in the situation, despite the bitterness of the dispute; perhaps his experience as an attorney for the railroads during the Pullman strike had given him familiarity with intense controversy. In any case, he gave a full and fair hearing to the issues.[37]

The hearing opened with arguments from the attorneys of both sides. Hough then produced about a dozen witnesses to testify on behalf of rectified whiskey. Some of the witnesses had been in business from before the Civil War. They came from all walks of the industry—some made equipment, some distilled, some rectified, some blended, some traded, some were stockholders, some were chemists. Collectively, they had a wide knowledge of the industry. They testified in some detail about whiskey making, which began with grain. Corn, wheat, barley, and rye were suitable grains, and different firms used differing proportions. The grain mixture was fermented, then distilled to create "low wines," which were distilled again at a different temperature to produce "high wines." High wines were refined further by running them through charcoal, which was called rectifying, or by distilling them a third time. The methods of distillation had improved from the original pot still, which had been used in the 1700s, to the continuous still, which came into being around 1880 and produced a more palatable distillate than the pot still. The distillate from the continuous still did not have to be run through charcoal and was known as neutral spirits. The distillate, whether run through charcoal or not, was then reduced to drinking strength, or "proof," by adding water. At this point, the product was usually colored by adding caramel or burnt sugar, although some brands, such as Imperial White Whisky, advertised their lack of color. Most consumers liked an amber colored drink, similar to the Irish and Scotch whiskeys. Small amounts of peach or prune juice were sometimes added for flavor. The final product of these processes, according to the witnesses, had been called *whiskey* by manufacturers, wholesalers, retailers, and consumers for as far back as anyone could remember.[38]

Straight whiskey was introduced shortly after the Civil War, when some distillers began to store high wines in a barrel for several years. Storage removed the disagreeable odor of the fusel oil, so that the high wines did not need to be filtered through charcoal. If the barrel were charred on the inside, the product would absorb a color similar to that of caramel. Straight whiskey had a strong flavor, which Wiley and other whiskey connoisseurs preferred. Others, however, liked the milder flavor of rectified whiskey or blended whiskey, which was a mixture of rectified and straight whiskeys.

There had never been much controversy about calling the rectified product *whiskey* until Wiley's agitation for a pure food law. Even some straight whiskey producers found Wiley's claims troubling. John Atherton, who manufactured Kentucky straight whiskey until he retired in 1899 and who no longer had a financial interest in the business, testified to Bowers:

> I must say now, in justice to myself, if you will permit me, that I have had a feeling that under previous rulings an immense injustice has been done to an immense branch of the business in the United States, without any possible good to result from it, giving old words new meanings and revolutionizing a business that men had conducted under the law ever since the internal revenue laws were established. I have no other reason for being here.[39]

To present the straight whiskey side of things, Taylor and Carlisle called various official chemists, most of whom were members of the National Association of State Food and Dairy Officials—Edwin F. Ladd of North Dakota, Richard Fischer of Wisconsin, Harry E. Barnard of Indiana, Joseph P. Remington, who edited the *Pharmacopoeia,* and Edward H. Jenkins. Employees of the Bureau of Chemistry—L. M. Tolman, Harris E. Sawyer, and Wiley himself—were also called to the stand. All of them said that they did not consider neutral spirits reduced to potable strength to be whiskey. Wiley was adamant; "I would say," he testified, "that this material which I have just described [neutral spirits] is not whiskey and never has and never will be."[40] They argued that the product made from neutral spirits did not have enough byproducts to be genuine whiskey. According to them, only straight whiskey had enough fusel oil and other congeneric products to be called whiskey. Although they acknowledged that the product produced from neutral spirits had been widely traded as whiskey both by itself and when blended with straight whiskey, they argued that the consumer did not know that he was buying neutral spirits and therefore fraud was being committed.

Richard Fischer pointed out that maple sugar and beet sugar became sucrose and were indistinguishable from one another if they were sufficiently refined. At that point, he went on to say, it was impermissible to call a sugar made from maple syrup *maple sugar* because it was indistinguishable from any other highly refined sugar. Only if enough by-products were left in the product to distinguish it from other sugars could it be called *maple sugar.*[41] This argument seems to have persuaded Bowers. He began to think of neutral spirits as pure alcohol, distinct from whiskey.

The idea that whiskey had to have fusel oil and other impurities was an idea recently introduced to the whiskey debate by Wiley. When some manufacturers of whiskey began aging their distillate in a barrel, everyone assumed that aging in a barrel oxidized the fusel oil, because it removed the objectionable odors of fusel oil from high wines, just as rectifying did. Then a British chemist, Philip Schidrowitz, analyzed the straight distillate and discovered, to the surprise of everyone, that fusel oil did not oxidize when left in a charred wooden barrel. He had informed Wiley of this in the summer of 1905. The new information had forced Wiley to do an about-face. Whereas before Wiley had insisted that whiskey could not contain more than .025 parts of fusel oil per 100 parts of ethyl alcohol, faced with Schidrowitz's information he decided that whiskey must have a *minimum* of fusel oil. He set no definite minimum, but he was sure that genuine whiskey had to contain more fusel oil than rectified whiskey or neutral spirits. Wiley's about-face is clear evidence that he was using chemistry to justify his preconceived notions of whiskey. Had he adhered to the standards he set prior to 1905, Schidrowitz's chemical analysis would have led Wiley to conclude that only a rectified distillate was entitled to the name *whiskey*.[42]

Schidrowitz's analysis also contradicted the argument of Fischer, that neutral spirits were pure alcohol. According to Schidrowitz, neutral spirits were not merely ethyl alcohol. In fact, the term *neutral spirits,* he said, was misleading. He preferred the term *grain whiskey* because he had compared neutral spirits made from molasses with those made from grain and had concluded that they were "very materially different." The fusel oil, acids, ethers, and esters that remained in neutral spirits, he pointed out, gave the distillate enough flavor to tell whether it was made from molasses or grain or fruit. When he had compared the distillate obtained from the pot still with the distillate from the continuous still, he had found them to be very little different. Straight whiskey processes took out about 90 percent of the substances found in the mash, whereas neutral spirit processes took out about 95 percent.[43]

After five weeks of hearings, during which he mediated between the views of straight whiskey producers and the rectified whiskey producers, Bowers wrote his decision, which he submitted to Taft on 24 May 1909. The decision agreed with Wiley's views and with previous rulings by Bonaparte; straight whiskey was entitled to the name *whiskey* but rectified whiskey or neutral spirits was not. Although he acknowledged that neutral spirits reduced to proof with water had been known to the trade and to the public as whiskey, he felt that consumers did not know what they were getting. Therefore, the product should not be called whiskey. Unlike Bonaparte, Bowers was willing to permit blends of neutral spirits and straight whiskey to be called whiskey. He reasoned that neutral spirits were practically pure ethyl alcohol, ethyl alcohol was the main component of straight whiskey, and thus adding neutral spirits was not an adulteration as long as the blended product contained enough by-products to be called whiskey.[44]

The press inaccurately reported Bowers's decision as a defeat for Wiley and the straight whiskey men. The anti-Wiley *American Food Journal* reprinted Bowers's opinion in full and described it as the "last crushing defeat of Dr. Wiley.... Three misses in a ball game entitle a man to the bench," the journal observed, although it predicted no benching for Wiley, because "he has long been unable to distinguish between fame and notoriety and no doubt welcomes each additional finding of the unsoundness of his views as another opportunity to bathe in the limelight."[45]

Oddly, Edmund Taylor also thought that the decision went against Wiley. On 8 June, he sent a telegram to Wiley that read, "Bowers decides for rectifiers. Opinion made public. Weak and vulnerable [news]papers dwell on several of you." Bowers and Wiley, however, saw the decision in a different and more accurate light. Bowers had been impressed by Wiley during the hearings and had written to him, "While it was my duty, and it certainly was my single purpose, to reach a conclusion which ... seemed right, I should have regretted very much any outcome greatly different from your own position. If I may say so, I learned to like you very much through the hearings, and I did not fail to get an insight into the earnestness and energy and value of your own good purposes and work." Bowers had gone on to lament that "no popular misapprehension concerning the outcome of any judicial controversy has often been more fundamental or entire than in the case of the whiskey report." For his part, Wiley later wrote, "I was impressed with the conviction that he was earnestly seeking the truth. Three-fourths of his decision was in harmony with my own views, so that I believe that he was at least three-fourths right."[46]

The Taft Decision

All the parties to the Bowers hearing took exception to the decision Bowers rendered. Taft felt that the universal dissatisfaction was a sign that the decision was a good one and agreed to hear the exceptions before he issued instructions on the decision. Unlike Roosevelt, who had acted hastily on the Bonaparte decision, Taft acted with deliberation. He held two days of hearings on 28 and 29 June. Wiley did not appear at the hearings. Instead, William Frear represented the position of official chemists. The attorneys for all parties, Carlisle, Taylor, Hough, Maxwell, Armstrong, Lucking, and Choate, were also present. After listening to the arguments of both sides, Taft read the testimony presented at the Bowers hearings. He then deliberated for six months and finally rendered his opinion on 27 December 1909. The opinion began with a summary of the purpose of the Pure Food and Drugs Act and the controversy over whiskey. This was followed by a synop-

sis of the history of whiskey making in the United States with special emphasis on improvements in distillation methods. Taft's grasp of the subject
revealed the close attention that he had paid to the testimony given to
Bowers. Taft judged neutral spirits to be the result of an improved production technique, the continuous, or patent, still, which took out slightly more
of the by-products than did running through charcoal or barrel aging.
However, he felt the improved production technique left the product substantially unchanged. Thus, he concluded that all methods of manufacture
resulted in whiskey.

> After an examination of all the evidence it seems to me overwhelmingly
> established that for a hundred years the term "whiskey" in the trade
> and among the customers has included all potable liquor distilled from
> grain; that the straight whiskey is, as compared with the whisky made
> by rectification or redistillation and flavoring and coloring matter, a
> subsequent improvement, and that therefore it is a perversion of the
> pure-food act to attempt now to limit the meaning of the term "whis-
> key" to that which modern manufacture and taste have made the most
> desirable variety.[47]

While recognizing that there had been fraud in the whiskey industry, Taft
noted, "these frauds did not consist in palming off something which was not
whiskey as whiskey, but in palming one kind of whiskey as another and
better kind of whiskey." This type of fraud could be stopped by requiring
each kind of whiskey, rectified, straight, or blended, to be identified on the
manufacturer's label.[48]

The January issue of the *American Food Journal* ran the full text of the
Taft decision along with a sampling of editorial opinion from across the
country. Although the sample was no doubt biased, the editorials praised
the decision for its sound reasoning and good sense. The normally pro-
Wiley *American Grocer,* in a comment typical of the editorials, said, "It
[Taft's decision] will clear the atmosphere, dispel the fogs and clouds that
have hung over the execution of the National Pure Food Act, and we trust
put an end to radical and technical definitions and rulings, scientific rather
than in conformity to long-established commercial precedents. It is based
on common sense and not on technical terms."[49]

If the Bonaparte decision had been a stunning victory for Wiley, the
Taft decision was a crushing defeat. The widespread praise of the decision
made it impossible for Wiley to continue his public campaign against the
manufacturers of rectified whiskey. The sheer force of a presidential opinion
made it impossible for him to continue his campaign within the administra-

tion. After five tumultuous years, the whiskey controversy was finally dead; Wiley had failed. Twenty-five years later, Wiley's resentment of Taft's decision was still evident. Although Wiley never criticized the substance of the decision, he did blame it for the "sweeping victory" of prohibition a few years later, and he intimated that Taft's overruling of Bowers was responsible for Bowers's death in 1910.[50]

Wiley also accused Taft of overturning an 1876 decision of Taft's father, Alfonso, who had ruled that alcohol could not be shipped under the name *whiskey,* thus recognizing that alcohol and whiskey are not the same thing. Wiley claimed that the 1909 decision denied this distinction by saying that neutral spirits were whiskey. However, neutral spirits and commercial alcohol, neither of which was pure ethyl alcohol, were shipped at higher proof than whiskey. Consequently, greater precautions had to be taken against inflammability, and railroads charged a higher price to ship alcohol than to ship whiskey. It would have been a material misrepresentation for a firm to ship alcohol under the name of whiskey. All this is perfectly consistent with both Taft decisions. Thus, Wiley's assertion, like many of his claims in the whiskey controversy, misleads and misrepresents, to the detriment of someone else's reputation.[51]

Taft's decision was not entered as a food inspection decision immediately. Instead, the secretaries of agriculture, treasury, and commerce collaborated on formulating a decision that was based on Taft's ruling. The official decision was issued as Food Inspection Decision 113 on 16 February 1910. It superseded all earlier decisions and was essentially the same as Taft's, although somewhat more liberal in defining what could be called whiskey.

Although some controversy over whiskey continued, it was minor. A year or so after Decision 113, Hiram Walker issued a pamphlet entitled *A Plot Against the People,* which criticized Wiley strongly but not very effectively. Around the same time, George W. Wickersham, Taft's attorney general, ruled that Canadian Club did not have to be labeled *blended whiskey.* Wiley's friends continued to praise him as a man of honor and courage. Joseph Remington, who had testified on the side of straight whiskey at the Bowers hearings, described him as a man "who has by superhuman courage faced innumerable enemies, yea, even those of his own household." Wiley himself later complained about Decision 113 in his book *History of a Crime.* Still, all this activity was a footnote. Decision 113 carried out whatever worthwhile intentions were in the 1906 law: It required various kinds of whiskey to state on their labels what they were, and it did so without giving one segment of the industry a competitive advantage over the other.[52]

CHAPTER 8

Sulphur and Benzoate of Soda

Food Inspection Decision 76

Preserving food by freezing, drying, smoking, salting, and pickling has been known for centuries. Nineteenth-century science contributed the use of chemicals to food preservation. The newly discovered chemical preservatives frequently surpassed traditional methods in effectiveness, but, being the product of laboratory experimentation, they were suspected by the public of being unhealthful.[1]

The pure food movement objected to chemical preservatives and dyes. The names for these chemicals were technical and sometimes frightening to the chemically uninitiated. A coal tar derivative did not sound like something that should go into the human body, yet most modern dyes were made from coal tar. In this atmosphere of doubt, the consumer naturally questioned the safety of additives. Harvey Wiley's Poison Squad experiments caught the public eye because they provided information to the consumer about mysterious chemical preservatives. Wiley began these experiments already convinced that preservatives were harmful, because he confused spoilage with digestion. If a chemical slowed down spoilage, reasoned Wiley, then it must *ipso facto* interfere with digestion.[2]

The uncertainty about preservatives played into Wiley's hands. If preservatives were commonly recognized as safe and effective, there would be less need for a pure food bill. Wiley's political ambitions may not have determined his ideas about preservatives, but they certainly prevented him from acting like a scientist. By 1904 he was condemning preservatives, even though his studies of the subject were not complete. And he was not the only one eager to exploit consumer ignorance about preservatives—so were business firms. Many of them claimed purity for their products, a claim that connoted superiority without saying anything very definite. Any manufacturer could make this claim, even if his product contained preservatives. Firms could not easily exploit a production process that avoided the use of preservatives, because very few companies listed preservatives on their labels. Where such listing did occur, as with the Curtice Brothers of Rochester, New York, it was because state law required it.[3]

A food law that required the listing of all ingredients on the label would probably have encouraged the production of foods without preservatives;

companies would have been able to secure some advantage by demonstrating that their product lacked a preservative that other products contained. However, this advantage would have been offset by the greater expense of foods without preservatives since consumers on a tight budget paid close attention to price.

The first ruling on preservatives under the new law was Food Inspection Decision 76, issued 18 June 1907. It permitted the use of salt, sugar, wood smoke, potable distilled liquors, vinegar, and some spices without giving notice on the label. Pending further investigation, the use of saltpeter was also allowed. The decision prohibited the use of boric acid, borax, and salicylic acid. Special provisions were made for the use of sulphur dioxide and benzoate of soda.[4]

Sulphur dioxide was allowed for the 1907 season as long as the amount did not exceed 350 milligrams per kilogram, of which not more than 70 milligrams could be in a free state. This standard was arrived at by examining a large number of food products purchased on the open market and taking an average. No experiments were made to determine how much sulphur was necessary to preserve various foods or what its health effects were. From the sulphur samples taken from the open market, it was clear that there was no uniform practice. The 350-milligram level may have been adequate for some purposes, such as preserving wine, but inadequate for others, such as preserving dried fruit.[5]

Under Decision 76 there would be no prosecutions during 1907 for the use of benzoate of soda in quantities less than one-tenth of a percent. The decision added that, in the opinion of the Food Inspection Board, benzoate of soda was harmful, and its use would not be allowed after 1907. Until that time, if a firm used either sulphur dioxide or benzoate of soda, the label had to say so. Manufacturers who used either preservative were not allowed to use the guarantee clause. The Food Inspection Board argued that putting the guarantee on the package might mislead the consumer, who could interpret the guarantee to mean that the food was pure. Of course, the guarantee was not meant for the consumer, and by law it did not certify that a product was either safe or pure. The guarantee only protected the seller from prosecution. However, the board seemed to recognize that the mere presence of the guarantee was likely to influence consumers.

To the extent that the guarantee clause led consumers to believe that they were buying pure food, the guarantee possessed commercial value. This commercial value could be granted or denied by the Food Inspection Board. Denying the users of benzoate of soda and sulphur dioxide the use of the guarantee discriminated against these firms.[6]

Even before Food Inspection Decision 76 was made public, California fruit dryers were objecting to any ruling that limited the amount of sulphur used to preserve fruits. Governor Gillett of California telegraphed President Roosevelt asking for the postponement of any ruling. He followed this with a letter saying that it "has been found absolutely necessary and has been the custom from the inception of this industry to subject a large portion of this product to the fumes of sulphur in order to preserve its character and keeping qualities." He argued it would be impossible to market dried fruit without the use of sulphur. In the judgment of people connected with the industry, the governor warned, the limit of 350 milligrams would destroy the industry.[7]

Roosevelt turned the protest over to the Department of Agriculture. Wilson was not in Washington, but Assistant Secretary of Agriculture Hays assured the governor that the department was in the process of thoroughly investigating the question and had dispatched two men to California to conduct further investigations. However, Hays did not offer to set aside the ruling until the investigation was completed.[8]

California fruit growers found Hays's response unsatisfactory. They sent petitions to Secretary Wilson asking him not to enact the regulations on sulphuring fruit. While he was touring the West with his son Jasper, Wilson found himself confronted by unhappy fruit growers in California. He turned to McCabe for advice. McCabe assured Wilson that the department was acting properly, and that there was no intention to enforce the regulation until more investigations were conducted.[9]

Hays also assured Roosevelt, who was still receiving protests from California fruit growers, that the department was not going to do anything to hurt the industry. He explained that the situation was more complicated than the use or nonuse of sulphur. Small California growers favored the regulation because their fruit required less sulphur to process and they could meet the standards. It was the large growers, who resoaked and resulphured their fruit, that were objecting to the standards, said Hays. He added that it was not the intention of the department to hold the fruit producers to a 350-milligram standard during the current packing year. After hearing from Hays, Roosevelt approved the department's policy.[10]

Wilson was informed of the president's approval prior to his arrival in California, where the fruit growers were eager to meet with him. Following his meeting with the growers, Wilson told them to continue their established practices for the time being. They would not be prosecuted under the law. Wiley, on his return from Europe, only mildly complained about not enforcing Decision 76.[11]

Years later, this episode would be used to demonstrate James Wilson's sellout to commercial interests. He was described by one critic in the 1930s as "technically ignorant and socially indifferent" because of his decision on sulphured fruit. A Ralph Nader study in 1970 described the incident by saying, "The first political intervention came within two months. Secretary of Agriculture James Wilson resolved a controversy about the use of sulphur in dry fruits by relying on the good will of industry and balancing industry economic interest against public health interest." Leaving aside the fact that this issue occurred more than a year after the law was passed and six months after the law went into effect, we should note that no such trade-off between public health and industry interest was ever established. Other than Wiley's Poison Squad experiments, which were hardly conclusive, there was no evidence that sulphuring dried fruits harmed health. Moreover, the process made fruits available to the family diet throughout the year. There had been no complaint from consumers that dried fruits were detrimental to their health.[12]

Wiley, however, thought that sulphur in its various forms was damaging to health. On his return from France he made public statements to that effect. Yet he did not object to the importation of French wine, which contained sulphur; he argued that French wines should not be required to list sulphur dioxide on their labels. When Wiley then tried to enforce the sulphur labeling requirement against U.S. firms, Dunlap objected to enforcing a law against American products while exempting imports. Wiley also took other steps that favored French wine producers: he tried to stop American wine producers from using names such as Sherry, Port, Burgundy, and Champagne and recommended that domestic wines substitute American names or else refer to themselves as Burgundy Type, Sherry Type, and so on.[13]

Benzoate of Soda

The disagreement over sulphur dioxide was minor compared to the controversy over benzoate of soda. This dispute created sharp conflict between Wilson and Wiley. It was the straw that broke Roosevelt's confidence in Wiley, and the issue that undercut Wiley's standing in the scientific community. The conflict encompassed more than a chemical preservative; at stake was who would enforce the food law.

Following the passage of the 1906 act, Wiley increasingly interpreted it as a grant of power to enforce the law as he saw fit. Together with a small group of agricultural chemists, state food officials, and commercial interests, Wiley used the benzoate of soda issue to amass public support and discredit his superiors.

Few foods contained benzoate of soda when the food law went into effect in 1907. It was mainly used in condiments, sauces, and pickles. The most widely used product containing benzoate of soda was catsup. Once exposed to the open air, catsup quickly spoiled. Prior to 1905 all catsup makers used preservatives to delay spoilage; manufacturers knew of no other way to preserve their product.

The term *catsup* (or *ketchup* or *catchup*) referred to a variety of sauces that had in common the use of tomatoes as a base. Even the use of tomatoes was a relatively recent American invention. Food historians trace the evolution of catsup from a blend of fish brine and spices to sauces made of walnuts, mushrooms, and cucumbers. Raymond Sokolov has suggested that Indian mango pickle, Chinese oyster sauce, and Mexican lime-cured ceviche may all be varieties of catsup. The first American catsup recipe to include tomatoes was in Mary Randolphs's *The Virginia Housewife,* published in 1824. It remained a home-made product until after the Civil War, when firms began to produce and market it commercially.[14]

By 1907 a bewildering number of catsups were available on the market. A study by the Dairy and Food Commission of Pennsylvania in 1912 examined 142 different brands. The brand names included SunShine, Hirsch's, Home Made, Waldorf, Wagner's, Highland, Blue Label, Yacht Club, Loudon's, Heinz, Somerset Club, and Surprise. All of them used tomatoes, vinegar, spices, and a sweetener, but the recipes differed substantially. Acidity and sweetness showed wide variation, as did the spices. The result was a range of sauces that varied in flavor, sweetness, and tartness. In addition to their own brands, many companies produced catsup on contract for wholesalers, jobbers, and retailers who had their own brand names and sometimes their own recipes. These conditions produced a highly competitive market and a wide variety of choice for the consumer. Some of the inexpensive catsups were produced as by-products, and some used the core and peelings of tomatoes, which cut down on costs.[15]

Most of the brands were local or regional. Only Heinz, Columbia, Blue Label, and a few others were nationally distributed and advertised. Establishing a national brand was not easy, and their prices were higher than prices of the local brands. Often, grocers received a larger markup with local products, so they would commonly recommend local brands over national brands or would simply fill the customer's order with a local brand.

In a market with so many brands, firms competed by differentiating their product. Each firm wanted customers to insist on their brand from the grocer. Heinz differentiated its product with a national campaign that advertised purity. It also tried to enhance the image of its product by enlisting the aid of the Chief Chemist of the Department of Agriculture.[16]

Wiley tested benzoate of soda on the young men of the Poison Squad. Testing was conducted during the spring and early summer of 1904. In all, twelve men were tested. Of these twelve, one had also participated in the experiment with sulphurous acid, nine had been involved in the salicylic acid experiments, and one participated in the borax experiment, all within six months of the benzoate of soda test. Wiley, when asked if using new men might not have been better, replied "No, I think they were tougher, it would be more difficult to make them sick the second time."[17]

The questionable use of the same subjects was compounded by the preexisting health problems of some. For example, one young man had asthma, headaches, a rapid heartbeat, goiter, and malaria. He also had a persistent sore throat, which was treated with quinine, and slight but chronic nephritis (inflammation of the kidneys). Yet, at the end of the experiments with benzoate of soda, he said he felt in good condition and an examination showed his nephritis had cleared up.[18]

When most of those taking benzoate of soda developed fevers, Wiley discontinued administering the preservative. Several of them had colds, sore throats, headaches, nausea, and dry throats. Wiley did not examine his subjects to see if some illness were causing the symptoms, nor did he have a control group. These were rather large oversights; the District of Columbia Health Department recorded an epidemic of grippe during 1903 and 1904, and grippe exhibited the same symptoms that Wiley recorded. Based on this experiment, Wiley concluded that benzoate of soda caused weight loss, a decrease in red blood cells, an increase of hippuric acid in urine, and damaging of the kidneys.[19]

In the summer of 1904, Wiley publicly announced that his experiment had convinced him that benzoate of soda was harmful. The results of the experiment, however, were not compiled and published until 1908, four years after the experiment took place. Wiley blamed the delay on the amount of work involved. Wiley's published experiments coincided with advertising claims by H. J. Heinz that it could now produce catsup that did not require preservation with benzoate of soda.[20]

In the meantime, based on Wiley's Poison Squad experiments, Food Inspection Decision 76 was issued on 18 June 1907. It permitted the use of benzoate of soda up to one-tenth of a percent through the 1907 season, provided that notice was given on the label. After 1907 benzoate of soda could no longer be used. According to Wiley, the intervening period gave companies adequate time to "adjust their manufacturing process so they no longer needed to use preservatives."[21]

Wiley casually assumed that preventing spoilage without preservatives was a simple matter, but it had not been. The Heinz Company had worked on the problem for several years before finding a solution in the spring of 1907. Sebastian Mueller wrote to Wiley on 8 May, saying,

we have finally and fully satisfied ourselves, through the results of our
experiments in putting up Ketchup without a preservative, that our
Ketchup may safely be sent in bottles as large as full net pints and that it
will keep perfectly for a period of not less than four weeks under
ordinary conditions, with only such closures for bottles as are in common use among Ketchup makers generally. . . . We believe that this
statement will be of particular interest to you and regret that we did not
feel sufficiently confident as to justify quite so broad an assertion on the
occasion of our recent call at your office, on which occasion we desired
to keep well within the bounds of known facts and to introduce nothing
in the slightest degree speculative.[22]

Before passage of the law, Wiley told benzoate of soda users that the
law would only require them to list benzoate of soda on the label. The news
from Heinz enabled Wiley to change his strategy. Now benzoate of soda
could be banned. Wiley convinced Dunlap, McCabe, and Wilson that
benzoate of soda was harmful and should be outlawed, and companies using
the chemical were given a year to eliminate it from their product.[23]

Decision 76 was ideal for Heinz, who already produced a product free
from chemical preservatives. Other manufacturers were not so fortunate;
they had not yet discovered Heinz's secret. This gave Heinz a competitive
advantage.[24]

Wiley in his autobiography tells the story of a catsup maker who claimed
that he could not produce his product without a preservative. Wiley assured
him that he could, and sent an expert to his factory to show the man how.
According to Wiley, success quickly followed. The real story is somewhat
different. The manufacturer was Charles F. Loudon of Terre Haute, Indiana;
the man sent to assist him was special agent Dr. Arvill W. Bitting. After trying
to figure out how to preserve catsup without benzoate of soda on his own and
failing, Bitting visited the Heinz plant. He was of course denied entry into the
catsup-making area. By November 1907 Bitting had not yet produced a
catsup that would keep for more than a few days after being opened. Bitting
would say later, "I did not know at the time how difficult it was to sterilize
catsup . . . our first year's work was not altogether satisfactory."[25]

Eventually Bitting, with the assistance of his wife Katherine, successfully
imitated the Heinz process. The secret was to increase the acid content, add
additional sugar to cover the increased tartness, and thicken the liquid.
According to Bitting, the acid content of Heinz was close to 3 percent, a level
high enough to retard spoilage. The thicker body was needed to keep air
from easily mixing with the product. High acidity and thick body delayed
spoilage for several weeks after the package was opened.[26]

After several months of waiting for Bitting to show him how to produce catsup without a preservative, Loudon grew anxious. His catsup did not meet the requirements of the law. He joined a group of other manufacturers, who met with Secretary Wilson to ask for a delay in the prohibition of the use of the preservative. Wilson forwarded their request to Wiley, who showed little sympathy. When Loudon complained that the product did not keep long enough after opening, Wiley responded, "I see no reason why a bottle of catsup should last thirty days after it is opened—this is entirely too long a time." But keeping-quality was important to the consumer, especially the low-income consumer who could not afford to have her food spoil. Wiley seemed to forget that not everyone dined at the Cosmos Club, where the keeping-quality of condiments was of little concern to the diner. Wiley once refused to use Blue Label catsup served him at the Willard Hotel in Washington because it contained benzoate of soda. The Willard switched brands, and the manufacturer of Blue Label complained to Secretary Wilson that Wiley was exceeding his authority and interfering with Blue Label's sales.[27]

After being refused by Wiley, Loudon and the other manufacturers asked for a special hearing before Secretary Wilson. Wiley contacted Sebastian Mueller of the Heinz Company and informed him of the hearing. He suggested that Heinz and other manufacturers who did not use benzoate of soda attend the hearing, but not let anyone know that he had suggested it. Wiley also said that he would be pleased to hear from Heinz personally as well as officially on the matter. The Heinz Company was more than willing to accommodate; they employed press agents to report favorably on Wiley and to attack his opponents. Wiley also used his contact with Heinz to bypass Wilson and exert influence on Roosevelt and Taft.[28]

The Remsen Board

Roosevelt became involved in the benzoate of soda dispute because of complaints from catsup makers and their Washington representatives. He held a hearing on preservatives in January 1908. Following the hearing, Congressman James Sherman of New York suggested the appointment of a special group of scientists to examine the issue. After meeting with Secretary Wilson and discussing the matter with his cabinet, Roosevelt decided to appoint a board of scientific experts.[29]

Establishing a board of leading scientists to resolve the ambiguity surrounding the use of preservatives seemed prudent and politically expedient. Roosevelt hoped that his decision would satisfy Wiley and his followers while not alienating the users of preservatives. The board was quickly appointed. Ira Remsen, renowned chemist and president of Johns Hopkins University, was chosen to head it. The other members of the board were Dr. Russell H. Chittenden, known as the father of physiological chemistry in the United States, Dr. John H. Long, professor of chemistry at Northwestern University, Dr. Christian A. Herter, professor of pharmacology at Columbia University and one of the original directors of the Rockefeller Institute for Medical Research, and Alonzo E. Taylor, professor of pathology at the University of California. Following Herter's death in 1910, Theobald Smith, professor of pathology at Harvard and a director of the Rockefeller Institute, was appointed to the board. This group was respected both for its scientific accomplishment and for its integrity. No one was suspected of ties to commercial interests.[30]

Rather than welcome this board of distinguished scientists in the confidence that his own research would be confirmed, Wiley perceived them as a threat to his authority. He suspected the board had been established to overturn his work. To defend himself, he felt compelled to criticize the Remsen Board. This of course meant challenging both Wilson and Roosevelt. Several of Wiley's supporters, including the Heinz Company and members of the National Association of State Food and Dairy Officials, joined the attack on the Remsen Board and Secretary Wilson. The August 1908 convention of the National Association of State Food and Dairy Officials at Mackinac Island, Michigan, provided the opportunity. In his opening address, E. F. Ladd of North Dakota, president of the association, verbally attacked Wilson, saying that he had given in to special interests by establishing the Remsen Board. Ladd also criticized Wilson's refusal to support the association's committee to establish uniform food standards.[31]

Before adjourning, the convention passed a resolution condemning Wilson. Wiley's longtime supporters M. A. Scovell of Kentucky, William Frear of Pennsylvania, and E. H. Jenkins of Connecticut were active in passage of the resolution. Some members of the association objected to the resolution, saying that it was improper to publicly condemn a cabinet official without giving him an opportunity to defend himself. The resolution received wide press coverage. Wilson was outraged. He was not able to prove that Wiley was behind the attack, but he believed that, at the least, Wiley should have defended him and the Department of Agriculture. Wiley, fearing Wilson might ask for his resignation, solicited letters from Scovell and Ladd saying that he had defended the secretary. Wilson did not ask for Wiley's resignation, but his animosity toward him increased.[32]

Meanwhile, the dispute over benzoate of soda continued. The pro-Wiley press called the Remsen Board agents of food-dopers and fakers. The Century Syndicate, an interest group financed by the Royal Baking Powder Company, hired Orville LaDow to work on a press campaign that attacked Wilson and the Remsen Board. LaDow wrote to Wiley, "If you have any doubt of our resources and efficiency, ask Gompers what we did to him recently." The Association for the Promotion of Purity in Food Products, a group made up of Heinz, Beechnut, and the Columbia Conserve Company, hired William Wolf Smith, who was at one time used by the National Wholesale Liquor Dealers Association. Smith, known around Washington as Poker Bill, had a thriving press bureau. Smith's bureau sent news items out to newspapers that did not have Washington correspondents. Poker Bill shaped the news to meet the needs of his clients. He managed to obtain space in the Capitol building by virtue of being secretary of the National Board of Rifle Practice, a group made up of military officers with the assistant secretary of war as its president. This gave his press notices an aura of authority considerably out of proportion to Smith's position. Because of earlier personal antagonism, Wiley did not approve of hiring Smith. He did not, however, object to Smith and LaDow's campaigns against Secretary Wilson.[33]

Wiley organized more sophisticated attacks through such muckraking journalists as Samuel Hopkins Adams and Mark Sullivan. To rebut the assaults on Wiley by the *American Food Journal,* Wiley supporters began the *American Pure Food and Drug Journal* on 1 January 1909. Edited by J. N. Garfunkle and located in Cincinnati, it claimed that its mission was to assist in the enforcement of the nation's pure food and drug laws. Dr. Charles L. A. Reed and John Uri Lloyd, both close associates of Wiley, were listed as contributing editors and the bulk of advertising was from the members of the Association for the Promotion of Purity in Food Products. The evils of benzoate of soda dominated both advertisements and articles. The journal apparently did not have a wide circulation; after the first year it went into decline and publication ceased in 1911.[34]

The *National Food Magazine* (formerly *What to Eat*), published out of Chicago by Paul Pierce, had more influence. The magazine advocated food regulation and was aimed at upper-middle-class women. It printed advice on food, meals, and service as well as reporting on etiquette and the fashions of the rich. In 1905 the magazine had been critical of Wiley, but by 1907 it had become a strong supporter. The conversion was accompanied by a plethora of advertisements from the H. J. Heinz Company. In 1909 Pierce became the secretary of the Association for the Promotion of Purity in Food Products, and his magazine became a voice for those who opposed benzoate of soda.[35]

National Food and other magazines portrayed Wiley as an incorruptible official and a defender of the public's health. They also cried wolf repeatedly, darkly warning that Dr. Wiley was about to be dismissed because of the evil influence of cheats, liars, and dopers. Press campaigns were launched against Secretary Wilson and the Remsen Board. The secretary was variously described as old, incompetent, and corrupt. The Remsen Board was accused of serving the same corrupt interests that wanted to discredit Dr. Wiley. Few historians have recognized that the source of these campaigns was the commercial interests benefiting from Dr. Wiley's opinions.[36]

Wiley's opponents also used the press. Journals such as *Leslie's Weekly,* the *American Food Journal,* and the *National Druggist* and newspapers such as the *San Francisco Chronicle* and the *Boston Traveller* criticized Wiley and defended preservatives. They were less effective than Wiley's coterie because their commercial ties were usually on the surface.

With Taft's election in 1909, the Heinz Company saw an opportunity to replace Wilson as secretary of agriculture, preferably with Dr. Wiley. L. S. Dow, a company representative, wrote Wiley that "An inquiry of a personal nature has come to me from an important, influential source, asking for reasons why Secretary Wilson of the United States Department of Agriculture should not be re-appointed to his present Cabinet position by Mr. Taft." Wiley furnished information that Dow assured him would remain confidential.[37]

Removing Wilson was only half the task. The other half was to get Wiley appointed. To enhance his reputation, a movement was started to back Wiley for the Nobel Prize. The attempt made little progress. Although many chemists admired Wiley's efforts for pure food, few thought that Wiley's contributions to chemistry were substantial enough to warrant a Nobel Prize. In the end, the attempt to oust Wilson and enthrone Wiley failed. Wilson was popular with farmers and Taft duly reappointed him. However, the attempt to make Wiley secretary of agriculture further angered Wilson and eroded his support for Wiley.[38]

The Remsen Board's report on benzoate of soda was published by the Department of Agriculture as "Report 88" in early 1909. It reversed Wiley's findings, which had been published in Bureau of Chemistry Bulletin 84 in 1908. The report was immediately criticized. Remsen's experiments, like Wiley's, fed benzoate of soda to groups of young men. Investigators conducted three separate studies, and each concluded that benzoate of soda was not harmful. The study was flawed in some of the same ways as the Wiley study; it had no control group and it did not study long-term effects. But the Remsen study was more comprehensive and less subject to variation, and it should have been more convincing, even to Wiley. However, Wiley held fast to his belief that benzoate of soda was harmful and should be outlawed. Over his objections, the secretaries of agriculture, commerce, and treasury issued Food Inspection Decision 104 allowing the use of benzoate of soda.[39]

Wiley was aware that the scientists on the Remsen Board were among the most eminent in the country. He knew that he would elicit scant support if he attacked them directly. He chose instead an oblique method, asserting that benzoate of soda should be prohibited because it could be used to cover up inferior or spoiled ingredients. The Remsen Board had not investigated this issue, so Wiley could continue to argue for the prohibition of benzoate of soda without directly challenging the findings of the board. However, Wiley did criticize the decision for benefiting unscrupulous food manufacturers. The users of preservatives replied that the law already prohibited the use of spoiled ingredients, and that the benzoate of soda was not as effective at hiding rotten ingredients as vinegar and sugar were.[40]

Showdown in Denver

By now Wilson was fully familiar with Wiley's tactics. He began countermoves of his own to discredit Wiley and restore his own reputation. A showdown came in 1909 at the National Association of State Food and Dairy Officials' convention in Denver. Wilson attended the meeting and made sure that his supporters did too. He insisted that members of the Remsen Board be there to defend their work. He wrote President Taft that there was a plan afoot to discredit the Remsen Board, but that it would not succeed.[41]

The Wiley forces also planned carefully for the meeting. The Heinz Company was particularly active in organizing criticism of benzoate of soda. They made arrangements with Paul Pierce of the *National Food Magazine* to pay D. R. Lucas, a defector from Dr. Herter's benzoate of soda experiments, to testify against the use of benzoate at Denver. Wiley encouraged Heinz to pay for Lucas's trip to Denver.[42]

Despite Wiley's efforts, Wilson carried the day. The convention endorsed the Remsen Board's findings on benzoate of soda, and they installed a platform of officers who supported Wilson. He wrote President Taft, "We smashed the whole program, turned things end for end, endorsed the Referee [Remsen] Board and its findings . . . and all interested in it." He went on to give his personal opinion of Wiley. Wilson likened Wiley to Gifford Pinchot, but said, "still there is a wide difference between him [Pinchot] and Wiley. Pinchot is a foolish gentleman, Wiley a mischief making, low bred fellow. Pinchot was unduly exuberant; Wiley is a consummate hypocrite."[43]

In the same letter Secretary Wilson asked Taft to "Consider whether you think it is wise to permit me to call for his resignation." Taft at the moment was caught up in the conflict between Pinchot and Secretary of Interior Ballinger. He gave Wilson a weak and discouraging response: "I

shall have to knock some heads together when I get back to Washington
after my trip. There is too much of a disposition to charge people with bad
faith, and too great encouragement to newspaper controversy." Taft's decision to keep Wiley would eventually lead to Wilson's condemnation. Years
later, Taft criticized Wilson for not controlling his department. However, it
was Taft, not Wilson, who was unwilling to discharge Wiley in 1909.[44]

Benzoate of Soda in Court

Having lost the fight over benzoate of soda at the national level, Wiley
moved the arena to his native state, Indiana. A fierce contest arose when the
Indiana State Board of Health prohibited the use of benzoate of soda. Wiley
worked closely with Representative Downey of the Indiana legislature, with
J. N. Hurty, the state food and drug commissioner, and especially with
Harry Everett Barnard, the state chemist. Barnard was a member of Wiley's
joint committee on standards and a loyal follower. When Hurty moved up
to head the State Health Department, Barnard became Indiana state food
and drug commissioner.[45]

Indiana law allowed the state to prohibit the use of additives to food if
they were deleterious to health. Based on the opinions of Wiley, Commissioner Barnard prohibited the use of benzoate of soda in products sold in
Indiana. Williams Brothers of Detroit and Curtice Brothers of Rochester,
two leading catsup-makers who both used benzoate of soda, asked the U.S.
Court for the District of Indiana to issue an injunction restraining the
Indiana Health Department. The court refused to grant a temporary injunction, but referred the case to a mastery in chancery. Here both sides gathered
their forces to testify. Before the proceedings were over, five thousand pages
of printed testimony would be taken and a great deal of maneuvering went
on behind the scenes.[46]

Wiley saw this as an opportunity to "make the fur fly." He was confident of victory in his home state and said of the event, "it will be a circus."
Wiley intended to be ringmaster. Later, in a deposition, he would say that he
knew little of what was going on at the trial, but this was less than candid.
He worked closely with Barnard and with Indiana's attorney general, James
Bingham, through every stage of the proceeding. He sought and obtained
support from Heinz and from the Association for Purity in Food. Heinz sent
its own experts to testify and provided funds to pay for others.[47]

Secretary of Agriculture Wilson saw the case as an attempt by Wiley
and his allies to attack the Remsen Board and, by implication, the administration of the law by President Taft. Wilson therefore made sure that members of the Remsen Board testified. Remsen was reluctant to do this, particu-

larly on behalf of the companies challenging the authority of the State Board of Health. He called the case a "nuisance" and wished the board could stay out of it. He told fellow board member Dr. J. H. Long, "I am sure the country would be better off, and the Administration, if the other insurgent should be dismissed. Things will never be right there until he is." President Taft encouraged Wilson's opposition to Wiley. He told Wilson, "I hope you hit them hard." Yet he refrained from dismissing Wiley or intervening to limit his activities. Evidently he feared another Pinchot affair.[48]

Sending the board members to testify in the Indiana case was only part of Wilson's strategy. He also kept Wiley from testifying. Attorney General Bingham went directly to President Taft in an attempt to get Wiley sent to Indiana, but Wilson told the president that if he sent Wiley he should expect the Remsen Board to resign. Taft refused to send Wiley.[49] With this avenue blocked, Wiley worked with Barnard and Bingham to have himself subpoenaed. After receiving the subpoena, Wiley went to McCabe, the solicitor for the Department of Agriculture. Feigning concern about Wilson's reaction if he testified, Wiley sought McCabe's opinion on whether or not he had to honor the subpoena. If approval was given, there could be no retaliation for what he said. This ploy, too, was defeated. McCabe informed Wiley that, since he was not testifying to facts, but rather as an expert witness, he was not required to honor the subpoena. Wiley did not testify in Indiana, but Wilson agreed that his deposition could be taken in Washington. Wiley would later use the episode as evidence that the administration was inhibiting him from telling the truth about preservatives. Other staff from the Bureau of Chemistry also gave testimony, but only after the court ordered them to do so. The court order was meant more to embarrass the secretary than to protect the staff from reprisals, which they claimed might result from challenging the official position of the department.[50]

Reprisals against those who opposed him were part of Wiley's arsenal. He had recently impugned the integrity of Dr. Edward Kremers of the University of Wisconsin. During the Indiana trial, Wiley wrote to a member of the university's Board of Regents, Magnus Swenson, attacking Kremers for testifying in support of benzoate of soda. He claimed that Kremers was selling his testimony for money and that he was a proven enemy of pure food, public health, and the general welfare. Kremers denied having been paid and stated that he supported pure food legislation and official government policy. He added, "I have been an advocate of rational pure food not of frenzied pure food. I am confident that the cause of pure food and drugs will not be advanced by unscientific reasoning any more than underhanded scheming." The self-righteous moral tone that Wiley invoked against paid experts only applied to those experts whose views differed from his. He did not object to experts paid by Heinz or other commercial interests who supported his position.[51]

Wiley's deposition for the trial was long and rambling. He related his Poison Squad experiments in detail. He emphasized his belief that all preservatives were harmful. He also asserted that benzoate of soda covered up the use of rotten, spoiled, and inferior ingredients. The charge that benzoate of soda could be used to mask the use of spoiled ingredients became a main issue at the trial. Arvill Bitting testified about his research on catsup making. He found that spoiled tomatoes could be covered up whether or not a firm used benzoate of soda, but he believed that masking spoiled tomatoes was more common among benzoate of soda users than it was among other firms.[52]

The testimony of Katherine Bitting could have decided the controversy, but she was ignored by both sides. Bitting explained that it was possible, with the use of a microscope, to ascertain the quality of the tomatoes used in making catsup. She could determine whether the tomatoes were fresh or decomposed. If microscopic examination disclosed the quality of the ingredients, then under the provisions of the 1906 law forbidding the use of spoiled ingredients the product could be seized, whether or not it contained a preservative. This is precisely the practice that would be adopted in the future, but only after Burton J. Howard of the Bureau of Chemistry presented similar information in a bulletin published in 1917. Katherine Bitting has never received recognition for her pioneering work in determining the quality of food by microscopic analysis.[53]

The makers of catsup also testified at the Indiana trial. On behalf of H. J. Heinz, Sebastian Mueller told of how the firm had developed a catsup that did not require a preservative. It was based on a recipe obtained from a woman in Pennsylvania. Heinz adapted this home-made recipe for commercial trade and stopped using preservatives in mid-1907. Charles Loudon, the catsup maker of Wiley's story, testified that he had adopted the process that Bitting had eventually developed. He had found it advantageous to quit using benzoate of soda because all the publicity had given preservatives a bad name. He did not believe that the chemical was harmful, but he quit using it for commercial reasons.[54]

The court, after reviewing the thousands of pages of testimony, decided against the plaintiffs, the two manufacturers who had sought an injunction against Indiana authorities to bar them from using benzoate of soda. Since there was no clear scientific evidence one way or the other as to hazard or safety, the state of Indiana had the authority to prohibit the use of the preservative. The decision was appealed, upheld in circuit court, and appealed to the Supreme Court. Before the high court reached a decision, the parties to the suit reached an agreement and the case was dropped. During the process of appeal, Indiana changed its ruling and permitted the use of preservatives, including benzoate of soda. Indiana health officials would conform with federal practice. However, many manufacturers of catsup, in response to the bad publicity about preservatives, quit using them.[55]

CHAPTER 9

Corn Syrup and Coca-Cola

Among the products that were a part of what James Harvey Young has called the "big, bombastic issues" were corn syrup and Coca-Cola. Today, corn syrup, in a variety of forms, is added to nearly everything requiring a sweetener. It not only sweetens and adds calories to a food, it also preserves, retards crystallization, extends shelf life, and provides what the food industry calls mouth feel. It is safe to eat, except for those concerned with excessive sugar consumption and persons allergic to corn. Today's consumer thinks nothing about its presence in foods. However, at the time the pure food bill passed, corn syrup generated a great deal of controversy, much of which was stirred up by Wiley.[1]

Coca-Cola also came under Wiley's scrutiny. Why he chose to prosecute a soft drink company at a time when Americans were using a variety of habit-forming drugs has always been something of a mystery. Why his superiors allowed him to proceed against the company has also been puzzling. The case was expensive, requiring legal and technical experts even before going to court. It also absorbed a great deal of Wiley's and his bureau's energy, but no health issue of any consequence was at stake. Except for a minor Supreme Court ruling on what constituted a food additive, the case's prosecution accomplished nothing of value to the consumer or the conduct of the food business.

Corn Syrup or Glucose?

In 1811, seeking a substitute for gum arabic, a water-soluble gum that is used in the manufacture of adhesives, inks, pharmaceuticals, and confections, G. S. C. Kirchoff, a Russian chemist, accidentally overheated some starch in a diluted acid solution and discovered a sweet, viscous substance. Further experimentation revealed the substance was a compound of the sugars dextrose and maltose along with dextrin, a partially converted starch. Excited by the discovery, research chemists rapidly began to convert potato, corn, and other vegetable starches to sugar. The sweet substance was named *glucose*, a word derived from the Greek *gleukos*, which means sweet new wine. The substance's first commercial success came during the Napoleonic wars, when the British blockade prevented sugar from reaching Europe.

Although glucose substituted for cane sugar during the blockade, it could not compete with cane sugar once the blockade was lifted. Government subsidies to sugar beets further hindered the development of the glucose industry in Europe.[2]

In the United States, Cicero J. Hamlin founded the American Glucose Company in 1866 and started producing glucose in a converted vinegar factory. Alone in the field, Hamlin enjoyed substantial profits until competitors entered the market in the 1870s. Because producers kept the manufacturing process secret, it was rumored that animal parts were used in the production process. It was also widely believed that glucose, if not an outright poison, was detrimental to health. In 1882, Congress introduced a bill to tax and regulate the sale and manufacture of glucose. The bill proposed a tax of ten cents per pound (or one dollar per gallon) of glucose. The bill did not pass, but Congress commissioned the National Academy of Science to study the wholesomeness of the product. The academy appointed a committee of leading scientists, including Charles F. Chandler, Wolcott Gibbs, Ira Remsen, William Brewer, and George Barker, to conduct the investigation. They found no evidence to support the claim that glucose, even when consumed in large quantities, was inferior to cane sugar in healthfulness. Although glucose companies distributed the findings of the committee and succeeded in overcoming most of the food manufacturers' prejudice against the product, the general public remained wary. Thus, the market for glucose depended on its being less expensive than sucrose, which was possible because of the high tariffs on cane sugar imported from tropical areas. At the same time, however, the Bureau of Chemistry was spending large sums of money on research to aid domestic sucrose producers. Government officials justified both the import tariff and the subsidies to domestic sucrose producers as a way to promote self-sufficiency in sugar production. Although glucose obviously had the potential to achieve this goal, it was not regarded as a way to become self-sufficient in sugar production.[3]

Even so, because of its low price, the demand for glucose expanded. By 1885, glucose manufacturers were attempting to establish a pool to limit production. The attempt did not last long; distrust and suspicion undermined the effort, and a period of sharp competition followed. By the end of the depression of the mid-1890s, several small producers had been driven out of the market, and others had suffered large losses. The return of prosperity found only a dozen companies still producing glucose. Hoping to benefit from the resurgent economy, these companies developed a scheme to monopolize the glucose market. While the scheme brought immediate profits to the promoters and paid high dividends for the first two years, new producers continued to enter the market and thus drove down profits. Each new wave of glucose producers was followed by an attempt to form a new cartel, each of which failed. In 1906, however, the Corn Products Refining Company was formed under the leadership of Edward Thomas Bedford, who was also a director of the Standard Oil Company, a member of Standard Oil's executive committee, and a highly skilled manager. Bedford had first become involved with glucose in 1901 as the president of the New York Glucose Company in Edgewater, New Jersey. In an attempt to consolidate the glucose producers, the Corn Products Company, a holding company, bought 49 percent of the New York Glucose Company. Controlling interest in the company remained in Bedford's hands. Like its predecessors, however, the Corn Products Company was unable to control the glucose market and soon failed. A new consolidation, the Corn Products Refining Company, was formed with Bedford at its head. The company controlled over 85 percent of the glucose production in the country.[4]

Bedford brought to the glucose industry the skills and knowledge that he acquired at Standard Oil. He created a well-organized, efficient company, and he introduced new market strategies. Convinced of glucose's value, he saw the possibilities for a direct market to consumers, but he knew that a name change was necessary to overcome consumer resistance. As a result, he began to market his product as "corn syrup." By 1906, corn syrup was the predominant ingredient in table syrups and was the sweetener favored by producers of low-cost jams and jellies. The amount of glucose produced annually was 1,350,000 barrels, nearly five times the amount of domestically produced sucrose. It was advertised as the product of the golden grain. Slogans such as "better than honey for less money," and "the great spread for daily bread" helped win over consumers. Corn syrups were soon outselling maple syrup and syrups made from sugar cane by a five to one margin. One representative of the corn products industry went so far as to suggest that cane sugars, when added to corn syrups, were an adulterant.[5]

Calling a Spade a Shovel

As the debate over food standards grew more intense, old myths about glucose began to show up in the popular press. It was frequently listed, along with coal-tar dyes and preservatives, as one of the poisons in the nation's food. Cartoons showing skeletal figures representing death from food adulterations frequently referred to glucose as one of the adulterants.[6] In defense of their product, glucose producers pointed out that white sugar from cane, beet, or sorghum was as artificial as glucose, since both products required mechanical and chemical processing. They could have pointed out that glucose appears naturally in fruits and honey just as sucrose appears naturally in sugarcane and beets.[7] These responses, however, should have been unnecessary, because by this point food officials knew glucose was neither dangerous nor poisonous. Most state laws recognized the product and permitted it to be called corn syrup, although labeling it as cane or maple syrup or trying to pass it off as honey was illegal.[8]

Bedford and other producers knew that any law requiring them to call their product *glucose* would hurt sales, but they did not anticipate any problems under a national food law. In 1903, the food standards committee of the Association of Official Agricultural Chemists, which was headed by Wiley, had recognized corn syrup as a synonym for commercial glucose. By November of that year, the secretary of agriculture had published the standard in Circular No. 10. A revision of the standard, published in December 1904 in Circular No. 13, still considered corn syrup synonymous with glucose.[9] Thus, glucose producers were taken by surprise when new standards, published a few days after the Pure Food and Drugs Act passed, proclaimed corn syrup to be an unacceptable term. Jobbers and wholesalers of corn syrup began to cancel orders, saying they had received word from the Bureau of Chemistry that it would no longer be proper to label the product *corn syrup*. Bedford was shocked. Writing to Wilson, he said, "I cannot believe that so serious an injury would be done to our business without due notice." In response, Wilson wrote, "There has been nothing decided along that line, and you may have a hearing anytime you desire."[10]

While Wilson may not have decided anything, Wiley had. On 28 February 1907, prior to any hearing, he wrote Bedford, "We have now a large mass of documentary testimony in regard to glucose, the proper name by which it shall be called." Bedford promptly contacted both Wiley and Wilson, saying that it was unfair to decide the proper name for the product without first allowing its manufacturers to present their case.[11] Soon after, the Board of Food and Drug Inspection was formed. Bedford was pleased with the appointment of the board, feeling that he now had a chance for a fair hearing. In June, he filed a brief that argued the secretary of agriculture's 1903 and 1904 standards had recognized *corn syrup* as a proper term. The brief quoted Wiley's book, *Foods and Their Adulteration,* in which he had said that glucose was wholesome and referred to it as corn syrup. The brief also pointed out that the corn syrup industry was a large purchaser of American corn and that anything that hurt the corn syrup industry would hurt the American farmer.

The board did not rule immediately. Wiley left for France in July and did not return until September. In the interim, the Corn Products Refining Company gathered further evidence, including testimony from leading chemists and food experts, that *corn syrup* was a proper name for its product. Although the company requested a hearing, it did not receive one until Wiley's return.[12] The hearing was finally held on 30 September 1907. Wiley took the position that *corn syrup* was not the proper term because the refined juices of the corn stalk already had a claim to that name, even though, as he himself noted, corn stalk juice was not a product of commerce. He also insisted that glucose was not a syrup as defined by the official food standards. These standards defined *syrup* as the "product made by purifying and evaporating the juice of a sugar-producing plant, without removing any of the sugar." Bedford and the Corn Products Refining Company promptly pointed out that refiner's syrup (the residue left after the crystallized sugar was removed during the processing of sugarcane) did not fit the definition given in the standards. This point would become a fatal flaw in Wiley's position, but the Corn Products Refining Company was not yet aware of the importance of the definition.[13] While Wiley admitted that refiner's syrup did not meet the definition, he claimed that he had opposed the acceptance of that term in the first place. With Dunlap and McCabe supporting Wiley's position, the board decided that corn syrup was not a satisfactory synonym for glucose.[14]

In response, the Corn Products Refining Company contacted members of Congress and bombarded President Roosevelt with letters from corn growers and business interests, all of whom warned of the adverse effects that the decision would have on agriculture and business. The company then prepared additional briefs and asked for an additional hearing. Wilson presided over the hearing, which took place on 5 December 1907. The animosity between Bedford and Wiley quickly surfaced during the hearing. Bedford complained that Wiley had sent out letters saying that corn syrup was not a proper name for glucose before an official ruling had been issued. Wiley replied that he had been offering only his personal opinion. Bedford argued that a ruling against the name *corn syrup* would so damage sales that irreparable harm would be done to the corn producers of the country. Wiley's response was perhaps more revealing than he intended: "We are all interested in the prosperity of agriculture, but we can show you, Mr. Secretary, that the glucose industry has been a positive injury to agriculture. It has almost bankrupted the bee keeping interests in this country; it has almost bankrupted the maple syrup industry of this country; it has almost bankrupted the cane syrup industry of this country; it has almost bankrupted the sorghum syrup industry of this country."[15] Wiley, the old sugar hand, had just revealed the particular elements of American agriculture that he favored; corn producers were not among them.

It was Charles F. Chandler, a chemist representing the Corn Products

Refining Company, who raised the issue of refiner's syrup contradicting the official standards definition of syrup. Wiley replied, "this definition of refiners syrup was put in at the request of Dr. Weichmann, the chemist of the Sugar Refining Co. I do not think we were in entire harmony. My associates thought because it was known to the trade and had been known to the trade for years by that name, and known to the public by that name, it distinguished it from the term syrup."[16] Having said that much, Wiley continued to cling tenaciously to his objections to the name *corn syrup*. Of course, these objections had not surfaced until the middle of 1906, when it seemed likely the pure food bill would become law, and he was working with Arbuckle and the sugar refiners on the creation of the New York Sugar Trade Laboratory (see chap. 5). This was a clear conflict of interest, which Wiley did not disclose to his superiors or to the public.

Chandler's testimony made it quite evident to Wiley that allowing corn syrup in the earlier standards and permitting sugar producers to use the term "refiner's syrup" was a weakness in his position. On 27 December, Wiley wrote to William Frear that "we unwisely and unwittingly allowed to creep into our standards those for glucose or corn syrup as synonymous terms. This fact is now used against us and with some effect. . . . Another thing we should regret is that in a moment of weakness we permitted Weichmann and the sugar trust to have us put in the definition of refiners' syrup." Frear reminded Wiley that "Your letter of June 3, 1903, which was the basis of further correspondence with the Committee, suggested the use of the term 'corn syrup' but did not use 'glucose syrup.' " He also reminded Wiley that he had not dissented when the committee approved the definition of refiner's syrup.[17]

Following the hearing, Wilson allowed the Corn Products Refining Company to submit further evidence and briefs. At the same time, he allowed Wiley to submit his own brief and asked McCabe and Dunlap to do the same. Wiley's brief was over a hundred pages long and included more than technical or chemical matters. Among other things, Wiley charged the Corn Products Refining Company with watering its stock. While this accusation was true of the company's predecessors, under Bedford, the company had reduced the ratio of stock to assets by over one-third, which improved the company's fiscal position considerably.[18]

Wiley also included in his brief letters from food officials and chemists who supported his position. He had obtained these in response to a letter that he had sent out soliciting opinions. The letter said that the secretary of agriculture had requested opinions, which was not true. Wilson was not even aware of Wiley's letter until Bedford brought it to his attention. In the letter, Wiley had summarized his objections to the name *corn syrup*, which naturally elicited responses sympathetic to his point of view. Even so, not all food officials agreed with him. Charles Baskerville, for example, said *corn syrup* and *glucose* were synonymous but added, "This is simply a difference of opinion, Old Fellow. I think you are wrong this time, whereas you are almost always right."[19]

The Dunlap and McCabe briefs indicated a change in their position on this issue. Both now favored allowing glucose to be sold as corn syrup, just as sucrose was sold as sugar. Dunlap argued that the product was a syrup as the term was understood by most people. Continuing with this argument, he said that since glucose was made from corn, it was entitled to be called corn syrup. According to him, the name was "not deceptive, misleading or false" and thus was not a violation of the Pure Food and Drugs Act.

McCabe's brief raised the question of the change in standards between December 1904 and June 1906. He argued that nothing had changed in the industry between those dates that would have called for a change of definitions: "Without any evidence to the contrary, it must be assumed that the change in the 1906 standards whereby the term 'corn syrup' was eliminated, was dictated by the personal opinions of the gentlemen who composed the committee." He went on to argue that the food standards committee was never authorized to fix names for food products. The committee's task, said McCabe, was "to determine standards of purity; that is, they were to select a product which by common usage was recognized by a certain name and determine the physical and chemical characteristics this product should have when sold under that name." McCabe concluded by saying that he had changed his mind because he found the briefs submitted by the Corn Products Refining Company convincing and that it was not fair "to saddle a pure, wholesome and nutritious, unadulterated, distinctly American product with a name which will prevent its sale."[20]

As he had with whiskey, President Roosevelt became embroiled in the corn syrup controversy. This time, however, he did not turn the matter over to his attorney general; he requested a meeting with Wilson to discuss the issue. Having looked over the materials available, Roosevelt concluded that glucose was a syrup, that it was made from corn, and that consequently it should be allowed to be called *corn syrup*. He was reported to have said, "You must make the manufacturers call a spade a spade, but don't make them call it a damn shovel."[21] Roosevelt would later cite the corn syrup episode as one of the reasons for his loss of confidence in Wiley. He knew of Wiley's support for the sugar industry. In fact, only the intervention of Wilson had kept Roosevelt from dismissing Wiley when he had earlier testified against lowering the tariff on Cuban sugar, a policy that Roosevelt favored. Roosevelt probably attributed Wiley's opposition to corn syrup as nothing more than an extension of his paternalism toward the sugar industry.[22]

Guerrilla Warfare

Officially, the episode ended on 13 February 1908, when the secretaries of agriculture, commerce, and the treasury signed Food Inspection Decision 87, which stated, "In our opinion it is lawful to label this sirup as Corn Sirup." Wiley, however, did not accept the ruling and, a few weeks after the decision in a speech before the International Congress of Mothers, said:

> I have spoken of maple syrup as an important food product. Other table syrups should also be carefully scrutinized in regard to their purity. We have in this country abundant supplies of syrup-making materials to provide for all the table syrup needed. The maple grove, the sorghum field and the cane field are ready to furnish all the table syrups that we need. There is no necessity any longer, if there ever has been, of using glucose as a basis of a table syrup.
>
> By itself it is not palatable nor is it eaten as a syrup. . . . The table syrup of this country would be vastly improved if glucose were eliminated from their composition, and there is substituted for this mixed mess the pure products of the maple grove, the sorghum field and the cane field.[23]

While these comments were clearly intended to undermine the glucose industry, they were also a warning to McCabe, Dunlap, and Wilson; overturning Wiley's opinions would produce repercussions outside the halls of the Department of Agriculture.

Both the pro-Wiley press and Wiley himself in his correspondence used Bedford's past association with Standard Oil to discredit the Corn Products Refining Company. They claimed that the giant oil company was the true owner and manager of the glucose company. Wiley also claimed that the owners of Standard Oil owned *Leslie's Weekly*, a publication fond of criticizing Wiley.[24] By this time, Wiley viewed the Corn Products Refining Company as an archenemy of pure food. He was convinced that the company not only controlled *Leslie's* and cooperated with the manufacturers of rectified whiskey but also was behind the *American Food Journal*, which was virulently anti-Wiley. Wiley had originally believed that the journal represented the manufacturers of rectified whiskey, but over time he added other manufacturers to his list, including the Corn Products Refining Company. He even sent postal inspectors and food inspectors to spy on the magazine staff and to find out who was behind the publication. Although he could not prove it, he remained convinced that the glucose producers were behind the journal's attacks.[25]

While gaining the Department of Agriculture's permission to use the term *corn syrup* on labels helped sales of glucose to manufacturers and jobbers, pure food regulations still considered corn syrup, used as a sweetener, to be an adulterant. As a result, the presence of corn syrup had to be listed on a product's label. Food Inspection Decision 66, on the other hand, allowed sucrose to be added to products without being listed on labels. It was argued that the sweet taste was sufficient to tell the consumer that sucrose was present. In fact, F.I.D. 66 gave sucrose the sole right to be called sugar. Glucose producers objected to both rulings for years, arguing they were unfair and discriminatory. In 1912, Bedford wrote to Wilson, "We claim, therefore, that they [corn sugars and syrups] should have the same rights as are accorded to the sugar and syrup produced from cane, beets or sap of the Maple tree." He went on to add, "It is our contention that our products, wherever used or desired to be used, shall have exactly the same rights as any other sugar or syrup." The protests were ineffectual and the glucose industry spent the next thirty years fighting to undo the discriminatory regulation put in place by F.I.D. 66.[26]

Even after he left government service in 1912, Wiley fought any change in the regulation favoring sugar. Using his column in *Good Housekeeping*, he urged readers to write to their congressmen opposing any change in the law. He also testified in congressional hearings against efforts by the corn refining industry to overcome the discriminatory regulations. Indeed, his opposition lasted until the end of his life. The last column he wrote for *Good Housekeeping* just a few months before his death in 1930 was devoted to opposing a bill that would have given glucose the same exemptions granted to sucrose. He still argued that sucrose was nutritionally superior to glucose and that glucose was harmful to human health.[27]

Coca-Cola on Trial

Perhaps the most famous product charged with violation of the pure food act during Wiley's tenure was Coca-Cola. In 1909, alleging that the product contained free caffeine (caffeine that is added to a product during manufacture), which made it injurious to health, the federal government filed a libel to condemn forty barrels and twenty kegs of Coca-Cola. The libel went on to accuse the product of using caramel as well as other coloring and flavoring substances to conceal damage or inferiority. It also charged that Coke was misbranded because its name implied that the product contained coca and cola when it contained no cocaine and little, if any, cola. Because, according to the government's complaint, the label also depicted images of the coca leaf and the cola nut, which suggested that these products were present, it was a false and misleading design regarding the substances and ingredients contained in the product. The comprehensiveness and gravity of the charges meant that the existence of the Coca-Cola Company was threatened.

The trial was held in March 1911 in Chattanooga, Tennessee.[28] Wiley attended with his bride of a few weeks, the noted feminist Anna Kelton. The couple lodged in a hotel room overlooking the post office, which also housed the courtroom where the trial was held. When the chief chemist was not conferring with experts and lawyers, the couple socialized with friends and those eager to meet the renowned Dr. Wiley. The newlyweds even made a journey to Lookout Mountain, Chattanooga's famous landmark, on a day when Wiley was free from his duties. Anna clipped out the daily newspaper reports, collected photographs of the area, made sketchy notes of the day's activities, and wove them together into a scrapbook of the combined trial and honeymoon.[29]

Wiley viewed the trial as a moment of glory and triumph. Years later he wrote of the difficulties he had encountered in bringing Coca-Cola to court. He told of the evidence that he had gathered on Coca-Cola's addictive properties and of how the secretary of agriculture had tried to stop the prosecution until Fred Loring Seely, an Atlanta newspaperman, had threatened to expose the secretary's interference. Even then, Wiley noted, the trial was held in Chattanooga, a town that he claimed was in the pocket of Coca-Cola. Wiley complained that Wilson and his vassals, McCabe and Dunlap, had acted to protect Coca-Cola by forcing him to hold the trial in a place where he was unlikely to win.[30] Wiley's rendering of history misled his readers. It was Wiley who had directed inspectors to look for shipments of Coca-Cola in eastern Tennessee. He had done so because he wanted to bring the case before Judge Edward T. Sanford, a former assistant attorney general who had prosecuted food and drugs cases. Wiley had met Sanford and considered him friendly to his interpretation of the Pure Food and Drugs Act.[31]

The president of Coca-Cola, Asa Candler, was angered by what he saw as an arbitrary attack on his law-abiding business. He characterized the government's evidence as "rat, rabbit, and frog." Only the support that he had received from numberless good people, said Candler, could " 'extract to a large extent the bitterness from the cup that has passed to my lips by ill meaning people during the past two years.' " His son, Charles Howard

Candler, blamed the case on the "overzealous notoriety-seeking of Dr. Harvey W. Wiley and his associates, who were too prone to use their authority for bureaucratic oppression." Charles Howard Candler believed the emotional stress caused by the need to protect his good name had led to his father's decision to retire early.[32]

Pretrial Maneuvers

By the time of the trial, Coca-Cola was the nation's most popular soft drink. The firm sold nearly five million gallons of syrup annually, which brought in revenues of more than six million dollars. The driving force behind its success was Asa Candler, an Atlanta pharmacist who had purchased the rights to the product from John Styth Pemberton, another Atlanta pharmacist, in 1888. Pemberton, the creator of several proprietary products, had developed Coca-Cola when cocaine was endorsed by the medical community. For a time, medical doctors believed that cocaine was a miracle drug that could kill pain and stimulate the nervous system without causing harmful side effects. President McKinley, Sarah Bernhardt, Thomas Edison, Sigmund Freud, three popes, and the fictional detective Sherlock Holmes all endorsed cocaine mixtures.[33]

Although Pemberton never put more than a trace of cocaine in his product, he used the drug's reputation as a brain stimulant to promote his product as a treatment for fatigue. He advertised it as a "brain tonic," a kind of intellectual medicine. It sold well, but Pemberton lacked the vision to make it a great success. In ill health and in debt, he sold his interest to Candler who soon realized that Coca-Cola's appeal was as a beverage, not as a medicine. Candler enhanced the flavor and began the successful promotion of Coca-Cola as a soda fountain soft drink. From the beginning, he sought a broad-based national market and thus promoted the product as a refreshing beverage for everyone.[34] When the government taxed his product as a proprietary medicine, Candler fought the case and won the return of his tax payments. Government experts at that time had testified that the product contained minute traces of cocaine, but they had drawn this conclusion not from chemical analysis but from the fact that the concentrated syrup numbed the tip of the tongue.[35]

In the first years of the twentieth century, the public's attitudes toward cocaine changed rapidly. Experience with the drug had shown that it could be habit forming. It was also alleged to cause crime and sexual excess. Candler decided to remove all traces of cocaine from the drink and use instead an extract of the coca plant free from the notorious alkaloid. Taking advantage of the growing prohibitionist movement, he began to promote the beverage as a temperance drink. However, rumors that the product contained alcohol led the U.S. Army to prohibit it on military bases. Candler disputed the claim, and in July 1907, the army asked the Department of Agriculture to analyze Coca-Cola's ingredients.[36] The company was already in communication with the Bureau of Chemistry; in February 1906, it had sent the bureau a gallon of syrup for examination. Wiley had turned it over to the chief of his drug laboratory, Dr. Lyman F. Kebler, for analysis but had informed Coca-Cola that it was against departmental rules to reveal the results of the analysis to the company. At the time, Wiley thought that the product contained cocaine.[37]

By 1907, newspaper articles were reporting that Wiley was criticizing soft drinks for containing cocaine. Candler wrote to Wiley, explaining that Coca-Cola contained no cocaine and only a small amount of caffeine, which gave the product a "mild stimulative character, the same as a light tea." He added that the use of caffeine did not result in the development of a habit. Whether he knew it or not, Candler had just waved a red flag at Wiley. As early as 1902, Wiley had claimed that free caffeine was similar to strychnine and morphia. By 1906, although he had no scientific evidence for his claims, he was comparing it to such habit-forming drugs as opium and cannabis indica.[38] His distinction between free caffeine and the caffeine in tea and coffee was about as well-founded as his claims that wearing hats caused baldness and that pasteurizing milk destroyed its value as a food; but his position as head of the Bureau of Chemistry gave his speculations currency and respectability.[39]

In closing, Candler said, "We feel confident that we have greatly benefitted the American public in originating this form of a non-alcoholic harmless beverage and all the reports pouring in from every section of this country agree in the appreciation of our effort."[40] Wiley, the connoisseur of wine and straight whiskey, responded to the temperance argument with a terse statement denying any responsibility for the statements attributed to him in the press. He then wrote, "In regard to the particular virtues of your preparation Coca Cola, I may say frankly that I have heard many complaints of the Coca Cola habit, apparently without any beneficial effect. I am totally unable to agree with your statement that the consumption of caffeine as a drug is no more reprehensible than the use of tea and coffee."[41]

By the time Wiley received the army's request to analyze Coca-Cola, he knew that Coca-Cola contained no cocaine and only a trace of alcohol. However, he delayed issuing a report while he sought to prove that caffeine added to a product was harmful to human health.[42] In the interim, officials in Bureau of Chemistry spoke out against soft drinks and the use of free caffeine. Responding to letters asking about the ingredients in Coca-Cola, they refused to give out information but did issue damaging statements. In July 1907, Lyman Kebler, responding to an inquiry from *Collier's Magazine,* wrote, "the information transmitted to another department of government is confidential and can therefore not be made public," but added, "we would like to ask whether in your opinion it would be conducive to health for persons of all ages to drink from ten to twenty-five and even forty glasses of a beverage containing as much caffeine as an ordinary cup of coffee?"[43]

Wiley now had Coca-Cola in his sights. The Bureau of Chemistry criticized its labels because they read "guaranteed under the pure food and drug law of 1906," rather than the technically correct "food and drugs act." In fact, on this minor technicality, the bureau threatened the company with loss of its guarantee. The firm quickly complied with the required change. Nevertheless, it soon found Lyman Kebler and other federal inspectors on its doorstep. Although Candler showed them his factory from "cellar to top," he knew that his company was a target of food regulators.[44]

In September 1907, John Candler, Asa's brother, met with Wiley and the other members of the Board of Food and Drug Inspection in Washington, D.C. His talk with Wiley was congenial, and afterward a mutual friend told Candler that Wiley had acknowledged that there was no cocaine in Coca-Cola. According to his friend, however, Wiley had also said that he might charge the company with misbranding because the label implied that the product contained cocaine. Candler complained to McCabe. The company was willing, he said in a September letter, to place a statement on labels declaring that the product contained no cocaine. The Candlers had no doubts about Wiley's animosity toward their product, but his fervor mystified them.[45]

Wiley's enmity toward the firm may have been increased by the company's switch from the sugar company of his friend and supporter John Arbuckle to Henry Havemeyer's American Sugar Refining Company. Between 1898 and 1901, Arbuckle Brothers were involved in a costly trade war with Havemeyer's company. Although they settled the trade war, the two companies were never on friendly terms. When Coca-Cola switched from Arbuckle to American Sugar in 1903, Wiley found himself in a position to retaliate. Coca-Cola's support of prohibition may have also stimulated his dislike. The company was rumored to have supported the prohibitionist movement financially so that Coca-Cola could be promoted as a temperance drink.[46] In any case, throughout September, the Bureau of Chemistry continued to imply, without undertaking a chemical analysis, that the product was addictive. In October, Wilson asked Wiley for the report, saying, "I have a large volume of correspondence in regard to Coca-Cola. Having Dr.

Kebler's report would relieve me of correspondence." The following day, Wiley sent a summary of the report to the secretary.[47]

Kebler's report showed that Coca-Cola contained no cocaine, a trace of alcohol, and a small amount of caffeine. Kebler also reported on the consumption of the beverage in the southern states. In seeking information on what he called the "coca cola habit," he discovered people in all walks of life were using it, "but those most addicted . . . are office people and 'brain workers.'" According to Kebler, the beverage was consumed not only by adults but also by children from four to six years of age. One physician reported, "the beverage is in some instances purchased at the fountain by the pitcher, taken home and consumed in the same way that beer is in some families." Officers at a military base reported that "in many cases soldiers consumed the beverage in undue amounts, particularly those persons who are addicted to the use of alcoholic beverages. The largest quantities are consumed after a prolonged alcoholic debauch." Kebler went on to say that a soda fountain dealer told him "that he frequently served Coca-Cola to soldiers who mixed same with whiskey and in this way produced what he termed a coca cola high-ball." The dealer also informed Kebler that "this mixture makes the soldiers wild and crazy." After summing up this anecdotal evidence of the dangers of Coca-Cola, Wiley concluded the report by saying that he was in the process of reviewing the literature dealing with caffeine and "studying the effects of caffeine as found in Coca-Cola on a number of individuals."[48]

Unable to substantiate any physiological or nutritional differences between free caffeine and natural caffeine, the caffeine found in coffee and tea, Wiley found it necessary to draw on the law that prohibited the addition of any deleterious substance to food and drink. The distinction was crucial for Wiley, who did not want to hurt the market for coffee and tea; his friend John Arbuckle was one of the leading importers and roasters of coffee.

Wiley was not alone in his belief in the deleterious effects of free caffeine. The chairwoman of the Medical Temperance Department of the Women's Christian Temperance Union, Martha M. Allen, whose efforts Wiley supported, published a pamphlet attacking the soft drink. Allen said that the soft drink contained cocaine and the caffeine and alcohol in the drink was deleterious to health.[49]

Wiley's attack on Coca-Cola also endangered the Monsanto Chemical Company, because Monsanto supplied the caffeine for Coke. The company was owned by John Queeny, who had testified before Congress in 1904 against Wiley's version of a pure food bill and had openly criticized Wiley's opinions on saccharin at the St. Louis Exposition. In 1907, Monsanto was still a small, struggling company that produced saccharin, caffeine, and a small number of other chemicals. Competition with German saccharin manufacturers kept the price for the sweetener low. Thus, Monsanto's survival depended on selling caffeine to the soft drink industry, particularly to Coca-Cola.[50]

To protect its financial interests, Monsanto hired Wiley's old nemesis, Warwick M. Hough. The firm disputed Wiley's opinions on saccharin and caffeine and joined in a campaign of criticism of the chief chemist. In late 1909 and early 1910, Monsanto circulated a sensational news report of an anti-caffeine speech Wiley had given to the Reformers' Conclave. The article, which originated in the Washington bureau of the *St. Louis Post Dispatch,* reported Wiley as saying that coffee drunkenness was more common than the whiskey habit and of equal or greater danger. In response, Monsanto called for the wholesale grocery trade to unite against Wiley.[51] Wiley received several copies of the circular from concerned businessmen who asked if he had made such statements. He denied the accuracy of the newspaper account but acknowledged that he had made the speech. He also attempted to discredit the report by pointing out that Monsanto was Coca-Cola's caffeine supplier.[52]

As Monsanto's circular spread, Wiley's response became harsher. In a letter to Edwin B. Pillsbury, editor of *Grocers' Magazine,* he said, 'I have never, either by precept or by practice, condemned the moderate use of tea or coffee." He added,

> The so-called soft drinks containing caffeine I consider objectionable in every respect. The number of victims of this habit of taking caffeine in soft drinks is very large throughout the South. In England, I have seen women who, if they were denied their tea at four o'clock, would become almost wild, and in this country I have known people who could not omit coffee or tea as usually taken without suffering from depression, headache, malaise, and a general feeling of discomfort.[53]

In another letter, this time to F. N. Barrett, editor of *American Grocer,* Wiley claimed:

> One has only to go through the South to see hundreds of victims of the Coca-Cola habit, and in England especially, the victims of the tea habit are almost as numerous as the female portion of the population. I have known many cases of persons so addicted to the use of tea or coffee that if they miss a single meal they are extremely unhappy and miserable and are usually subject to a severe headache. The evil influences of

these substances are well known to the physicians. I do not think I have intimated that people under the influence of tea and coffee would brawl, or quarrel, cuss and swear, maim, maltreat, attack and kill! The Monsanto circular discloses the desperate and despicable conduct of the opposition to my campaign for purity of food and drink.[54]

When Wilson asked about the accuracy of the *St. Louis Post Dispatch* account, Wiley acknowledged that he had delivered a speech in which he had said that the consumption of habit-forming drugs in soft drinks was a menace, especially to children, and that excessive coffee and tea consumption had ill effects. However, he attempted to discredit the account by pointing out that Monsanto was circulating the article and that the company had been investigated by his bureau, which had discovered that it manufactured caffeine, saccharin, acetphenetidin, and other chemicals.[55]

For all his efforts, Wiley found it difficult to proceed against Coca-Cola. In October 1908, he attempted to seize ten barrels and fifteen kegs of Coca-Cola shipped from Atlanta, Georgia, to Knoxville, Tennessee. Claiming that information on the pharmacology of caffeine was inadequate to justify seizure, Dunlap and McCabe, the other members of the Food and Drug Inspection Board, stopped the action.[56] In May 1909, he again tried to convince McCabe and Dunlap of the dangers of caffeine in soft drinks, especially Coca-Cola. In a memorandum to them, he said that Mrs. Hill, a member of the Washington, D.C., school board, was protesting the presence of attractive signs near school buildings that advertised Coca-Cola. She also complained that "school children are patronizing these places in large numbers and that if their parents knew the children were drinking caffeine they would be horrified."[57]

McCabe and Dunlap, however, continued to demand better evidence that Coca-Cola was dangerous to American children before proceeding. McCabe argued that if caffeine in Coca-Cola were ruled dangerous, the board would also have to rule that caffeine in coffee and tea was dangerous. Under Section 11 of the Pure Food and Drugs Act, such a ruling would require the Treasury Department to stop the entry of coffee and tea into the United States.[58]

After refusing to go along with Wiley in the spring and summer of 1909, McCabe and Dunlap altered their position in the fall of that year. Wiley later claimed that their change of heart resulted from a threat to expose their protection of Coca-Cola. This, however, seems unlikely for a number of reasons. First, it is doubtful that Wiley could have made his charges sound plausible, even with the aid of a muckraking press. Requiring evidence, as McCabe and Dunlap did, before beginning with a criminal proceeding hardly constitutes a cover-up. Second, McCabe and Dunlap had recently triumphed in the benzoate of soda controversy, and Wilson had sided with them. Indeed, in August, Wilson had sought permission from President Taft to ask for Wiley's resignation.[59] Third, the paper trail left by McCabe and Dunlap suggests that by allowing the charges against Coca-Cola to go to trial, the two men were hoping to discredit Wiley, whether or not he won the case. If he won, they felt certain that the Treasury Department would have to stop the importation of all tea and coffee into the United States. The resulting uproar would be blamed on Wiley and justify his dismissal. If he lost, he could be blamed for wasting resources on a frivolous issue while ignoring more dangerous drugs, such as cocaine, which were available in other beverages. Beneath the surface of the Chattanooga trial lay the hidden agendas of the government officials who administered the nation's food law.

The Trial

The central issue in the trial was whether or not free caffeine was a deleterious substance. The outcome depended on the testimony of expert witnesses, and neither side spared expense. The government spent over $50,000 prosecuting the case; Coca-Cola probably spent more. Candler hired many of the nation's leading experts to testify on behalf of his beverage.[60] McCabe, who hoped to keep Wiley from later saying the government had lost the case because he had not testified, urged Wiley to speak, saying that it would have a positive moral effect on the jury, but Wiley refused. He modestly claimed he did not qualify as an expert.[61] He did, however, complain about the scientists who testified for the other side. He accused them of selling their expertise to the highest bidder, which, he said, was often some crooked business interest that doped and poisoned food for profit.[62]

Among those testifying was John Queeny who spoke briefly on the total consumption of beverages containing caffeine in the United States. Many of the same distinguished scientists who had previously disputed Wiley's scientific claims—Victor Vaughan, Charles Chandler, and John Mallet, among others—testified for Coca-Cola. Dr. Kebler, H. H. Rusby, and Solis Cohen were among the government witnesses. In fact, the scientists testifying represented the nation's leading experts on food, drugs, and human physiology.[63]

During the trial, both sides engaged in surreptitious activity. Suspecting that someone was tampering with the jury, the government called in undercover agents to investigate. The agents concentrated on three jurors, eventually narrowing their suspicions to one who spent every evening in a bar getting drunk. The agents befriended the juror, hoping to persuade him to talk about what the jury was thinking. He refused several times, but the agents persisted, plying him with drinks and with promises of sex from a female agent. Finally, the man said that he, and probably the other jurors as well, were on the side of Coca-Cola; the jurors were not convinced that caffeine was harmful.

The jury never got to say which group of experts they believed because Coca-Cola's lawyers filed a motion to dismiss the case after the experts had testified. The company's lawyers argued that all of the ingredients contained in the beverage were an integral part of the product. Without any one of the ingredients, including caffeine, Coca-Cola would not be Coca-Cola. Therefore, they said, nothing, deleterious or not, was being added to the product, which was the legal issue. Judge Sanford agreed and dismissed the case. No decision was made on the harmfulness of caffeine. While there is no evidence that the dismissal was related to the information obtained from the jury member, there were distinct legal advantages to the government agreement to dismiss the case on a legal interpretation rather than having the jury rule in favor of Coca-Cola. A dismissal on a legal ruling would make it easier for the government to appeal, which it later did. At the same time, however, the dismissal undermined McCabe and Dunlap's efforts to discredit Wiley.[64]

Wiley had left Chattanooga before Judge Sanford dismissed the case. Needless to say, the verdict angered him. He refused to accept the ruling or to wait for the appeal. Indeed, he advised *Collier's* not to advertise Coca-Cola, saying that it was dangerous. Two years later in a letter to Norman Hapgood, he bitterly predicted what losing the case would mean.

> It will not be long before a milk dealer will discover that by adding a grain or two of caffeine to his milk it will become more popular which will drive his competitors into similar practices, and soon we will have our bread and our meat treated in the same way. It will open wide the flood gates to drug addiction in our foods through which the muddy waters of wealth and greed will rush.[65]

Because the dismissal left the issue of caffeine unresolved, the government could do little but pursue the case through appeal. In 1916, the Supreme Court ruled that the component parts of a compound food were subject to the law and remanded the case to district court. Coca-Cola then settled the case with the Justice Department. The company changed its formula, reducing the amount of caffeine, and then claimed that retrying the case was unwarranted because any conclusions reached would not apply to the new formula. It forfeited any claim to the forty barrels and twenty kegs and paid the cost of the trial. Judge Sanford accepted the plea and ended the case. The company was never again charged with adding a deleterious substance to its beverage.[66]

The facts do not justify Wiley's prosecution of Coca-Cola, and certainly his actions were not a wise use of the Bureau of Chemistry's resources. While the effects of caffeine needed investigating and the public needed informing, Wiley and Kebler were so prejudiced that they could not offer a scientific judgment. Indeed, Wiley's motives for prosecuting Coca-Cola are suspect; as in the other major issues that arose during his tenure, Wiley's purpose may well have been the desire to reward his friends and punish those who disagreed with him.

Meanwhile, Coca-Cola became a quintessential part of American life. The publicity surrounding the charges and the trial did not slow down the growth of sales. American consumers, who by now knew the product, did not think it was dangerous. There were many stronger drugs readily available, including beverages that contained cocaine. By the 1950s, growing worldwide sales led some to view Coca-Cola as one aspect of American imperialism, and even today, nothing is more American than a hamburger and a Coke. Despite the dire predictions of Wiley, no great calamity seems to have followed his loss at Chattanooga. The ladies of England still drink their tea, Americans their coffee, and children caffeine-free milk.

CHAPTER 10

Administrative Dominance under President Taft

Following Taft's election in November 1908, the *Christian Herald* published a series of articles on the most important tasks facing the new administration. In his contribution to the series, Wiley urged the administration to enforce the Pure Food and Drugs Act as Congress had intended. He accused the Roosevelt administration of aiding and abetting in the emasculation of the food law by ruling in favor of unscrupulous corporations and by appointing unthinking scientists who supported cheaters and poisoners. The most important task before the new administration, he said, was to "remove this stigma" from the enforcement of the pure food law. According to him, the same interests that had opposed the law's passage in the first place were now fighting its enforcement. "Under the guise even of favoring the law," he said, they had "cut its heart out and emasculate[d] its requirements." If he were given free reign, he went to say, it "would be noticed that vested interests could no longer control legislation or execution of laws."[1]

Although such administrative measures as the Board of Food and Drug Inspection and the Remsen Board had restricted Wiley's authority during Roosevelt's presidency, they had not controlled his use of the popular press or his personal denunciations of particular products and firms. Within the administrative constraints imposed by Wilson and Roosevelt, Wiley had still enjoyed considerable latitude. Under Taft, however, the atmosphere in which Wiley worked deteriorated, primarily because Wilson, angered by the attempts to oust him, deliberately diminished Wiley's autonomy. No longer did Wilson see Wiley as an honest but overly zealous reformer who was prone to poor judgment. Instead, Wilson saw him as a hypocrite, a term he used to describe Wiley to Taft, and sought to discredit him. Indeed, he wanted to remove him from office.

Bureaucratic Power Struggles

Following Taft's election, Wiley found himself increasingly on the defensive: Wilson did his best to undermine Wiley's support among state food and dairy officials; Dunlap and McCabe would not support him on the Board of Food and Drug Inspection; more and more of the controversial issues were handed over to the Remsen Board for decisions. Within the new administration, Wiley's credibility and actions were sharply questioned. Only his skillful use of the press kept him from being dismissed.

One of Wiley's most effective press campaigns came shortly after his defeat at the 1909 Denver convention of state food and dairy officials. Following that convention, Samuel Hopkins Adams had published an attack on Wiley's opponents in *Hampton's Magazine*. Adams pronounced the Pure Food and Drugs Act dead. It could not stand against the formidable array of food tricksters out to drug, poison, cheat, and deceive the consumer, he wrote. President Roosevelt and Secretary of Agriculture Wilson, he went on to say, had given in to these interests by establishing the less-than-honest Remsen Board to overrule the upright Wiley. Wiley's critics in the food industry, according to Adams, endangered the public by selling adulterated food and medicine. The article combined Wiley's arguments with the skills of an accomplished muckraking journalist.[2]

Wiley's opponents did not defend themselves well against the criticisms in the press. Thinking that it was beneath the dignity of the Board, Remsen refused to enter into a public controversy with Wiley. Although he and other members of the board had testified at the Indiana trial on benzoate of soda, their testimony was not widely reported. Eventually, Remsen would recommend that future boards should be established through the National Academy of Science in order to protect the reputations of the board's scientists from attack by hucksters and muckrakers.[3] Attempts to discredit Wiley within the administration were more effective. In early 1910, McCabe asked Wiley why so little action had been taken against misbranded drugs. McCabe argued that these drugs presented a greater danger to the consumer than the minor food issues that were receiving so much attention. He objected to Wiley's practice of permitting patent medicines to display a guarantee number and accused Wiley of having made a deal with the drug producers to not enforce the law.[4]

To stop what he viewed as blatant abuse of the law against drugs, McCabe sent an agent around to apothecaries in Washington, D.C., to purchase proprietary medicines that listed curative powers on their labels. Dr. Greene's Nervura, for example, claimed to be a "blood and nerve remedy." The product's label read, "For nervousness, poor blood, malaria, female weakness, mental depression, apoplexy, St. Vitus Dance, dyspepsia, constipation, and afflictions of the nervous system. Guaranteed under the Food and Drugs Act of June 30, 1906 and guaranty filed with Secretary of Agriculture, at Washington, D.C., Serial No. 150." McCabe's agent sent this and other items with similar claims to the Bureau of Chemistry, asking the bureau to analyze the products and take appropriate action.[5]

Wiley responded that there were some 25,000 such items being sold in the country and that the bureau's drug division lacked the money and personnel to pursue every violation of the law. McCabe retorted that there could not possibly be 25,000 nostrums on the market, but even if there were and all of them could not be investigated, certainly the most dangerous and egregious false claims could be prevented. In support of McCabe, Dunlap wrote a memorandum to the food inspection board that said, "The greatest expenditure of energy, not to say money, in the enforcement of the Food and Drugs Act has been markedly in the line of foods, and to judge from the results, mostly along lines of preventing and prosecuting for fraud in which the question of public health has not been involved. . . . Quite the reverse appears to be true with drugs. The least expenditure of energy, and the least results have been obtained when they have been the most needed." Rejecting Wiley's explanation for this state of affairs, Dunlap continued, "Money has not been lacking, but it has apparently been turned into the food control rather than to drugs. . . . the condition of the drug market, as indicated by the Chairman, is so appalling, that this Board is guilty of criminal negligence if it does not take immediate steps to bend its energies to the protection of the public against dangerous nostrums rather than along lines where the question of the public health is less actively protected than is the pocket book."[6]

It was not primarily a concern for public health that led Dunlap and McCabe to criticize Wiley for his lack of drug enforcement. The flurry of memorandums on lax drug enforcement was part of a broad attempt by the administration to discredit Wiley. Together, McCabe and Dunlap were hoping to force Wiley's resignation or to have him dismissed. After 1908, much of their energy was devoted to a bureaucratic struggle with Wiley. By 1910, both sides were expending so much energy fighting each other that enforcement of the law had become a sideshow to the bureaucratic power struggle.

General Order No. 140

The Agricultural Appropriation Act of 1910 struck a substantial blow against Wiley. McCabe managed to have inserted into the act a phrase that placed the control of whom to prosecute in the office of the solicitor. Presented to Congress as a means of gaining legal control over the troubled Forest Service, the phrase simply said, "Hereafter the legal work of the Department of Agriculture shall be performed under the supervision and direction of the Solicitor."

Using the Department of Agriculture's General Order No. 140, which was based on this phrase and placed all authority over legal actions, including those brought under the Pure Food and Drugs Act, in the hands of the solicitor, McCabe brought the administrative mechanisms for enforcement of the Pure Food and Drugs Act under his direct supervision.[7] The Board of Food and Drug Inspection was now limited to conducting hearings. A report on all products obtained by food inspectors was to be forwarded to McCabe. Even if the Bureau of Chemistry determined that a product was not misbranded or adulterated, a report explaining the bureau's decision had to be sent to McCabe. If the Board of Food and Drug Inspection determined that a product was misbranded or adulterated, it was up to McCabe to decide if there were sufficient evidence for the board to hold hearings. After a hearing, the board was required to return its findings to McCabe, who would then decide if the case should be prosecuted. It was McCabe alone who would choose the witnesses and communicate with the Justice Department about the case. Under the terms of General Order No.140, only the direction of inspectors was left in Wiley's hands.[8] Of course, Wiley was angered by this turn of events, but there was little he could do. Without prior approval from Wilson, he was prohibited from contacting members of Congress, from publishing in the popular press, and from speaking in public. Although, with the cooperation of L. S. Dow of the Heinz company, he attempted to induce Congress to investigate the enforcement of the pure food law, his attempt failed.[9]

McCabe and Dunlap also took action against Wiley's supporters. Two of Heinz's products, India Relish and Mandalay Sauce, were brought before the Board of Food and Drug Inspection on the grounds they were mislabeled; India Relish was not from India and Mandalay sauce was not from Mandalay. Wiley refused to take action against the products, even though he had charged Holland Gin and other firms with using inaccurate geographical designations. In response, McCabe and Dunlap drew up a seizure order for each product and surreptitiously slipped the orders into a stack of papers awaiting Wiley's signature. Both men were aware of Wiley's habit of signing a large number of papers at one time without bothering to read them. He would assign one person the task of handing him the papers and another the task of removing them. He thus unknowingly signed seizure orders for India Relish and Mandalay Sauce.

Five cases of India Relish were seized in Washington, D.C., and the company was brought to court, but before the case was heard, another court dismissed the charges against Holland Gin, holding that the geographical name was generic. Since the case against India Relish involved the same issue, it too was dismissed. The case against Mandalay Sauce was also dropped, but only after the case was rediscovered in the office of the U.S. attorney in Pittsburgh where it had been lost for several years. Before either case was dropped, however, Wiley provided officials of the Heinz Company with inside information to help them defend themselves against the charges brought by his agency.[10]

The offensive against Wiley was carried out primarily by McCabe, and it was not without its lighter moments. Wiley frequently spent his spare time on his farm in northern Virginia. Each fall he would bring back apples from the farm and pass them around to his employees. In the fall of 1910, McCabe picked out a few bad apples and sent them to the bureau's laboratory, which naturally found them to be spoiled. Upon receiving the report, McCabe cited Wiley for interstate transportation of impure food.[11]

The Rusby Incident

Slowly Wiley found his political base slipping away from him. He had lost the whiskey wars; he had lost the benzoate of soda battle; and Wilson had soundly defeated him at the Denver convention of state food and dairy officials. After the Denver convention, Wiley did not attempt to regain control of the association nor did he attend its annual convention held in New Orleans in 1910, which had unity as its dominant theme. Nearly all of the members of the organization, including R. M. Allen, agreed to put the disputes of the past behind them. Although Commissioner Emery of Wisconsin wanted to fight on the old issues, the majority of the organization agreed to support the Pure Food and Drugs Act and Secretary Wilson.[12] Faced with the opposition of Wilson and the attendant loss of support from within the Department of Agriculture and the State Food Officials, Wiley more than ever had to rely on the public for support. Fortunately for him, the public proved to be a solid friend.

In the spring of 1911, the payment of Henry H. Rusby of the New York College of Pharmacy, one of the experts at the Coca-Cola trial, became grounds for charges against Wiley. Rusby had been employed by the Bureau of Chemistry to examine drugs brought through the port of New York. Originally, he had been paid twenty dollars per day, but in the spring of 1909, his pay was lowered to nine dollars per day, the legal maximum established by Congress for classified scientific investigators. Because Rusby was not willing to continue his services at the lower rate, Wiley devised a plan to put him on an annual salary. Under Wiley's plan, Rusby would be paid sixteen hundred dollars per year and would be expected to work eighty days per year. Wiley took his plan to Wilson, who approved it.

While Wiley was honeymooning in Chattanooga during the Coca-Cola trial, Dunlap, who had been left in charge of the Bureau of Chemistry, discovered correspondence between assistant chemist Bigelow, Lyman Kebler, head of the drug laboratory, and Rusby, which revealed that the scheme was simply a means to get around the nine-dollar limit.[13] He realized that this could be construed as a violation of the law and conferred with McCabe and Wilson, who decided to use the correspondence as grounds for dismissal of Wiley. They referred the matter to the Department of Agriculture's personnel committee, of which McCabe was a member. The committee questioned Rusby, Kebler, Bigelow, and Wiley, then issued a report saying that Rusby should be dismissed, Kebler demoted, and Bigelow and Wiley given a chance to resign. Wilson took the report to a cabinet meeting and recommended Wiley's dismissal. The case was turned over to Attorney General George W. Wickersham, who had offered to review it from the legal standpoint. Although Wickersham decided that the agreement with Rusby was illegal and merited "condign punishment," he said the accused were entitled to an opportunity to respond.[14]

Wiley was on his Virginia farm at the time Wickersham's opinion was released. When Bigelow delivered the news, Wiley reportedly yelled, "Victory! victory! victory!" A guilty verdict from so prominent a figure as the attorney general of the United States does not usually elicit a triumphant response, but Wiley had his eyes fixed on a larger picture. The muckraking press had claimed repeatedly that there was a conspiracy between certain members of the Department of Agriculture and various business interests that wanted to continue poisoning and cheating the American consumer. Wiley knew that Wickersham's opinion would attract widespread public attention and believed that the public outcry would induce a congressional investigation, which would enable him to expose his detractors.[15]

As Wiley had predicted, news of the possibility that he might be dismissed soon spread across the nation, and the strength of his support began to reveal itself. Letters poured in to President Taft and Secretary Wilson. *Oil, Paint, and Drug Reporter* magazine wrote that this was the time to expose the cabal of corrupt officials and unethical businesses that wanted to overthrow Wiley. Ralph W. Moss of Indiana, chairman of the House Agriculture Committee, called for an investigation, saying, "We propose to find out, if possible, what influences are back of the movement to oust Dr. Wiley. It is my idea there should be a thorough investigation of the administration of the Food and Drug Act."[16]

The stage was now set for Wiley's vindication. Congressman Moss was favorably disposed toward his native son, and Wiley's popularity gave the press a story with mass appeal. Congressional hearings that revealed the persecution of Wiley by venal officials would splash across the headlines of

America's newspapers. All Congress needed to do was to expose the corruption of the food dopers and their cohorts in the Department of Agriculture.

Bringing charges against Wiley based on the Rusby affair revealed the lengths to which Wilson, McCabe, and Dunlap were willing to go to oust him. In the first place, the damaging correspondence was between Bigelow and Rusby, not Wiley and Rusby. Indeed, Wiley could have placed the blame for trying to circumvent the law on his assistant chemist. That he chose not to shows a quality that Wiley displayed throughout the food campaign; he was consistently loyal to those who supported him. In the second place, it was easy to argue that the Bureau of Chemistry was simply trying to secure the services of a competent expert. The law that lowered wages to nine dollars per day made it impossible to secure competent chemists. Circumventing an unrealistically low wage by entering into annual contracts was common practice in the Department of Agriculture; the technique had been used when establishing the Remsen Board. Singling out Wiley for prosecution was vindictive, and it reveals how far working relations between Wilson and Wiley had deteriorated.

From the opening gavel, the investigation favored Wiley, who worked closely with Congressman Moss. Not only did Wiley supply Moss with information, he also told him which areas to investigate and what questions to ask. While the witnesses who testified before the committee were not represented by lawyers, two distinguished attorneys, Henry E. Davis and former congressman William Hepburn, represented Wiley and directed much of the questioning. The tone of the questioning made it seem as if the witnesses, not Wiley, were under investigation; Moss had made clear that the hearings were less about Wiley than about the enforcement of the Pure Food and Drugs Act. Despite this sympathetic stage, the plot that emerged from the testimony was not one of corrupt officials. Wilson, the elderly secretary of agriculture, McCabe, his loyal solicitor, Dunlap, the university chemist, and Ira Remsen, the distinguished president of Johns Hopkins University, could not convincingly be portrayed as corrupt. Wiley was unable create an image of a venal cabal, as he had confidently claimed. Furthermore, there was no evidence of corrupt businessmen controlling the enforcement of the law. In fact, the most credible evidence on this score was the influence that Arbuckle, Heinz, and Taylor had exerted on Wiley, but Wiley's lawyers astutely steered questioning away from his connections with these business firms. Wiley himself volunteered nothing; for once he was silent, even about whiskey.[17]

What did emerge from the hearings was a picture of bureaucratic squabbling over how the law should be administered and who should administer it. As the real issues had none of the criminal conspiracy or corruption that Wiley had promised, the newspapermen who remained in Washington through the heat of August found their ardor cooling. *Oil, Paint, and Drug Reporter,* which had earlier clamored for an exposé, now simply said, "It is manifest that conditions of strong prejudice have existed on both sides. It will be necessary to bring about a general reorganization of the service if the law is to be effective."[18]

The report of the Moss Committee was finally issued on 22 January 1912. It was not the report that Wiley had hoped for. It did not reveal any large scandal, nor did it reveal conspiracy with commercial interests to prevent Wiley from enforcing the law. All in all, the report was a disappointment to Wiley.[19]

Although the Moss report received the unanimous vote of the committee, it did so only after considerable compromise. Congressman Moss himself did not agree with all of it. This became evident during the debate on agricultural appropriations early in 1912. Moss blamed Wilson for mismanaging the pure food law and proposed eliminating the Remsen Board until Congress passed a law specifically authorizing it. However, he was immediately challenged by Edwin Higgins of Connecticut and Charles H. Sloan of Nebraska, both of whom defended Wilson. Higgins, quoting from the *American Food Journal,* openly doubted Wiley's honesty and called for an investigation of him. Both men claimed that Moss's speech was unfair, unnecessary, and contrary to the findings of his own committee.[20]

It was during these appropriation hearings that Joseph Cannon, the former Speaker of the House, defended Wilson and commented on the passage of the Pure Food and Drugs Act in 1906. His speech, while primarily a defense of Wilson, showed his dislike for Wiley and his suspicion that Wiley had directed a public campaign against him in 1906. Even James R. Mann, who was a friend of Wiley and a longtime supporter of pure food legislation, corroborated that Cannon had worked for passage of the bill in 1906. Mann also said that Wiley was wrong about the Remsen Board and the authority of Wilson. Mann, while acknowledging Wiley's contribution to the pure food law, explained to his colleagues, "the law does not provide that Dr. Wiley or anyone else at the head of the Bureau of Chemistry shall have the final say as to prosecution for violation of the law. . . . The Remsen Board and the Bureau of Chemistry are only advisory as to whether the government should attempt the prosecutions."[21]

It did not take long for Attorney General Wickersham, regarded by some as having the political savvy of an ox, to realize that the Rusby issue was too minor to justify the dismissal of Wiley. This left Taft, whose administration was already on the defensive over the dismissal of Pinchot the year before, to cope with the political problems caused by the bungled attempt to dismiss Wiley. Not wishing to provide more fodder to his political enemies,

Taft waited until the Moss hearings were completed, then issued, in his judicial manner, a long document exonerating Wiley. He may have wished that he had followed Wilson's advice to dismiss Wiley a year earlier, but he could not do so now. He would later blame Wilson for the whole incident.[22]

Because the congressional hearing had revealed there were systemic problems in the Department of Agriculture's enforcement of the Pure Food and Drugs Act, Taft's statement exonerating Wiley did not confine itself to the Rusby affair: "The broader issues raised by the investigation, which have a much weightier relation than this one to the general efficiency of the Department, may require much more radical action than the question I have here considered and decided." While some interpreted this statement to mean that Wiley would be given a free hand to enforce the law as he saw fit, the only immediate result of the hearings was to change the composition of the Food and Drug Inspection Board. McCabe resigned and was replaced by Roscoe E. Doolittle, a Wiley supporter who had previously directed the bureau's laboratory in New York. Although this gave Wiley firm control over the board, Dunlap remained in place and Wilson still insisted on approving the board's actions. Furthermore, as department solicitor, McCabe continued to decide whether or not to prosecute. Thus, the administrative change did not substantially increase Wiley's control over enforcement of the law.[23]

Most of the daily press cheered Taft's decision to drop the charges against Wiley. Wiley's critics, however, felt that the real issue had not been explored and demanded that Congress investigate Wiley's connections with special interests. While there was little support for this position by the public or in Congress, the feeling was shared by Wiley's opponents in the government.[24]

Final Straws

As far as Wiley was concerned, the release of the Moss report did nothing to strengthen his position. Furthermore, at the conclusion of the agricultural appropriation hearings that year, the House provided funds for the Remsen Board for the following year, and an attempt to delete the salary of Solicitor McCabe failed. A public dispute over baking powder made it abundantly clear that Wiley's situation would not improve.

The Baking Powder Dispute

On 27 February 1912, the daily papers carried a report, based on documents given to the United Press Association by someone within Bureau of Chemistry, that Wiley and Doolittle of the Board of Food and Drug Inspection had voted to abate a case against a cream of tartar baking powder that contained lead. The press speculated that the case had been abated because of Wiley's close association with the Royal Baking Powder Company, also known as the Baking Powder Trust. Wiley was known to be a friend of William MacMurtie and other high officials in the company.

In defending himself, Wiley argued that the amount of lead was very small, that it resulted from the manufacturers' use of lead tanks, and that he was following the decision of the attorney general not to prosecute cases in which ingredients were added until the courts had reached a decision on Coca-Cola case. His defense, however, was inconsistent with his actions on other occasions. Even in small amounts, lead was harmful, and Wiley had often condemned products that contained small amounts of substances that he felt were harmful, such as benzoate of soda. By his own publicly proclaimed standards, he should have voted to have the baking powder taken off the market or at least to have the presence of lead listed on the label.[25]

Suspecting that Dunlap had supplied the documents to the press, Wiley demanded that Wilson remove Dunlap from the Board of Food and Drug Inspection. When Wilson refused, Wiley offered his resignation. On 15 March 1912, Wilson accepted it. In a statement to the press, Wiley outlined the reasons for his resignation. He could, he said, better carry out the purifying of food and drugs—the work closest to his heart—by leaving government service. His superiors in the department, he averred, had undermined his work and prevented the Bureau of Chemistry from doing the job assigned to it by law. After saying that the bureau was authorized to examine foods and refer companies that broke the law to the court for prosecution, he went on to accuse commercial interests of controlling his superiors and derailing the process. He cited as examples whiskey, benzoate of soda, sulphurous acid, and glucose. He could no longer bear to work side by side, he said, with those who falsely accused and harassed him. He complained that nothing was done to change the conditions under which he worked despite his exoneration by a congressional investigation and by the president of the United States. He concluded by saying that he would continue to work for the interest of the people against those forces that wanted to cheat and poison them.[26]

Although Wiley had decided to resign before the Moss report was released, his statement expressed his growing frustration with his position. He had been vindicated of the Rusby charges, but his situation within the Taft administration was substantially the same. By now, his superiors were well aware of his tactics and were intent on opposing him. Furthermore, although he was prosperous, he felt the need for more income. He was sixty-six years old, recently married, and soon to be a father. He had already accepted an offer from *Good Housekeeping* and would soon begin rounds on the Chautauqua speaking circuit.

Fading Commercial Support

There was another reason for Wiley's resignation—he was losing his commercial supporters. The whiskey industry was putting aside its differences to fight prohibition. Differences between Wiley and the Heinz Company were growing. The publicity against benzoate of soda and other preservatives had given the company the commercial edge it wanted. A continuation of the battle held little advantage for Heinz and the distinct possibility of an investigation into its connection with Wiley, which could be damaging. Heinz was also inclined to support the presidential bid of Theodore Roosevelt, whom Wiley believed was responsible for his troubles. Finally, John Arbuckle, a longtime friend, fell seriously ill. He died only a few days after Wiley offered his resignation.

Without strong commercial support, Wiley knew that his prospects as chief chemist were not promising, whatever the outcome of the 1912 election. Although he had been a lifelong Republican, he realized that a Taft victory or the return of Roosevelt would probably mean his dismissal. He had some hope that a Democratic victory might vault him into the secretary of agriculture's chair, but he must have realized that this possibility was remote. Still, his resignation left him free to campaign, and his political support was valuable because of his large following among the public. Indeed, only days after his resignation he met with Roosevelt at the request of the former president. Wiley, however, had no intention of mending fences and attacked Roosevelt prior to the meeting. Taft also made several attempts to gain Wiley's endorsement but to no avail. Finally, in October 1912, in a bitter speech denouncing Roosevelt for undermining the pure food law, Wiley declared his support for Woodrow Wilson. While his support was welcomed, it brought him only a thank-you from the victorious president-elect.[27]

For many years after his resignation, Wiley wrote a column in *Good Housekeeping*, spoke out on food issues, and testified before Congress, but he was never again the force that he was as chief of the Bureau of Chemistry. In time, he became lost in refighting old enemies and past issues that were no longer of concern to the American public. But if his shadowboxing was irrelevant to the policy of his day, it still had its significant effects, as did nearly everything in which Wiley involved himself. Because his opponents were no longer on the scene, his attacks went unanswered, and by being unanswered, became the accepted interpretation of events. Wiley's repeated criticisms, which continued for twenty years after his resignation, contributed to the enduring myth that he was the nation's defender of purity and health.

In the wake of his resignation, Wiley left behind in the Bureau of Chemistry a group of men who believed in their mission as overseers of the purity of the nation's food and drugs. Many state and local food officials, however, remained bitter over the years of conflict and the attacks on their integrity that had occurred during his stewardship. At the 1912 Seattle convention of the National Association of State Food and Dairy Officials, R. M. Allen and Harry Barnard led an effort to pass a resolution recognizing Wiley for his contribution to pure food. The resolution was defeated; the professional group who best knew and understood Wiley's work refused to honor him.[28]

Conclusion

Wiley tendered his resignation on 29 February 1912, after twenty-nine years as head of the Bureau of Chemistry and six years as the chief enforcement officer of the Pure Food and Drugs Act. After his departure, a quieter bureau settled in to administer a law that, with minor amendments, would serve as the federal law regulating food and drugs until the passage of the Food, Drug, and Cosmetic Act in 1938. In 1928, the Department of Agriculture created a special unit to enforce the 1906 pure food law. The Bureau of Chemistry, then on its way to organizational extinction, was joined with the Bureau of Soils. In time, the new enforcement unit would move out of the Department of Agriculture to become the Food and Drug Administration, which, more than half a century after its creation, still administers federal food and drug law.

At the time of his resignation, Wiley could point to several achievements. Under his direction, his bureau had grown impressively. In the numbers of its employees and in the size of its budget, the bureau was fifteen times as large in 1912 as it had been in 1883. From a routine testing lab known mainly to sugar producers, it had become recognized throughout the nation as the leader in the fight for pure food. Wiley could also take some credit for the passage of the 1906 Pure Food and Drugs Act. He brought together an effective coalition of business interests and government officials, including many expert chemists, and won over influential segments of the press and the public. Having done so, he used this coalition to exert pressure on Congress. In short, he did everything necessary to bring about passage of a law and to give himself a large measure of control over its enforcement.

While ultimately Wiley was not victorious in deciding the big, bombastic issues in his favor, we should not underrate what he did achieve. By persuading Roosevelt and Attorney General Bonaparte to adopt his views on the subject, he almost overturned what had been called whiskey for over a century in the United States. In working to do this, he won a crucial victory in a district court and convinced a thoughtful solicitor general to adopt his definitions. It was simply bad luck that a judicially minded politician from Ohio, the center of the rectified whiskey industry, was elected president in 1908. Had it not been for Taft, Wiley would have conferred on Old Taylor and other pot distillers exclusive title to the name *whiskey*.

Although Wiley's rulings on corn syrup and benzoate of soda did not get as far as his ruling on whiskey, he nevertheless had an impact. Because of his efforts, corn syrup had to be listed on food labels. Thanks to the Remsen

Board and President Roosevelt, benzoate of soda won the right to be used as a preservative and to be used in conjunction with the guarantee clause, but the unfavorable publicity surrounding it led many manufacturers to discontinue its use. While Wiley did not win his case against Coca-Cola or succeed in banning the addition of caffeine to soft drinks, he did succeed in bringing Coca-Cola to trial. Ultimately, the court required the company to sign a consent decree and to bear the expenses of its legal defense. Similarly, although he was unable to enforce his 350-milligram sulfur dioxide limit on dried fruits, he did get the limit officially adopted.

If these achievements were short-lived, his success in building a reputation for honesty and purity has been very long-lived indeed. His resignation has been widely interpreted as a triumph for fraud and corruption. Throughout his tenure as chief enforcer of the food law and for generations after, much of the press and public has viewed him as the defender of pure food, honestly labeled. Harvey Levenstein reports that food reformers of the 1930s "saw themselves as continuing the crusade against dangerous drugs and food additives, begun by the recently deceased chemist Dr. Harvey Wiley."[1]

Wiley's image has been an integral part of the historical interpretation of the Pure Food and Drugs Act. Mark Sullivan's *Our Times,* Oscar Anderson's *The Health of a Nation,* and Robert Crunden's *Ministers of Reform,* as well as Wiley's own *History of a Crime* and *Autobiography,* portray him and his supporters as defenders of honesty and purity, while his opponents are depicted as agents of food dopers and cheaters. More recently, Mark Pendergrast concludes that "above all else, Wiley mounted a moral crusade against fraud and vice," and Paul Van Riper says that Wiley was an "outstanding moral exemplar in his own day as he deserves to remain in ours."[2]

The emphasis that Peter Temin (*Taking Your Medicine*), Donna J. Wood (*The Strategic Use of Public Policy*), James Harvey Young (*Pure Food*), and others have given to commercial interests in the passage of the Pure Food and Drugs Act has provided some corrective to the interpretation of Wiley's role in administering the food law. According to these studies, firms that supported the act to obtain a commercial advantage were no more concerned with public health and purity than their rivals were. To use Wood's phrase, a goodly measure of the activity that underlay the passage of the national food bill was simply the strategic use of public policy.

Studies of Wiley's situation within the Department of Agriculture and his ambitions for his bureau have also improved understanding of the food law and at the same time modified the image of Wiley as a food reformer. As A. Hunter Dupree has pointed out, the sugar industry was too narrow a base on which to maintain the Bureau of Chemistry, let alone expand it. Wiley's

concern over food adulteration was in large measure an effort to stave off
the steady encroachment of other bureaus within the Department of Agriculture. While bureau-building may not be incompatible with championing the
public interest, neither is it the same.

When the patina of public-spirited reform is removed, we find that the
cumulative interaction of commercial and bureaucratic competition led to
the passage of the Pure Food and Drugs Act in 1906. These two competitive
forces, rather than consumer health or business fraud, also account for
Wiley's actions as a regulator of food and drugs. He joined forces with
particular government officials and business interests because they helped
him to secure passage of the law and control over its administration. M. A.
Scovell, R. M. Allen, William Frear, Old Taylor, H. J. Heinz, and Arbuckle
Brothers all stood to benefit from a food law enforced by Wiley. They thus
worked together toward that common end. However, this alliance of necessity led to conflict with other business interests—glucose makers, Coca-
Cola, Monsanto Chemical, and manufacturers of rectified whiskey, among
others. It also led to conflict with state food officials, with reputable scientists such as Ira Remsen, and with Wiley's superiors in government—
particularly James Wilson, Theodore Roosevelt, and William H. Taft—
whenever they disagreed with him. The conflicts were not contests between
good and evil, or purity and adulteration, or honesty and fraud. They were
contests over who would benefit and lose from regulatory activity.

The competitive process produced little in the way of general benefit,
despite the widespread belief that Wiley served the public interest. His
enforcement of the act did not improve the health of the consumer, the
plane of competition among producers, or the honesty and integrity of
government officials. If anything, Wiley's enforcement worsened the ability
of consumers to make informed judgments about food and drugs. His
claims about the healthfulness of various foods and preservatives were not
well-founded. He produced no sound evidence that rectified whiskey was
more harmful than straight whiskey, that catsup without benzoate of soda
was more healthful than catsup with it, that 350 milligrams of sulfur dioxide
in dried fruit was the proper limit, that syrup made with sucrose was more
nutritional than syrup made with glucose. In fact, some of his claims—that
rectified whisky coagulated the protoplasm, that preservatives hindered the
digestive process, that added caffeine was more deleterious than naturally
occurring caffeine, that sucrose was healthier than glucose—were exaggerated even at the time that he made them, and they certainly have not stood
the test of scientific advance.

The attempt to label rectified whiskey as imitation misled the consumer; drinking straight, rather than rectified, whiskey did not improve

consumer health, nor did it reduce fraud. Requiring whiskeys to list the percentages of esters, aldehydes, and amyl, butyl, and propyl alcohols would have increased the amount of information available to consumers, but it is doubtful that this information would have been particularly useful to the average whiskey drinker. To the extent that it would have been useful, it would have discouraged the use of straight whiskey, which contained more of the poisons, and thus encouraged an effect opposite to the one sought by Wiley. Requiring glucose but not sucrose to be listed on food labels also distorted consumer judgment, leaving the impression that the consumer was making a healthier choice when selecting sucrose rather than glucose. The Coca-Cola case had similar misleading effects on consumers, some of whom came to believe that ingesting caffeine from coffee or tea was healthier than ingesting it from soft drinks. In short, none of the issues to which Wiley devoted the lion's share of his enforcement efforts furthered the interests of the consumer in any significant way.

The use of the guarantee label also misled consumers by creating the impression that food so labeled was pure or healthful. Food Inspection Decision 76, which prohibited the use of the label for products containing benzoate of soda, is a case in point; it implied that catsup without the preservative was more healthful than catsup with it. Had Wiley made use of Katherine Bitting's discovery that spoiled ingredients could be detected by microscopic analysis, he would have taken a noteworthy step toward ensuring the purity of foods. Unfortunately, his desire to outlaw the preservative deflected his attention from this important discovery.

The firms that Wiley opposed were not shady operations designed to bilk the consumer. They were reputable firms that were as forthright in their commercial and political dealings as the firms that Wiley supported. Thus, there was no significant improvement in the plane of competition under Wiley's enforcement of the law. The manufacturers of rectified whiskey did not try to palm their products off as straight whiskey, nor did they try to brand straight whiskey as fraudulent or inferior. Unlike Edmund Taylor, who worked with Wiley behind the scenes, they openly hired Warwick Hough to represent them. Coca-Cola did not represent its product as containing cocaine, nor did it try to hide the presence of caffeine. John Queeny of Monsanto and Asa Candler of Coca-Cola publicly opposed Wiley, while coffee and sugar magnate John Arbuckle quietly offered Wiley favors. Catsup manufacturers who used benzoate of soda relied on the expert scientific work of Ira Remsen and his colleagues to claim that the preservative produced no detectable harm to health. Heinz, on the other hand, secretly hired public relations agents to aid Wiley.

Wiley's claim to have served the public interest through exemplary moral conduct is equally dubious. While he criticized others for their ties to business interests, he himself was as guilty of commercial favoritism as Roosevelt, Taft, or Wilson. Ira Remsen and his colleagues on the Remsen Board were more objective and disinterested in their research than Wiley. The state food officials who opposed Wiley were no more corrupt than Allen or Scovell. Many of them opposed Wiley because they resented his manipulation of their organization.

While the image of Wiley as an unalloyed champion of purity is consistent with both a public interest theory of regulation and a capture theory of regulation, our interpretation of his actions is not consistent with either theory. The public interest, as we have pointed out, was scarcely present in Wiley's enforcement of the law, nor does it seem fair to say that business interests captured Wiley or Wilson or Roosevelt or Taft. Indeed, it would be just as true to say that business interests were captured by government officials. Our interpretation is, however, consistent with an economic theory of competitive processes. This theory, which is more general than the capture theory, views regulation as the outcome of two competitive processes: one that takes place among firms, and one that takes place among government officials. Firms are motivated by the desire for increased profits; government officials by the desire to expand their budgets and power. Both processes are economic in the sense that businessmen and government officials exercise their entrepreneurial abilities to alter control over scarce resources that have alternative uses.

Like the capture theory of regulation, the theory of competitive processes implies that regulation will serve particular business interests, although these interests do not usually include an entire industry. The complex of business interests that benefit from regulation usually spans various industries and creates fissures within each industry. The roles of Heinz, Old Taylor, Arbuckle Brothers, Blue Label, the manufacturers of rectified whiskey, Coca-Cola, Monsanto, and the American Medical Association in regulatory battles illustrate this principle.

In the theory of competitive processes, regulation also serves political interests. Again, these interests do not usually constitute a monolith. Elected officials serve particular constituencies, who keep them in office. Politicians will support regulation that benefits the most important of their constituents. While these constituents can be commercial interests, they can also be members of the voting public who hold particular moral or political attitudes. The actions of Roosevelt and Taft, Aldrich and Cannon, and the Congress as a whole reveal the attempts of elected officials to satisfy particular constituencies. The result of these contending constituencies was the passage of a food bill that evaded taking a position on divisive issues.

The competitive theory also explains and illustrates the use of regulation to serve the interests of bureaus. Bureaus compete for funds from the legislature; they exert influence on senators and congressmen in their attempts to gain funds and change laws to their benefit. As with business firms, bureaus rarely constitute a monolithic interest group, as the actions of Wilson, Wiley, and state food officials clearly demonstrate. Members of a bureaucracy can also try to persuade the public of the rightness of their cause. Ideas, including moral sentiments and appeals to the public interest, are often a crucial element in this process. The ideas can range from carefully researched conclusions that are presented in a balanced manner to the most biased and misleading propaganda. The Remsen Board, Kathleen Bitting, and some of the Food Bulletins represent careful research; Wiley's pronouncements on whiskey and catsup represent one-sided propaganda. More importantly, Wiley's ability to convince the voting public that he was fighting fakers and dopers was a crucial element in his strategy to build his bureau. His bureau would have been reduced to performing relatively unimportant chemical analyses and soon swallowed by bigger and more successful bureaus had he not successfully advanced this idea. The vital role of ideas in regulatory outcomes has been neglected in economic theories of regulation. Viewing regulation as the outcome of competitive processes gives ideas and moral sentiments their rightful place in the theory of regulation. In fact, it is scarcely an exaggeration to say that the competitive regulatory process is primarily a process of persuasion.

The theory of regulation based on competitive processes does not rule out the possibility that regulation can serve the public interest. In seeking regulation, it is possible for businessmen, bureaucrats, and politicians to identify problems and to offer solutions that improve the general weal. Since events are the outcome of competitive processes, the rules that govern the competition will determine whether the outcomes will primarily serve the general good or special interests. The rules that govern market competition usually produce the result of serving the general good; such competition lowers costs, improves quality, encourages technological innovation, and brings advances in management, marketing, finance, and accounting. The cumulative effect of this competition is gradually to raise standards of living, even though particular groups are sometimes hurt by such competition as progress occurs in fits and spurts.

The competitive processes of regulation may produce the same effects, as long as the rules of the competitive process conform to those general principles that have produced so much benefit in the market realm, that is, so long as regulation is confined to identifying, securing, and otherwise facilitating right of property. Although right of property has a conservative and backward-looking element to it, the competitive process is dynamic and forward-looking. The process will throw up new problems for solution and create opportunities for expanding and refining property rights. By helping to establish rights in new and unfamiliar settings, regulation can help to further the public interest. However, regulation can also be used to abrogate existing property rights and thus undermine the very system that it is supposed to promote. The administration of the food and drugs act under Wiley illustrates how real this danger is.

Thomas K. McCraw has put forward the proposition that the design of regulation should fit the economic conditions of the industry being regulated. In many respects, the Pure Food and Drugs Act met this requirement. The consumer valued help in making more informed choices about food, drink, and drugs; the law required disclosure and prohibited fraud. A judicious implementation of such a law could have eased the task of the consumer and raised the plane of competition among producers. Certainly, Wiley had the opportunity to assemble respectable groups of scientists to study the effects of preservatives, dyes, and other food additives. He could have worked with leading researchers to uncover the nutritional requirements of human health; he could have systematically studied the effects of patent medicines on persons who regularly used them and promoted discoveries that detected spoiled ingredients. He could have worked with government officials and industry leaders to develop a consensus of acceptable practices and standards. Had he engaged in these kinds of activities, he might well have reduced ignorance and fraud, informed the consumer, and made a lasting contribution to food and diet in America. Instead, his secret dealings with businessmen, his commercial favoritism, his antagonism toward those who disagreed with him, and his attempts to give his prejudices the force of law subverted potentially serviceable regulation. That personal opinion and special interest can masquerade as objective science and public good, thereby corrupting even potentially useful law, reveals one of the chief dangers of regulation in democratic society.[3]

Notes

Introduction

1. *Washington Post,* 5 June 1991, A3.
2. *Time,* 15 July 1991, 52–59.
3. *Newsweek,* 27 May 1991, 46–53.
4. *Advertising Age,* 20 January 1990, 58; Wiley Papers, Box 97, 1910.
5. *Newsweek,* 1 July 1991, 45.
6. *Washington Post,* 6 May 1991, A10.
7. Donna J. Wood, *Strategic Uses of Public Policy: Business and Government in the Progressive Era* (Marshfield, Mass.: Pitman Publishing, 1986); James Harvey Young, *Pure Food: Securing the Federal Food Law of 1906* (Princeton, N.J.: Princeton University Press, 1989).

Chapter 1

1. For a more detailed account of the parallel development between the theory and history of economic regulation, see Jack High, "A Tale of Two Disciplines," in *Regulation: Economic Theory and History,* ed. Jack High (Ann Arbor: University of Michigan Press, 1991), 1–17.
2. Arthur S. Link, *American Epoch* (New York: Alfred A. Knopf, 1955), 68; Claire Wilcox, *Public Policies towards Business,* 3d ed. (Homewood, Ill: Richard D. Irwin, 1966). For reviews of the history and theory of regulation see Thomas K. McCraw, "Regulation in America," *Business History Review* 49 (summer 1975): 159–83; Richard Posner, "Theories of Economic Regulation," *Bell Journal of Economics and Management Science* 5 (autumn 1974): 335–58; Robert Britt Horwitz, *The Irony of Regulatory Reform* (Oxford: Oxford University Press, 1989), chap. 2; Robert Tollison, "Regulation and Interest Groups," in *Regulation: Economic Theory and History* (Ann Arbor: University of Michigan Press, 1991), 59–76.
3. Gabriel Kolko, *The Triumph of Conservatism* (New York: Macmillan, 1963), 57–58; George J. Stigler, "The Theory of Economic Regulation," *Bell Journal of Economics and Management* 2 (spring 1971): 3; see also Gabriel Kolko, *Railroads and Regulation* (Princeton, N.J.: Princeton University Press, 1965); Paul MacAvoy, *The Economic Effects of Regulation: The Trunk-line Railroad Cartels and the Interstate Commerce Commission before 1900* (Cambridge: MIT Press, 1965).
4. Richard H. K. Vietor, "Businessmen and the Political Economy: The Railroad Rate Controversy of 1905," *Journal of American History* 64 (June 1977). Sam Peltzman, "The Economic Theory of Regulation a Decade after Deregulation," in *Brookings Papers on Economic Activity,* ed. Martin Neal Baily and Clifford Winston (Washington, D.C.: Brookings Institution, 1989), writes, "The specific conclusions Stigler reached bear the imprint of the then accumulating evidence in favor of some form of the C[apture] T[heory]. Indeed his article comes across as an effort to rationalize those results" (174).

5. Morton Keller, "The Pluralist State," in *Regulation in Perspective,* ed. Thomas K. McCraw (Cambridge: Harvard University Press, 1981), 94; Ralph W. Hidy, "Business History: Present Status and Future Needs," *Business History Review* 44 (winter 1970): 50. See also K. Austin Kerr, *American Railroad Politics, 1914–1920* (Pittsburgh: University of Pittsburgh Press, 1968).

6. James Buchanan and Gordon Tullock, "Polluter's Profits and Political Response: Direct Controls versus Taxes," *American Economic Review* 65 (March 1975): 139–47.

7. The conflict over coal scrubbers is described by Robert Crandall, *Controlling Industrial Pollution: The Economics and Politics of Clean Air* (Washington, D.C.: Brookings Institution, 1983). Other examples of high cost producers winning regulatory battles are given by Richard H. K. Vietor, *Environmental Politics and the Coal Coalition* (College Station: Texas A&M University Press, 1980); A. P. Bartel and L. G. Thomas, "Direct and Indirect Effects of Regulation: A New Look at OSHA's Impact," *Journal of Law and Economics* 28 (April 1985): 1–25.

8. In general, higher cost firms can win these regulatory conflicts as long as $n < P/(P - S)$, where n is elasticity of demand for the industry and $P/(P - S)$ is an index of productive efficiency. For a more detailed discussion of these theoretical considerations, see Jack High, "Can Rents Run Uphill?" *Public Choice* 65 (1990): 229–37; Tollison, "Interest Groups and Regulation," 64–66.

9. Quoted in Thomas K. McCraw, *Prophets of Regulation* (Cambridge: Harvard University Press, 1984), 269.

10. For the history of airline deregulation, see Stephen Breyer, *Regulation and Its Reform* (Cambridge: Harvard University Press, 1982), 317–40; Thomas K. McCraw, *Prophets of Regulation,* 265–99; Richard H. K. Vietor, "The Hubris of Regulated Competition," in *Regulation: Economic Theory and History,* ed. High, 27–36.

11. See Eugene Lewis, *Public Entrepreneurship: Toward a Theory of Bureaucratic Political Power* (Bloomington: Indiana University Press, 1980), 228.

12. William J. Baumol, "Entrepreneurship in Economic Theory," *American Economic Review* (May 1968). See also James Buchanan, "What Should Economists Do?" *Southern Economic Journal* 30 (January 1964): 213–22; Israel Kirzner, *Competition and Entrepreneurship* (Chicago: University of Chicago Press, 1973), 8; Robert Herbert and Albert Link, *The Entrepreneurs* (New York: Praeger, 1982), 51–52; Mark Casson, *The Entrepreneur* (New York: Barnes and Noble, 1982), 9–13.

13. See also Salisbury, "An Exchange Theory of Interest Groups," *Midwest Journal of Political Science* (1969): 21. The relevant work on bureaucratic entrepreneurship includes Richard Wagner, "Pressure Groups and Political Entrepreneurs," *Papers on Non-Market Decision Making* (1966): 161–70; Robert Salisbury, "An Exchange Theory of Interest Groups," 1–32; Albert and Raymond Breton, "An Economic Theory of Social Movements," *American Economic Review* (May 1969): 198–205; Norman Frolich, Joe A. Oppenheimer, and Oran Young, *Political Leadership and Collective Goods* (Princeton, N.J.: Princeton University Press, 1971), 6; Eugene Lewis, *Public Entrepreneurship.*

14. Ludwig von Mises, *Human Action* (New Haven: Yale University Press, 1966), 253.

15. Israel Kirzner, *Discovery and the Capitalist Process,* 110.

16. Joseph Schumpeter, *The Theory of Economic Development* (Cambridge: Harvard University Press, 1934), 93–94. Frolich et al. write, "At the most general level, an

entrepreneur can be defined as an individual who seeks to make a profit from the supply of some good to members of a group." These goods can be either public or private, and supplied by either the market or the state. Lewis (1980, 9) says, "A public entrepreneur may be defined as a person who creates or profoundly elaborates a public organization so as to alter greatly the existing pattern of resource allocation of scarce public resources." Casson, *The Entrepreneur,* 24–25; Mises, *Human Action,* 253.

17. Mises, in *Bureaucracy,* writes, "Bureaucratic management means, under democracy, management in strict accordance with the law and the budget" (43). For an insightful history and analysis of bureaucracy, see Mary A. Yeager, "Bureaucracy," in *Encyclopedia of American History,* ed. Glenn Porter (New York: Charles Scribner's Sons, 1980), 894–926.

18. Fred S. McChesney, "Rent Extraction and Rent Creation in the Economic Theory of Regulation," *Journal of Legal Studies* 16 (January 1987): 102. McChesney effectively elaborates this theme in *Money for Nothing* (Cambridge: Harvard University Press, 1997). See also Thomas DiLorenzo, "Competition and Political Entrepreneurship," *Review of Austrian Economics* (1987): 66.

19. See William A. Niskanan, *Bureaucracy and Representative Government* (Chicago: Aldine-Atherton Press, 1971); Barry R. Weingast and Mark J. Moran, "Bureaucratic Discretion or Congressional Control?" *Journal of Political Economy* 91 (October 1983): 765–800.

20. Gary S. Becker, "A Theory of Competition Among Pressure Groups for Political Influence," *Quarterly Journal of Economics* 98 (August 1983): 392.

21. See Anthony Downs, *An Economic Theory of Democracy* (New York: Harper and Row, 1957), and Becker, "Competition Among Pressure Groups."

22. In *Capitalism, Socialism, and Democracy,* Schumpeter says, "The picture of the prettiest girl who ever lived will in the long run prove powerless to maintain the sales of a bad cigarette. There is no equally effective safeguard in the case of political decisions. Many decisions of fateful importance are of a nature that makes it impossible for the public to experiment with them at its leisure and at moderate cost. Even if that is possible, however, judgment is as a rule not so easy to arrive at as it is in the case of a cigarette, because the effects are less easy to interpret" (263).

23. See especially Richard Wagner, "Agency, Economic Calculation, and Constitutional Construction," in *The Political Economy of Rent Seeking,* ed. Charles Rowley, (Boston: Kluwer Academic Publishers, 1988).

24. A. Hunter Dupree, *Science in the Federal Government: A History of Policies and Activities to 1940* (Cambridge: Harvard University Press, 1957), 161–69; Charles E. Rosenberg, "Rationalization and Reality in Shaping American Agriculture Research, 1875–1914," in *The Sciences in the American Context: New Perspectives,* ed. Nathanial Reingold (Washington D.C.: Smithsonian Institute Press, 1979), 401–21.

25. A. Hunter Dupree, *Science in the Federal Government: A History of Policies and Activities to 1940,* (Cambridge: Harvard University Press), 161–69; Gladys Baker, Wayne D. Rasmussen, Vivian Wiser, and Jane Porter, *Century of Service* (Washington: USDA, 1963), 47–54.

26. Gifford Pinchot, *Breaking New Ground* (New York: Harcourt, Brace, 1947); James Penick Jr., *Progressive Politics and Conservation: The Ballinger-Pinchot Affair* (Chicago: University of Chicago Press, 1968), 2–5.

27. Public interest interpretations of the Pure Food Act can be found in Harvey Washington Wiley, *History of a Crime against the Food Law* (Washington, D.C.: H. W.

Wiley, 1929); Mark Sullivan, *Our Times,* vol. 2 (New York: Charles Scribner's Sons, 1927); Thomas A. Bailey, "Congressional Opposition to Pure Food Legislation," *American Journal of Sociology* 36 (July 1930); Steven Wilson, *Food and Drug Regulation* (Washington, D.C., 1942); Gerald Carson, "Who Put the Borax in Dr. Wiley's Butter," *American Heritage* 7 (1956): 58–63; Maurice Natenberg, *The Legacy of Dr. Wiley* (Chicago: University of Chicago Press, 1957); Oscar Anderson, *The Health of a Nation* (Chicago: University of Chicago Press, 1958); James Harvey Young, *The Toadstool Millionaires* (Princeton, N.J.: Princeton University Press, 1961); Young, "The Long Struggle for the 1906 Law," *FDA Consumer* (12 June 1981): 12–16; Young, ed., *The Early Years of Federal Food and Drug Control* (Madison, Wisc.: American Institute of the History of Pharmacy, 1982); Robert M. Crunden, *Ministers of Reform: The Progressive Achievement in American Civilization* (New York: Basic Books, 1982); James Harvey Young, *Pure Food: Securing the Federal Food and Drugs Act of 1906* (Princeton, N.J.: Princeton University Press, 1989). In chapter 12 of *Pure Food,* Young presents a thorough summary of the historiography of the Pure Food Act. Economists have devoted relatively little attention to food regulation. Francis A. Walker praised food regulation in "The Beef Trust," *Economic Journal* 16 (December 1906): 491–511, and Charles van Hise offers a public interest interpretation of the Pure Food Law in *Concentration and Control* (New York: Macmillan, 1912). Melvin Hinich and Richard Staelin give a theoretical justification of the public benefits of pure food laws in *Consumer Protection Legislation and the U.S. Food Industry* (New York: Pergamon Press, 1980); Caswell and Johnson examine firms' strategic responses to regulation, but take changes in regulation as independent constraints. Their strategic response to regulation, while important in its own right, is less relevant to changes in regulation than Donna Wood's strategic use of regulation, which makes regulation a strategic variable in the firm's planning. See Julie A. Caswell and Gary V. Johnson, "Firm Strategic Response to Food Safety and Nutrition Regulation," in *Economics of Food Safety,* ed. Julie A. Caswell (New York: Elsevier Science, 1991), 273–79, especially 279.

28. Harvey Washington Wiley, *History of a Crime against the Food Law.*

29. Arthur Kallett and F. J. Schlink, *100,000,000 Guinea Pigs* (New York: Grosset and Dunlap, 1935); James Turner, *The Chemical Feast* (New York: Grossman Publishers, 1970). For a recent conflict over labeling, see *The Washington Post,* 9 November 1992; *Business Week,* 23 November 1992.

30. Donna J. Wood, "The Strategic Use of Public Policy: Business Support for the 1906 Pure Food and Drug Act," *Business History Review* 59 (autumn 1985): 403–42; Wood, *Strategic Uses of Public Policy* (Marshfield, Mass.: Pitman Publishing, 1986); James Harvey Young, *Pure Food: Securing the Federal Food Law* (Princeton, N.J.: Princeton University Press, 1990).

31. A. Hunter Dupree and Peter Temin emphasize that the food law presented an opportunity for Wiley to build his bureau. See Dupree, *Science in Federal Government,* 176–83; Temin, *Taking Your Medicine: Drug Regulation in the United States* (Cambridge: Harvard University Press, 1980), chap. 1.

Chapter 2

1. Joseph Schumpeter, *Capitalism, Socialism, and Democracy* (New York: Harper and Row, 1942), chaps. 6 and 7.

2. Alfred Chandler, *The Visible Hand* (Cambridge: Harvard University Press, 1977), 234, 295–96, 328, 391–402.

3. Richard Osborn Cummings, *The American and His Food* (Chicago: University of Chicago Press, 1940), 113–15; Dan Morgan, *The Merchants of Grain* (New York: Viking Press, 1979), 49–50.

4. Daniel J. Boorstin, *The Americans: The Democratic Experience* (New York: Random House, 1973), 307–15.

5. Ibid.

6. Ibid.

7. Young, *Pure Food*, 108–13. However, the lead solder used in canning could result in health problems if it leached into the food.

8. Ibid., 106–13.

9. Earl W. Hayter, *The Troubled Farmer, 1850–1900: Rural Adjustment to Industrialism* (Dekalb: Northern Illinois University Press, 1968), 65–68.

10. Young, " 'This Greasy Counterfeit': Butter versus Oleomargarine in the United States Congress," Bulletin of the History of Medicine 53, no. 3 (1970): passim.

11. *Proceedings of State Dairy and Food Departments* (1904), 192.

12. Wood, *Strategic Uses of Public Policy*, 164–73.

13. *Proceedings of the Annual Conference of State Dairy and Food Departments* (1904), 192–98.

14. Wood, *Strategic Uses of Public Policy*, 164–73.

15. *Proceedings of the Annual Conference of State Dairy and Food Departments* (1904), 192–98.

16. Wood, *Strategic Uses of Public Policy*, 170–72.

17. Cummings, *The American and His Food*, 11–14; Harvey Levenstein, *Revolution at the Table: The Transformation of the American Diet* (New York: Oxford University Press, 1988), 3, 7.

18. Arthur M. Schlesinger, *Paths to the Present* (New York: Macmillan, 1949), 226–27.

19. The attitude toward fresh fruits and vegetables is not as farfetched as it seems. When irrigated with contaminated water, these foods easily pass along disease. Harvey Levenstein, *Revolution at the Table: The Transformation of the American Diet* (New York: Oxford University Press, 1988), provides an excellent discussion of the eating habits of the middle class in the late nineteenth century and its concern with quantity rather than quality.

20. Quoted in James C. Whorton, *Crusaders for Fitness: The History of American Health Reformers* (Princeton, N.J.: Princeton University Press, 1982), 48.

21. Cummings, *The American and His Food*, 43–47; Waverly Root and Richard de Rochemont, *Eating in America: A History* (New York: Ecco Press, 1981), 161–64; see also Gerald Carson, *Cornflake Crusade* (New York: Rinehart, 1957); Whorton, *Crusaders for Fitness*.

22. Harvey Levenstein, *Revolution at the Table: The Transformation of the American Diet* (New York: Oxford University Press, 1988), 60–71; Stephen Mennell, *All Manners of Food: Eating and Taste in England and France from the Middle Ages to the Present* (Oxford and New York: Basil Blackwell, 1985), 157–59.

23. Stephen Mennell, *All Manners*, 160; Cummings, *The American and His Food*, 21. Americans had come a long way from the days when Patrick Henry attacked Thomas Jefferson for his weakness for French food and when the Whig party could claim their candidate William Henry Harrison ate raw beef without salt, while Van Buren used

taxpayers' money to raise strawberries and cauliflower for his table. Cummings includes this verse from a campaign song:

> Let Van from his coolers of silver drink wine,
> And lounge on his cushioned settee.
> Our man on his buckeye bench can recline
> Content with hard cidar is he.

24. Elizabeth Ewen, *Immigrant Women in the Land of Dollars: Life and Culture on the Lower East Side, 1890–1925* (New York: Monthly Review Press, 1985), 174–75.

25. Irving Howe, *World of Our Fathers* (New York: Simon and Schuster, 1976), 67–70.

26. Harvey Levenstein, *Revolution at the Table*, 23–29.

27. Ewen, *Immigrant Women in the Land of Dollars*, 166–76.

28. *Proceedings of the Annual Conference of State Dairy and Food Departments* (1901), 338.

29. C. F. Langworthy, "Food and Diet in the United States," *Yearbook of the Department of Agriculture* (Washington, D.C.: USDA, 1907), 361–78.

30. Louise Boland More, *Wage-Earners' Budgets* (New York: Henry Holt, 1907), passim; Mary Kingsbury Simkhovitch, *The City Worker's World in America* (New York: Macmillan, 1917), passim.

31. Harvey Levenstein, *Revolution at the Table*, 60–71.

32. Ibid.

33. Glenna Matthews, *Just a Housewife: The Rise and Fall of Domesticity in America* (New York: Oxford University Press, 1987), 93–97, 105; see also David M. Katzman, *Seven Days a Week: Women and Domestic Service in Industrializing America* (New York: Oxford University Press, 1978).

34. Mark Sullivan, *Our Times*, 3:491.

35. Harvey Levenstein, *Revolution at the Table*, 86.

36. Matthews, *Just a Housewife*, 151.

37. Langworthy, *Food and Diet in the United States*, 364–73; Cummings, *The American and His Food*, 122–37.

38. Laura Shapiro, *Perfection Salad: Women and Cooking at the Turn of the Century* (New York: Farrar, Straus and Giroux, 1986), 209–13; Harvey Levenstein, *Revolution at the Table*, 72–85; Matthews, *Just a Housewife*, 151, 164.

39. Shapiro, *Perfection Salad*, 191–237.

40. Robert C. Alberts, *The Good Provider: H. J. Heinz and His 57 Varieties* (Boston: Houghton Mifflin, 1973); *Journal of Proceedings of the National Association of State Dairy and Food Departments* (1903), 532–34.

41. Young, *Pure Food*, 106.

42. James Harvey Young, " 'This Greasy Counterfeit': Butter versus Oleomargarine in the United States Congress, 1886," *Bulletin of the History of Medicine* 53, no. 3 (1970): 413.

43. Ibid., passim.

44. *United States Department of Agriculture, Bureau of Chemistry Bulletin Number 13*, Part I (Washington, D.C.: General Printing Office, 1887), 24.

45. *United States Department of Agriculture, Bureau of Chemistry Bulletin Number 13*, Part I (Washington, D.C.: General Printing Office, 1887).

46. William R. Pabst Jr., *Butter and Oleomargarine: An Analysis of Competing Commodities* (New York: Columbia University Press, 1937), 35.

Chapter 3

1. John Alfred Heitmann, *The Modernization of the Louisiana Sugar Industry, 1830–1910* (Baton Rouge: Lousiana State University Press, 1987), 117–20.

2. Ibid., 123.

3. Oscar Anderson, *The Health of a Nation* (Chicago: University of Chicago Press, 1958), 28, 35–37.

4. Ibid., 28.

5. Heitmann, *Sugar*, 125; Harvey Washington Wiley, *An Autobiography*, 176.

6. Heitmann, *Sugar*, 136–38, 145–46.

7. Ibid., 159–60.

8. Ibid., 166.

9. Terry S. Reynolds, "Defining Professional Boundaries: Chemical Engineering in the Early Twentieth Century," *Technology and Culture* 27 (1986): 699–701; Heitmann, *Sugar*, 151–53.

10. Terry S. Reynolds, "Defining Professional Boundaries," 702–3.

11. Alan I. Marcus, "Setting the Standard: Fertilizers, State Chemists, and Early National Commercial Regulation, 1880–1887," *Agricultural History* no. 1 (1987): 60; Kenneth Helrich, *The Great Collaboration* (Arlington, Va.: Association of Official Agricultural Chemists, 1984): 1–16; see also Charles E. Rosenberg, "Rationalization and Reality in Shaping American Agricultural Research, 1875–1914," in *Social Studies of Science* 7 (1977): 401–22.

12. Kenneth Helrich, *The Great Collaboration,* 11–15. Largely due to Wiley's support the proceedings of the Association of Official Agricultural Chemists were published annually as Bulletins of the Bureau of Chemistry until 1913.

13. Anderson, *The Health of a Nation,* 71–73.

14. Part 6 dealt with sugar, molasses and sirup, confections, honey and beeswax; part 7 with tea, coffee, and cocoa preparations; and part 8 with canned vegetables.

15. For a similar view on the capabilities of early food chemists see Mitchell Okun, *Fair Play in the Marketplace* (Dekalb: Northern Illinois University Press, 1986), x–xi.

16. Marcus, "Setting the Standard," 71; "Proceedings of the Tenth Annual Convention of the Association of Official Agricultural Chemists," *Chemistry Bulletin* 38, 1893.

17. Anderson, *The Health of a Nation,* 87–89.

18. Alfred C. True, *A History of Agriculture Experimentation and Research in the United States, 1607–1925,* U.S. Department of Agriculture and Research misc. pub. no. 251 (Washington, D.C.: General Printing Office, 1937).

19. Anderson, *The Health of a Nation,* 86–97.

20. Harvey Washington Wiley to G. L. Spencer, 28 July 1895, Box 5, Wiley Papers, Manuscripts Division, Library of Congress (hereafter cited as WP).

21. Wiley to Blanch, 5 November 1896, Wiley to G. L. Spencer, 5 November 1896, Wiley to Herbert Marlick, 3 February 1897, Wiley to W. B. Allison, February 1897, Box 5, WP.

22. Earley Vernon Wilcox, *Tama Jim* (Boston: Stratford, 1930); Clayton A. Coppin, "James Wilson and Harvey Wiley: The Dilemma of Bureaucratic Entrepreneurship," *Agricultural History* 54, no. 2 (spring 1990): 167–84.

Wiley wondered if Wilson's Scot heritage would make him overly frugal in appropriations for the department. Wiley to Herbert Marlick, 3 February 1897, Box 5, WP. Wilson was not frugal when it came to departmental appropriations, although he lived a spartan personal life. He spent little on lodgings or entertainment and saved nearly half of his salary. See David Houston, *Eight Years with Wilson's Cabinet, 1913–1920* (New York: Doubleday, 1926).

23. Wiley to the Honorable C. I. Long, 13 February 1897; Wiley to Henry T. Oxnard, 9 February 1987; Wiley to the Honorable Henry Casson, March 1897, Box 5, WP.

24. Wiley to Assistant Secretary Charles W. Dabney, 12 February 1897, Box 5, WP.

25. Wiley to the Honorable C. I. Long, 13 February 1897, Wiley to G. L. Spencer, 20 February 1897, Box 5, WP; Wiley to Secretary of Agriculture James Wilson, 30 July 1901, Box 7, WP.

26. Willard Lee Hoing, "James Wilson as Secretary of Agriculture, 1897–1913" (Ph.D. dissertation, University of Wisconsin, 1964), 23, 29–30; Wiley to E. B. Cowsill, 27 March 1897; Wiley to the Honorable A. M. Todd, 22 April 1897; Wiley to Professor Albert R. Leeds, 24 April 1897; Wiley to G. L. Spencer, 6 May 1897; Wiley to Henry Houston, 21 April 1897; Wiley to G. L. Spencer, 10 May 1897; Wiley to McElroy, c. 11–12 May 1897, Box 5, WP.

27. Williard Lee Hoing, "James Wilson as Secretary of Agriculture, 1897–1913," Ph.D. diss., University of Wisconsin, Madison, 37; Wiley to G. L. Spencer, 6 May 1897, Box 5, WP; Anderson, *The Health of a Nation*, 106.

28. Wiley to Secretary of Agriculture James Wilson, 19 April 1897, Box 5, WP.

29. Wiley to Secretary of Agriculture James Wilson, "Memorandum Relating to Conference Between Dr. H. W. Wiley and Doctors Atwater and True," 19 June 1897, Box 5, WP.

30. Hoing, "James Wilson," 59–61, 101–2; Hoing quotes Wilson's letter to John Myers, 15 March 1899, Wilson Papers; Anderson, *The Health of a Nation*, 123. For the story of the embalmed meat scandal see Margaret Leech, *In the Days of McKinley* (New York: Harper Brothers, 1959); Edward F. Keuchel, "Chemicals and Meat: The Embalmed Beef Scandal of the Spanish-American War," *Bulletin of the History of Medicine*, 48 (1974): 249–64; Anderson, *The Health of a Nation*, 128.

31. Boxes 6–8 of the WP contain detailed information on Wiley's activities outside the department; see also Anderson, *The Health of a Nation*, chap. 6. Wiley to Secretary of Agriculture James Wilson, 30 July 1901, Box 7, WP.

32. Wiley to Professor N. S. Shaler, 7 January 1902, Box 7, WP. See also Wiley to E. W. Hilgard, 15 February 1902, Box 7, WP.

33. Wiley to Clifford Richardson, 6 January 1902; Wiley to the Honorable James Wadsworth, 27 December 1901 and 30 January 1902, Box 7, WP. Wiley to E. W. Hilgard, 3 November 1903, Box 8, WP.

34. Wiley to E. W. Hilgard, 3 November 1903, Box 8, WP. As head of the California Experiment Stations, Hilgard had his own disputes with the Department of Agriculture. See Ronald L. Nye, "Federal vs. State Agricultural Research Policy: The Case of California's Tulare Experiment Station, 1889–1909," *Agricultural History* 57, no. 4 (1983): 436–49; Anderson, *The Health of a Nation*, 108–12; B. P. Galloway Memorandum, 10 July 1903, Box 599, Gifford Pinchot Papers, Manuscripts Division, Library of Congress (hereafter cited as Pinchot Papers).

35. B. P. Galloway Memorandum, 10 July 1903, Pinchot Papers.

36. Wiley would argue for the preeminence of the Bureau of Chemistry again in 1905 to the Keep Commission, but his arguments had little effect on the trend toward problem-oriented bureaus. Gifford Pinchot later wrote that Wiley's idea to centralize chemistry was "about as reasonable as to confine all typewriting in a single bureau."

See Pinchot Papers, 17 July 1903, Box 602. For further information on the Committee on Organization of Government Scientific Work, see Pinchot Papers, Boxes 598–601. For information on the Keep Commission, see Pinchot Papers, Boxes 602–603; See also Harold T. Pinkett, "The Keep Commission, 1905–1909: A Rooseveltian Effort for Administrative Reform," *The Journal of American History* 52, no. 2 (1965): 297–312; Forest Service, RG 75 Entry 28, National Archives; Gifford Pinchot, *Breaking New Ground* (New York: Harcourt, Brace, 1947), 311. For a summary of Wiley's view, see "Report of the Bureau of Chemistry for the Period Begun July 1, 1897 and Ending June 30, 1905," Box 199, WP.

37. Wiley to A. J. Wedderburn, 20 March 1899, Box 6, WP; Wiley to William Frear, 12 and 16 March 1898, Box 5, WP; Harvey W. Wiley, *An Autobiography,* 214; Anderson, *The Health of a Nation,* 123.

38. Wiley to William Frear, 12 and 16 March 1898, Box 5; Wiley to F. N. Barrett, 1 December 1901; 15 February 1902; 17 June 1902, Box 7, WP.

39. *Proceedings of the National Association of State Dairy and Food Departments, 1898–1904.* After 1904, proceedings of the association were published in *National Food Journal.*

40. Wiley to M. N. Kline, 26 January 1903; Wiley to F. N. Barrett, 17 June 1902; Wiley to M. A. Scovell, 23 January 1903; Wiley to Len. M. Frailey, 21 May 1903; Wiley to William Frear, 16 January 1903, Box 7, WP; L. M. Frailey to William Frear, 20 February 1903, William Frear Papers, Pennsylvania State University, State College.

41. Wiley to R. M. Allen, 2 April 1903, Wiley to J. W. Bailey, 2 April 1903, Box 8, WP.

42. Wiley to R. M. Allen, 1 May 1903; 9 May 1903; 6 July 1903; 8 July 1903; Wiley to F. N. Barrett, 9 May 1903; Wiley to Len. M. Frailey, 21 May 1903; Wiley to J. N. Hurty, 23 May 1903; Wiley to the Honorable P. J. McCumber, 23 May 1903; Wiley to the Honorable W. P. Hepburn, 23 May 1903; Box 8, WP.

43. Wiley to William Frear, Wiley to M. A. Scovell, Wiley to Len. M. Frailey, Wiley to A. C. Morrison, 30 June 1903, Box 8, WP.

44. *Journal of Proceedings of the Seventh Annual Convention of the State Dairy and Food Departments* (1903).

45. Ibid.

46. Ibid.

47. Ibid.

Chapter 4

1. Kenneth Helrich, *The Great Collaboration,* 16–26.

2. Harvey Levenstein, *Revolution at the Table,* 40.

3. *Journal of Proceedings of the Seventh Annual Convention of State Dairy and Food Departments* (Washington, D.C.), 512–14.

4. Ibid., 510, 538–39.

5. Additional information about the distillation of whiskey is contained in chapter 7.

6. Donna J. Wood, *Strategic Uses of Public Policy.*

7. R. M. Allen to Wiley, 21 May 1903, Bureau of Agricultural and Industrial Chemistry, RG 97, National Archives (hereafter cited as BAIC); Wiley to Taylor, 7 July

1903, Wiley Papers, Manuscripts Division, Library of Congress (hereafter cited as WP).

8. Taylor was quoting Wiley's testimony before the the the House Committee on Interstate and Foreign Commerce. See House Committee on Interstate and Foreign Commerce, *Hearing on Pure Food Bill,* 57th Cong., 1903.

9. *Proceedings,* 585.

10. For Wiley's early interest in straight whiskey, see W. H. Thomas to Wiley, 24 May 1907; Wiley to W. H. Thomas, 27 May 1907, File 2336, RG 97, BAIC; Malcom E. Washburn, *The Cosmos Club of Washington: A Centennial History, 1878–1978* (Washington, D.C.: Cosmos Club, 1978); Wiley to Dr. Alfred Springer, 13 November 1900; Wiley to Charles Richards Dodge, U.S. Paris Exposition Commission, 10 December 1900, letterbooks, RG 88, Files of the Food and Drug Administration (FDA), National Archives.

11. U.S. Department of Agriculture, Bureau of Chemistry, Bulletin 84 (Washington, D.C.: General Printing Office, 1904–8); Anderson, *The Health of a Nation* (Chicago: University of Chicago Press, 1958), 149–51.

12. H. W. Wiley, "Experimental Studies with the Poison Squad," Memorandum, n.d., Box 91, WP. For an extended discussion of Wiley's beliefs about preservatives, see his testimony before the House Committee on Interstate and Foreign Commerce, *Hearing on the Pure Food Bill,* 1906.

13. Anderson, *The Health of a Nation,* 149–52.

14. Ibid., 148; Young, *Pure Food,* 165; R. James Kane, "Populism Progressivism, and Pure Food," *Agricultural History* 38 (1964): 162.

15. The retaliatory nature of the legislation is evident in Wiley's discussions with the House Committee on Agriculture, *Hearings on Appropriations for the Department of Agriculture,* 1906, 311–13.

16. Young, *Pure Food,* 164. A debate between Hough and Wiley on this issue took place during the appropriations hearings by the House Committee on Agriculture in January 1906.

17. Wiley to Messrs. A. Overholt and Co., 10 October 1903, WP.

18. Anderson, *The Health of a Nation,* 159.

19. Ibid., 160.

20. Wiley to Warwick M. Hough, 2 January 1904, RG 97, BAIC.

21. Wily to the Honorable William Lorimer, 4 January 1904, RG 97 BAIC.

22. Wiley to Edmund W. Taylor, 11 January 1904, RG 88, FDA; Wiley to the Honorable P. J. McCumber, 21 January 1904, RG 88, FDA; P. J. McCumber to William Frear, 23 February 1904, William Frear Papers, Pennsylvania State University, State College (hereafter cited as FP).

23. Wiley to L. M. Frailey, 5 January 1904, WP; L. M. Frailey to William Frear, 27 February 1904, FP.

24. Wiley to Warwick M. Hough, 2 January 1904, RG 97, BAIC; Wiley to the Honorable P. J. McCumber, January 1904; Wiley to William Frear, 10 March 1904; Wiley to Percy T. Morgan, 4 March 1904, RG 88 FDA; Wiley to F. F. Gilmore, 9 March 1904, RG 88, FDA.

25. Wiley to Warwick M. Hough, 20 January 1904, RG 88, FDA; R. M. Allen to Wiley, 26 January 1904, RG 97, BAIC.

26. Wiley to William Frear, 15 February 1904, FP; Stanley Baron, *Brewed in Amer-*

ica: The History of Beer and Ale in the United States (Boston: Little Brown, 1962), 291–93; Frear to Gallus Thomann, 2 February 1904, FP.

27. Anderson, *The Health of a Nation*, 164–65.

28. Ibid., 161.

29. Young, *Pure Food*, 171.

30. Wiley to the Honorable P. J. McCumber, 27 January 1904, WP; Wiley to R. M. Allen, 25 February 1904, RG 88, FDA.

31. Wiley to R. M. Allen, 25 February 1904, RG 88 FDA; Wiley to M. N. Kline, 9 March 1904, RG 88 FDA.

32. Anderson, *The Health of a Nation*, 164; James Harvey Young, *The Toadstool Millionaires*, 226.

33. Wiley to R. M. Allen, 25 February 1904, RG 88, FDA; Wiley to William Frear, 28 March 1904, RG 88, FDA.

34. R. M. Allen to Wiley, 2 February 1904, R. M. Allen to Wiley, 18 February 1904, R. M. Allen to Wiley, 23 February 1904, R. M. Allen to Wiley, 29 January 1904, RG 97, BAIC.

35. Wiley to F. N. Barrett, 1 February 1904, Wiley to William Frear, 5 January 1904, Wiley to Edmund W. Taylor, 11 January 1904, Wiley to E. E. Slossen, 12 January 1904, Wiley to Percy T. Morgan, 4 March 1904, Wiley to R. M. Allen, 20 February 1904, RG 88 FDA.

36. As president of the fledgling company, which had not yet turned a profit, Queeny feared that the pro-sugar Wiley would discriminate against his product. See Dan J. Forrestal, *Faith, Hope, and $5000: The Story of Monsanto* (New York: Simon and Schuster, 1977), 11–20; Senate Report 1209, 58th Congress, 2d session, 108–11.

37. Wiley to the Honorable Weldon B. Heyburn, 30 April 1904, letter books, RG 88, FDA.

38. Wiley to R. M. Allen, 25 February 1904, Wiley to William Frear, 28 March 1904, Wiley to Miss Fanny Norris, 8 August 1904, Wiley to the Honorable Weldon B. Heyburn, 30 April 1904, Wiley to R. M. Allen, April 1904, RG 88, FDA.

39. Wiley to Alice Lakey, 10 May 1904, Wiley to Alice Lake, 7 June 1904, RG 88, FDA; William D. McKenzie, "The Consumers' League and Its Work for Pure Food," *American Food Journal* 1, no. 8 (August 1908): 8–12.

40. Wiley to Alice Lakey, 10 and 21 May 1904 and 7 June 1904, RG 88, FDA.

41. Wiley to R. M. Allen, 21 April 1904, Wiley to Edmund W. Taylor, 11 June 1904, Wiley to F. N. Barrett, 1 February 1904, RG 88, FDA.

42. Wiley to R. M. Allen, 19 April 1904, Wiley to William P. Hepburn, 30 April 1904, RG 88, FDA.

Chapter 5

1. Robert W. Ridell, *All the World's a Fair: Visions of Empire at American International Expositions, 1876–1916* (Chicago: University of Chicago Press, 1984), 154–59.

2. Henry Adams, *The Education of Henry Adams* (Boston: Massachusetts Historical Society, 1918), 259–61; Walter Lord, *The Good Years* (New York: Harper and Row, 1960), 93–94; Sullivan, *Our Times*, vol. 2 (New York: Charles Scribner's Sons, 1927).

3. Allen to Wiley, 16 November 1903, 7 December 1904, Bureau of Agriculture and Industrial Chemistry, National Archives (hereafter cited as BAIC).

4. National Association of State Food and Dairy Officials, *Proceedings* (Washington, D.C., 1904), 104.

5. Ibid., 185.

6. Ibid., 121–23.

7. Ibid., 161–68.

8. Ibid., 144–46.

9. Ibid., 148–52.

10. Ibid., 273–89. Hough printed his comments in a pamphlet entitled "The Truth About Whiskey."

11. Ibid., 296–97.

12. Ibid., 297.

13. Wiley to President, Wine and Spirit Trader's Society, 28 October 1904; Wiley to E. T. Fleming, 11 October 1904, FDA. Wholesale Liquor Dealers Association, Letter to Members, 14 May 1904, Files of the Food and Drug Administration (FDA), National Archives; Warwick M. Hough, "The Truth about Whiskey" (National Wholesale Liquor Dealers Association, 1904). Hough to Wiley, 11, 19, 28 October 1904, BAIC. Hough to Wiley, 11, 19, 28 October 1904, BAIC.

14. U.S. Senate Report No. 1209, 58th Congress, 2d session, 60; Wiley to J. H. Chinn, 21 March 1906; Wiley to Editor, *The Wine Trade Review,* 6 March 1905; Wiley to Fleming, 11 October 1904, FDA.

15. Jackson Tinker, "Who Killed the Pure Food Bill?" 572–73, 590.

16. Mark Sullivan, *Our Times* 531–32; Nathaniel W. Stephenson, *Nelson W. Aldrich* (Port Washington, N.Y.: Kennikat Press, 1930), 280, 464.

17. Warwick M. Hough to Wiley, 3 January 1905, BAIC; Wiley to Warwick M. Hough, 9 January 1905; Wiley to M. A. Scovell, 14 March 1905; Wiley to R. M. Allen, 8 March 1905, FDA. The speech was given on the first of April, and Wiley at first thought that the criticisms were part of an April fool's roast.

18. Willard Lee Hoing, "James Wilson as Secretary of Agriculture, 1897–1913" (Ph.D. dissertation, University of Wisconsin, 1964), 160–90. Henry Beach Needham, "Senate of Special Interests," *World's Work* 2 (January 1905), 7206–11; Allen to Wiley, 24 March 1905, File 16, RG 97, BAIC; Wiley to Editors, *Public Opinion,* 18 April, 1905; Wiley to William O. Bates, 16 April 1905; Wiley to H. N. Gardner, 18 April 1905; Wiley to Dr. Hugo Schwertzer, 13 April 1905; Wiley to Editor, *Collier's Weekly,* 27 May 1905; Edward Lowery, "The Senate Plot Against Pure Food," *World's Work* 10 (1905): 6215–17.

19. Wiley to Miss Elizabeth Foster, 2 March 1905; Wiley to E. W. Taylor, 6 May 1905, FDA; Anderson, *The Health of a Nation,* 190–93. Jonathan Wirtschafter, "The Genesis and Impact of the Medical Lobby: 1898–1906," *Journal of the History of Medicine and Allied Sciences* 13, no. 1 (1958): 15–49.

20. See the advertisements in the publication of proceedings for 1903 and 1904. The proceedings of the each year's convention were distributed the following year. Because of the disagreement over advertising, the proceedings were no longer published as individual volumes after 1905.

21. The proceedings of the 1905 convention were published serially in the *American Food Journal,* which began publication in 1906 with Meyers as editor. Both Allen and Wiley disputed the accuracy of Meyers report.

22. Eaton's remarks and the ensuing debate can be found in the first four issues of the *American Food Journal.* See National Association of State Food and Dairy Officials, "Proceedings of the National Association of State Food and Dairy Officials," *American Food Journal,* beginning in January 1906.

23. "Proceedings," *American Food Journal* 1 (June 1906): 1–32.

24. *American Food Journal* 1 (15 January 1906): 18.

25. Ilyse D. Barkan, "Industry Invites Regulation: The Passage of the Pure Food and Drug Act of 1906," *American Journal of Public Health* 75, no. 1 (January 1985): 18–25.

26. Mary Hinman Abel, *The Delineator* (September 1905–August 1906).

27. House Committee on Agriculture, *Hearings on Agriculture Appropriations,* 59th Congress, 1st session, 1907, 289–90.

28. Ibid., 290–92.

29. Ibid., 470–90.

30. Wiley to William Frear, 11, 19, 25 May 1906, BAIC. See also Wiley to E. H. Jenkins, 1 February 1906, FDA.

31. Wiley to E. W. Taylor, 24 October 1905, FDA; E. W. Taylor to Wiley, 23 November 1905, Anna Kelton Wiley Papers, Manuscripts Division, Library of Congress (hereafter cited as AKW).

32. W. Parmenter, "The Jungle and Its Effects," *Journalism History* 10, nos. 1–2 (1983): 14–17, 33–34; Sullivan, *Our Times,* 535–36; Anderson, *The Health of a Nation,* 166; Young, *Pure Food,* 192.

33. Richard McCormick, "The Discovery that Business Corrupts Politics: A Reappraisal of the Origins of Progressivism," *American Historical Review* 86, no. 2 (April 1981): 247–74; Anderson, *The Health of a Nation,* 180–94. Wiley memorandum, 3 April 1906, FDA.

34. Anderson, *The Health of a Nation,* 176–80.

35. National Wholesale Liquor Dealers Association, Letter to Members, 14 May 1904; Stephenson, *Nelson W. Aldrich,* 464; Anderson, *The Health of a Nation,* 181–85.

36. Anderson, *The Health of a Nation,* 181–82; *Hearings on Pure Food,* House Committee on Interstate and Foreign Commerce, 59th Cong., 1st sess., 1906, passim.

37. Wirtschafter, "The Genesis and Impact of the Medical Lobby," 15–49; James G. Burrow, *AMA: Voice of American Medicine* (Baltimore: Johns Hopkins University Press, 1963), 67–92; Wiley to George Simmons, 20 February 1906, Let. Book 178, #113; Wiley to George Simmons, 2 March 1906, Let. Book 178, #495.

38. Wiley to James R. Mann, 19 March 1906, RG 97, Let. Book 180, #305; Wiley to Geo. H. Simmons, 20 February 1906, Let. Book 178, #113; Wiley to Geo. H. Simmons, 2 March 1906, Let. Book 178, #495; Wiley to Samuel H. Adams, 12 March 1906, Let. Book 179, #476.

39. House Committee, *Hearings on Pure Food,* 322–40; Wiley to J. W. McCulloch, 9 June 1906, FDA.

40. Anderson, *The Health of a Nation,* 185–94. Wiley Memorandum, 3 April 1906; Wiley to Congressman Mann, 8 March 1906; Wiley to Dr. Charles A. L. Reed, 14 March 1906, FDA; Wiley to Allen, 8 February 1906, RG 97, BAIC.

41. *American Food Journal* 1 (15 January 1906): 10.

42. House Committee on Agriculture, *Hearings on Agriculture Appropriations,* 59th Cong., 1st sess. 1906, 206–13; *American Food Journal* (15 April 1906): 11.

43. House Committee, *Hearings on Pure Food,* 12–14, 283–300; Wiley to H. J. Heinz, Company, 14 February 1906, LB 177, #391, RG 97, BAIC.

44. House Committee, *Hearings on Pure Food,* 312–16.

45. Ibid., 14–18.

46. Wiley to H. J. Heinz Company, 14 February 1906, Letter Book. 177, #391, RG97, BAIC; Wiley to F. N. Barrett, Letter Book 179, #25, RG97, BAIC; Wiley to James H. Shepard, 6 April 1906, RG 88, FDA.

47. Burrow, *AMA,* 80.

48. Ibid., 82, note.

49. Wiley to R. M. Allen, 9 June 1906. For details concerning congressional action on the bill see Young, *Pure Food,* 253–62.

50. *Congressional Record,* 62d Congress, 2634–35.

51. *Congressional Record,* 62d Congress, 2641; Roosevelt to Joseph Gurney Cannon, 27 May 1906, Theodore Roosevelt Papers, Manuscripts Division, Library of Congress.

52. Martin L. Fausold, "James W. Wadsworth, Sr., and The Meat Inspection Act of 1906," *New York History* 51, no. 1 (1970): 42–61.

Chapter 6

1. Wiley would later write, "While a bureau is an important element in Government activities, it also affords an opportunity for ambitious directors (and all directors should be ambitious) to leave the base on which they are supposed to stay. I do not except even the bureau over which I presided for nearly thirty years from having at various times had attacks of this grasping disposition." Harvey W. Wiley, *History of a Crime against the Food Law,* 282.

2. John Braeman, "The Square Deal in Action," in *Change and Continuity in Twentieth-Century America,* ed. John Braeman, Robert H. Brenner, and Everett Walters (Columbus: Ohio State University Press, 1964), 35–80; Martin L. Fausold, "James W. Wadsworth, Sr., and the Meat Inspection Act of 1906," 43–61; James Harvey Young, "The Pig that Fell into the Privy: Upton Sinclair's *The Jungle* and the Meat Inspection Amendment of 1906," *Bulletin of the History of Medicine* 59 (1984): 467–80; Mary Yeager, *Competition and Regulation: The Development of Oligopoly in the Meat Industry* (Greenwich, Conn.: JAI Press, 1981), 197–205.

3. Hoing, "James Wilson as Secretary of Agriculture," 165–88.

4. Ibid., 178–79; *New York Herald,* 27 August 1905; Donald Witnah, *A History of the United States Weather Bureau* (Urbana: University of Illinois Press, 1961). On Wilson's management style, see Clayton A. Coppin, "James Wilson and Harvey Wiley: The Dilemma of Bureaucratic Entrepreneurship," *Agricultural History* 54, no. 2 (summer 1990): 166–79.

5. Hoing, "James Wilson," 180–81; Whitnah, *A History of the United States Weather Bureau,* 82–84, 102, 117; Harold T. Pinkett, "The Keep Commission, 1905–1909," 297–312.

6. Coppin, "James Wilson and Harvey Wiley," 166–79.

7. Wiley to J. W. McCulloch, 1 July 1906, RG 88, Files of the Food and Drug Administration; J. W. McCulloch to Wiley, 13 July 1906, Box 310, Anna Kelton Wiley Papers, Manuscripts Division, Library of Congress (hereafter cited as AKW). McCulloch suggested that Wiley not return the whiskey, but place it "in the charge of the Alexander young lady?" where Wiley could draw on it as needed. The Wiley papers contain

frequent references to his accepting small gifts of whiskeys, wines, hams, and maple syrups, both before and after passage of the law.

8. Clayton A. Coppin, "John Arbuckle: Entrepreneur, Trustbuster, and Humanitarian," *Market Process* 7, no. 1 (spring 1989): 11–15.

9. John Arbuckle to Wiley, 18 February 1907, Entry 8, File 203, RG 97, Bureau of Agricultural and Industrial Chemistry, National Archives.

10. Wiley to John Arbuckle, 19 March 1907, letterbook 279, Wiley to Arbuckle, 11 June 1907, letterbook, 310, box 9, Wiley Papers, Manuscripts Division, Library of Congress (hereafter cited as WP).

11. Charles A. Brown, "A History of the New York Sugar Trade Laboratory," Charles A. Brown Papers, Manuscripts Division, Library of Congress; Wiley to Arbuckle, 11 June 1907, letterbook, 310, box 9, WP.

12. The information on Maxwell Wiley is taken from numerous letters to and from Harvey Wiley in WP.

13. Herbert D. Ward to William H. Taft, 2 March 1909, series 5, file 4176, William Howard Taft Papers, Manuscripts Division, Library of Congress (hereafter WHT).

14. Memorandum, "Food Standard Committee, Importance of the Work," 1907, box 207, WP.

15. Memorandum from the Office of the Solicitor of the Department of Agriculture, 4 March 1907, entry 45, file 798, RG 16, Office of the Secretary of Agriculture, National Archives (hereafter cited as OSA).

16. The committee was made up of William Frear, chairman, E. J. Jenkins of Connecticut, M. A. Scovell of Kentucky, Richard Fischer of Wisconsin, H. E. Barnard of Indiana, H. A. Weber of Ohio, and Wiley. This was a carefully selected, pro-Wiley group.

17. American Food Journal (August 1906): 16.

18. James Wilson to Wiley, 24 July 1906, Box 60, WP; Wiley to Joseph W. Wheatly, 6 July 1906, Record Group 88, FDA. Wiley encouraged Wheatly to get himself appointed to the regulations committee by the treasury secretary. U.S. Department of Agriculture, *The Report of the Chemist for 1907* (Washington, D.C.: General Printing Office, 1908); *American Food Journal* (October 1906): 16; Wiley, *History of a Crime against the Food Law,* 78; Harvey W. Wiley, "Opening Statement by the Commission Appointed to Formulate Rules and Regulations for the Enforcement of the Food and Drugs Act," Box 190, WP; *American Food Journal* (October 1906): 5. At the same time that Wiley welcomed the participation of industry, he wrote to O. C. Schock, assistant dairy and food commissioner of Pennsylvania that he did not think that industry representatives should be part of rule and regulation making. Wiley to O. D. Schock, 4 April 1907, Entry 8, File 20, RG 97, BAIC.

19. Warwick M. Hough to Secretary James Wilson, 21 August 1906, Box 61, WP; Wiley to R. M. Allen, 13 August 1906, 401, Wiley to E. H. Taylor, 13 August 1906, 403, RG 97, BAIC.

20. North and Gerry to Wiley, 26 October 1906, Entry 8, File 11, RG 97, BAIC; Warwick Hough to Wiley, 4 October 1906, Box 61, WP; Warwick Hough to James Wilson, 27 October 1906, Entry 17, RG 16, OSA, Wiley to Gerry, 3 November 1906, RG 88, FDA; Wiley to M. A. Scovell, 23 November 1906; Wiley to R. M. Allen, 23 November 1906, RG 88, FDA; Warwick Hough to James Wilson, 6 November, 3 December, 22 December 1906, Box 61, WP.

21. The Department of Commerce's position is stated in a letter from secretary of commerce Oscar Straus to E. C. Johnson, secretary of the food manufacturers' association, 23 November 1907, Box 64, WP.

22. 59th Congress, *Hearings before the Committee on Interstate and Foreign Commerce of the House of Representatives* (Washington, D.C.: General Printing Office, 1906), 341–42.

23. House Committee on Agriculture, *Hearings before the Committee on Agriculture,* 59th Cong., 2d session, 1907, 266–70.

24. Ibid., 269–72; James Harvey Young, "From Oysters to After-Dinner Mints: The Role of the Early Food and Drug Inspectors," *Journal of the History of Medicine and Allied Sciences* 47 (1987): 31; House Committee on Interstate and Foreign Commerce, *Hearings before the Committee on Interstate and Foreign Commerce of the House of Representatives,* 59th Cong., 2d session, 1906, 341–42; House Committee on Agriculture, *Hearings,* 249, 276–77.

25. House Committee on Agriculture, *Hearings,* 254.

26. Ibid., 260.

27. Ibid., 278–79.

28. Wiley to M. A. Scovell, 6 March 1907, Letterbooks, RG 88, FDA.

29. Anderson, *The Health of a Nation,* 200–201; *American Food Journal* (15 November 1907): 6–7; Wiley to E. F. Ladd, 10 April 1907, Entry 8, File 1527, RG 97, BAIC.

30. Young, "From Oysters to After-Dinner Mints," 32; Anderson, *The Health of a Nation,* 213.

31. James Wilson to Wiley, 24 April 1907, Box 62, WP; Department of Agriculture General Order No. 111, 25 April 1907, Box 64, WP. Wiley would later say that Wilson arrived with Dunlap to announce that Dunlap would be Wiley's associate in February 1907, but Dunlap did not accept a position with the Department of Agriculture until April. Wiley must have confused the timing of events. Wiley, *History of a Crime against the Food Law,* 157; Frederick L. Dunlap to Wilson, 5 April 1907, Entry 17, RG 16, OSA.

32. Anderson, *The Health of a Nation,* 204; *American Food Journal* (15 August 1907): 20; Frederick L. Dunlap to James Wilson, 2 April 1907, White House to James Wilson, 5 April 1907, Entry 17, RG 16, OSA.

33. Wiley stated in a deposition taken by Curtice Brothers attorneys in 1911 that he thought that the board was created to overrule his decisions, Entry 17, RG 16, OSA; Wiley, *History of a Crime against the Food Law,* 154–60.

34. The details of this conflict can be followed in the letters sent to Wiley in France by Annie Pierce and W. D. Bigalow during June and July of 1907, Box 62, WP, and Box 311, AKW.

35. Wiley to William Frear, 3 June 1907, Entry 8, File 21, RG 97, BAIC.

36. *American Food Journal* (15 May 1907): 18; James Wilson to Wiley, 16 November 1908, Entry 8, File 1, RG 97, BAIC.

37. *American Food Journal* (15 August 1907): 18–20; Edmund W. Taylor to Wiley, 27 August 1907, Box 311, AKW.

38. *American Food Journal* (15 September 1907): 17; Needham to Wiley, 17 July 1907, Box 62, WP.

39. U.S. Department of Agriculture, Circular 21 (Washington, D.C.: General Printing Office, 1907); *American Food Journal* (15 May 1907): 18.

40. *American Food Journal* (15 September 1907): n.p.

41. A number of minor adjustments were made in the guarantee clause. See food

inspection decisions 60, 62, 70, 72, 83, 96, and 99. Food inspection decision 76 contains Wiley's reply to his critics. Food inspection decision 153, issued after Wiley left office, repealed the use of the guarantee clause.

42. James Wilson to Sunny Brook, 3 May 1907, Sunny Brook to James Wilson, 10 May 1907, Wiley to Sunny Brook, 17 May 1907, Sunny Brook to Wiley, 24 May 1907, copies of Sunny Brook labels, ads, and correspondence, Entry 8, File 2310, RG 97, BAIC. Wiley exhibited a far harsher attitude toward Coca-Cola for a simple error on a label, which said "Guaranteed under the Pure Food and Drugs Law" instead of "Guaranteed under the Food and Drugs Act."

43. James Harvey Young, *The Medical Messiahs* (Princeton, N.J.: Princeton University Press, 1967), 41. Wiley was a member of the revision committee and actively used his bureau's resources to assist in the revision until Secretary Wilson prohibited future use of the bureau's resources for this purpose.

44. Young, *The Medical Messiahs,* 6.

45. Ibid., 10–11.

46. Wiley to Samuel Hopkins Adams, 1 April 1907, Entry 8, File 2303, RG 97, BAIC. See also Wiley to George McCabe, 16 April 1907, Entry 8, File 2303, RG 97, where Wiley approves of a company calling itself the Asthema Cura Company, and Wiley to Samuel Hopkins Adams, 11 November 1907, Box 64, WP.

47. Young, "From Oysters to After-Dinner Mints," 32.

Chapter 7

1. Wiley to W. H. Thomas, 6 July 1906, RG 97, National Archives.

2. Warwick M. Hough to James Wilson, 21 August 1906, W. Hough to Wiley, 4 October 1906, Box 61, Wiley Papers (hereafter WP), Manuscripts Division, Library of Congress; W. Hough to J. Wilson, 27 October 1906, RG 16, National Archives; W. Hough to J. Wilson, 6 November 1906, W. Hough to J. Wilson, 3 December 1906, Box 61, WP.

3. Warwick M. Hough to James Wilson, 27 October 1906, Box 61, WP.

4. Chester A. Gwinn (Washington, D.C.: Government Printing Office, 1914), 36–37, has the text of food inspection decision 45; Warwick M. Hough to James Wilson, 26 October 1906, RG 16, National Archives.

5. Harvey W. Wiley, *History of a Crime against the Food Law,* 109, 111; Oscar Anderson, *The Health of a Nation,* 219–20 ; Wiley to R. M. Allen, 30 March 1907, Box 63, WP.

6. J. G. Schmidlapp to W. H. Taft, 14 December 1906, Entry 17, RG 16, National Archives; William H. Taft to Theodore Roosevelt, 19 December 1906, Entry 17, RG 16, National Archives. See also Thompson Distilling Co. to Senator Boris Penrose, 23 February 1907, Entry 17, RG 16, Fishel and Levy to Theodore Roosevelt, 13 March 1907, Entry 17, RG 16, George C. Dempsey to Theodore Roosevelt, Entry 17, RG 16, P. J. Bowlin Liquor Co. to Theodore Roosevelt, 2 March 1907, Entry 17, RG 16, Cornelius Dougherty to Theodore Roosevelt, 27 March 1907, Entry 17, RG 16, National Archives.

7. Bonaparte's opinion and Roosevelt's subsequent letter to Secretary Wilson comprise food inspection decision 65, issued 11 April 1907, reprinted and discussed in Gwinn, 51–60.

8. Gwinn, 57. See advertisements for claims made about the various kinds of whiskey.

9. Ibid., 56.

10. Ibid., 51–60; Joseph Bucklin Bishop, *Charles Joseph Bonaparte* (New York: Charles Scribner's Sons, 1922), 161–63. Bonaparte's flippancy was not unique to the whiskey case. Eric F. Goldman, *Charles J. Bonaparte, Patrician Reformer* (Baltimore: Johns Hopkins Press, 1943), 16, writes, "Few men in American public life have been as flippant, and none has shown a greater unconcern about who might be galled."

11. R. M. Allen to Wiley, 12 April 1907, J. N. Hurty to Wiley, 13 April 1907, E. H. Jenkins to Wiley, 17 April 1907, M. A. Scovell to Wiley, 20 April 1907, Wiley to E. H. Jenkins, 23 April 1907, William Frear to Wiley, 11 May 1907, Box 64, WP.

12. C. J. Bonaparte to R. M. Allen, 8 May 1907, R. M. Allen to Wiley, 10 May 1907, R. M. Allen to C. J. Bonaparte, 14 May 1907, R. M. Allen to Wiley, 14 May 1907, Wiley to William Frear, 17 May 1907, William Frear to Wiley, 22 May 1907, Box 62, WP.

13. Gwinn, 776–78.

14. *Memorandum on the "What is Whisky?" Controversy* (Washington, D.C.: Federal Alcohol Control Commission, 1935), 27.

15. John G. Capers to James Wilson, 26 November 1907, Box 62, WP.

16. Attorney General, "Marking and Branding of Spirit Casks," 11 January 1908, reported in Gwinn, 787.

17. Wiley, *History of a Crime against the Food Law,* 118–19.

18. Wiley to M. A Scovell, 14 December 1908, Box 69, WP. There are two similar letters to Scovell on this date. One is longer, contains more information, and is more conspiratorial than the other. The quotation is from the longer letter. On the appointment of the whiskey commission, which apparently took place in April, see Wiley, *History of a Crime against the Food Law,* 118–19, 132–35.

19. Attorney General, "The Labeling of Whiskey," 19 February 1909, reprinted in Gwinn, 797–800.

20. Gwinn, 798–99, contains Bonaparte's references to previous court cases. Gwinn, 390–91, reports on *U.S. v. Fifty Barrels of Whisky.*

21. See note 6.

22. The U.S. Circuit Court, Southern District of Ohio, Case No. 6403, "Original Bill," 4 August 1908, *The Fleischmann Co. v. Bernard Bettman et al.,* "Order Granting Temporary Injunction," Case No. 6403, 5 August 1908, 5, National Archives, Great Lakes Region.

23. Internal Revenue Order 723, *Marking Packages of Distilled Spirits,* Department Circular No. 33 (Washington, D.C.: Treasury Department, 1908), 2; see also *Memorandum of the "What is Whiskey" Controversy,* 41.

24. *The Union Distilling Co. v. Bernard Bettmann et al.,* "Original Bill" (10 August 1908), U.S. Circuit Court, Southern District of Ohio, Case No. 6407, National Archives, Great Lakes Region.

25. Wiley, *History of a Crime against the Food Law,* 113–15.

26. Ibid., 116

27. *The Union Distilling Co. v. Bernard Bettmann et al.,* "Application for Injunction Pendenti Lite," 3–4.

28. William Robins, *A Plot against the People* (Ontario: Hiram Walker and Sons, 1911), 36; *Proceedings Before and by the Direction of the President Concerning the Meaning of the Term Whisky* (Washington, D.C.: Government Printing Office, 1909),

814. Guido Marx presented Wiley's statement as chief chemist of the Columbian Exposition and Wiley's chemical analyses of all whiskeys, including Hiram Walker's, on 820–21.

29. Robins, *A Plot against the People*, 36–37; Entry 8, File 5358, RG 97 contains examples of the company's efforts to protect its brand name, including copies of advertisements it used.

30. J. B. Reynolds to Hiram Walker, 22 October 1906, Hiram Walker to James Wilson, 20 December 1906, File 5358, RG 97; Robins, *A Plot against the People*, 37.

31. Joseph H. Choate to Hiram Walker and Sons, 14 December 1906, Box 61, WP; Lucking to Hiram Walker, 14 December 1906, File 5358, RG 97, National Archives. On the career of Choate, see *National Cyclopedia of Biography*, vol. 9, 1159–62.

32. Hiram Walker and Sons to James Wilson (with enclosure), 20 December 1906, Entry 8, File 5358, RG 97, National Archives.

33. Hiram Walker and Sons to Wiley, 20 May 1907, 30 May 1907, Entry 8, File 5358, RG 97.

34. Wiley to Hiram Walker, 26 December 1906, Hiram Walker to Charles J. Bonaparte, 4 June 1907, Charles Bonaparte to Hiram Walker, 1907, Entry 8, File 5358, RG 97.

35. U.S. Solicitor General, *Proceedings by and before*, 3–4.

36. Ibid., 1244. *Proceedings* is the published testimony, along with Taft's order, Bowers's decision, exceptions to Bowers's decision, and Taft's decision.

37. William Frear to Wiley, 16 April 1909, Wiley to William Frear, 18 April 1909, Box 77, WP; *National Cyclopedia of American Biography*, vol. 22, 1932, 148.

38. For the organization and pricing practices of the whiskey industry, see Jeremiah Jenks, *The Trust Problem* (New York: McLure, Phillips, 1900); Werner Troeshen, "The Whiskey Trust and Exclusive Dealing" (University of Pittsburgh, unpublished ms.).

39. *Proceedings*, 223.

40. *Proceedings*, 838.

41. Ibid., 505–6.

42. Ibid., 843.

43. Ibid., 895, 939.

44. Gwinn, 828–29. Bowers's report is also contained in *Proceedings by and before* and is reprinted in full, with excerpts of the arguments of the attorneys, in the *American Food Journal* (15 June 1909): 10–15, 22–26.

45. *American Food Journal* (15 June 1909): 17.

46. Edmund H. Taylor to Wiley, 8 June 1909, Box 316, Anna Kelton Wiley papers, Manuscripts Division, Library of Congress; Lloyd Bowers to Wiley, 2 July 1909, Box 71, WP; Wiley, *History of a Crime*, 151.

47. Gwinn, 833.

48. Ibid., 834.

49. *The American Grocer* quoted in the *American Food Journal* (15 January 1910): 14. See also Anderson, *The Health of a Nation*, 224–26.

50. Wiley, *History of a Crime against the Food Law*, 151.

51. Ibid., 146; *National Cyclopedia of American Biography*, vol. 4, 24.

52. Gwinn, 129–30; William Robins, *A Plot against the People*; Carl M. Wilson to Wiley, 8 August 1911, Box 95, WP; Joseph Remington to Wiley, 29 October 1910, Box 81, WP.

Chapter 8

1. For information on early preservatives see Reay Tannahill, *Food in History* (New York: Crown, 1973).

2. Young, *Pure Food,* 112–13

3. Examples of Wiley's statements against the use of preservatives are in his speeches given at the International Pure Food Congress in St. Louis in 1904. An examination of advertisements and labels in the decade before 1906 shows that claims of purity were nearly universal.

4. Food Inspection Decision 76, "Dyes, Chemicals, and Preservatives in Foods." The first ruling on whiskey was issued in December 1906; it took six more months to issue a ruling on preservatives; "Memorandum To Accompany Food Inspection Decision 76, On Dyes, Chemicals, And Preservatives."

5. "Memorandum To Accompany Food Inspection Decision 76."

6. "Memorandum," F.I.D. 76; Food and Drug Regulation 9. The use of the Guarantee statement on labels was forbidden by F.I.D. 153, issued 5 May 1914. This decision recognized that such statements misled the consumer. McCabe to Wilson, 17 July 1907, RG 16, Entry 17, "Sulphur."

7. Telegram, Governor J. N. Gillett to President Roosevelt, 28 June 1907, RG 16, Entry 17, "Food Law"; Governor J. N. Gillett to President Roosevelt, 29 June 1907, RG 97, Entry 8, File 14451. Dried fruit at this time was more than the snack food it later became. Soaked and cooked, it competed against canned fruits for a place on the consumer's table.

8. White House to Secretary Wilson, 29 June 1907, RG 16, Entry 17, "Food Law"; Assistant Secretary Hays to Governor Gillett, 12 July 1907, RG 97, Entry 8, File 14451. Hays's response was probably prepared by McCabe.

9. Campbell Fruit Growers Union, 23 July 1907, RG 97, Entry 8, File 14451, McCabe to Wilson, 17 July 1907, RG 16, Entry 17, "Sulphur."

10. Hays to Roosevelt, 24 July 1907, Wm. Loeb Jr. for President Roosevelt to Hays, July 25, 1907, both RG 16, Entry 17, "Sulphur."

11. Anderson, *The Health of a Nation,* 209.

12. Arthur Kallett and F. J. Schlink, *100,000,000 Guinea Pigs* (New York: Grosset and Dunlap, 1935), 201–2; James Turner, *The Chemical Feast* (New York: Grossman Publishers, 1970), 109.

13. Anderson, *The Health of a Nation,* 225, 228. Also, see the Memoranda between Wiley and Dunlap from July 1909 to December 1909 on sulphur dioxide, Box 71, WP. Also see RG 88, FDA, Seizure 348.

14. Raymond Sokolov, "Sauce for the Masses," *Natural History* 93 (May 1984); Evelyn Zamula, "Tale of the Tomato: From 'Poison' to Pizza," *FDA Consumer* (July–August 1984).

15. A. W. Bitting, *Appertizing or the Art of Canning; Its History and Development* (San Francisco: The Trade Pressroom, 1937), 674. In this study, 36 used benzoate of soda, 106 did not. The chemical analyses did not show much difference in the brands; Wiley to the Secretary of Agriculture, 4 November 1908, RG 16, Entry 17, "Preservatives." This letter included an analyses of various catsups. Based on the reported sugar and acid content it can be determined that these products tasted substantially different from one another.

16. Robert C. Alberts, *The Good Provider,* 166–80.

17. Williams Brothers Co. et al., Complainants, vs. The Indiana Board of Health et al., Defendants, Circuit Court of the U.S. for the District of Indiana, copies of Testimony, 6 vols. are in Boxes 234–36, WP.

18. Ruth DeForest Lamb, "The Devil's Candle," Ph.D. diss., Vassar College Library, Poughkeepsie, New York, c. 1940.

19. Ibid.; H. W. Wiley, *Influence of Food Preservatives and Artificial Colors on Digestion and Health: Benzoic Acid and Benzoates,* Bureau of Chemistry, U.S. Department of Agriculture, Bulletin 84, part IV, Washington, D.C., 1908, 1294.

20. H. J. Heinz Company to W. D. Bigelow, 25 January 1907, RG 97, Ser. 8, File 3027; Sebastian Mueller to Wiley, 8 May 1907, 14 November 1908, RG 97, Ser. 8, File 3027.

21. F.I.D. 76 and accompanying memorandum.

22. Sebastian Mueller to Wiley, 8 May 1907, RG 97, Series 8, File 3027.

23. Wiley to C. L. Watrous, Iowa State Agriculture and Industrial League, 29 January 1906, RG 88, FDA, Wiley Letterbooks; Young, "The Science and Morals of Metabolism," explains the scientific and moral arguments used over the use of Benzoate Soda. Food Inspection Decision 76, 18 June 1907.

24. A. W. Bitting to Wiley, 4 October 1907, RG 97, Ent. 8, File 811.

25. Wiley, *An Autobiography* (Indianapolis: Bobbs-Merrill, 1930); Williams Bros. et al., "Testimony," vol. 3, 2617.

26. Bitting to Wiley correspondence detailing efforts to make catsup without the use of preservatives is in RG 97, Ent. 8, File 811. Bitting, writing in the 1930s, complained about the lack of varieties in catsup as early as 1912.

27. Charles F. Loudon to Wiley, 9 November, 22 November, 27 November 1907; Wiley to Loudon, 20 November 1907; all RG 97, Ent. 8, File 3449.

28. Wiley to Sebastian Mueller, care of Heinz Company, 21 October 1907, Box 66, WP. Mueller to Wiley 23 October 1907, Box 311, AKW, Manuscript Div., Library of Congress. The correspondence between Wiley and Heinz is extensive. It contains numerous plots and counterplots against users of benzoate of soda and against the Secretary of Agriculture. The correspondence is divided among the Bureau of Chemistry official records, the Wiley Papers, and the Anna Kelton Wiley papers.

29. William Loeb (Sec. to President) to James Wilson, 8 January 1908; James Sherman to Roosevelt, 10 January 1908; Loeb to Wilson, 11 January 1908, all RG 16, Correspondence, "Corn Syrup." Such a board had been considered by Congress but rejected. Wiley at the time opposed such a board. In a letter to George Simmons he wrote, "The board to determine wholesomeness is a bad piece of work, intended, if possible, to handicap the Secretary of Agriculture and prevent him from carrying out his convictions." Wiley to George Simmons, 19 March 1906, RG 88, FDA, Wiley Letterbooks.

30. A complete record of the official correspondence establishing the Remsen Board is in the *Hearings on Expenditures in the Department of Agriculture* (Washington, D.C.: General Printing Office, 1911). Lamb, "The Devil's Candle," 95.

31. Wiley, Testimony in Williams Brothers et al., passim; Wiley testimony, *Expenditures in the Department of Agriculture 1911,* passim; Graham Lusk, "The Remsen Board and Dr. Wiley," *Medical Record,* 9 December 1911; *American Food Journal* (15 August 1908).

32. *American Food Journal* (15 August 1908): 11. The Wiley papers hold extensive correspondence between Wiley and Scovell, Frear, and Jenkins. Also see the William Frear Papers; Anderson, *The Health of a Nation;* M. A. Scovell to Wiley, 13 August

1908, Box 66, WP; Ladd to Wiley, 13 August 1908. Ladd sent two different letters with slightly different versions of what happened; Box 67, WP.

33. Orville LaDow to Wiley, 9 January 1909; Wiley to LaDow, 12 January 1909, Box 71, WP. It is not entirely clear who was paying the Century Syndicate; Oscar Anderson says it was the Royal Baking Powder Company, but other evidence points to Heinz. See Lamb, "The Devil's Candle," 109–11.

34. *American Food Journal,* 1909–11. The Library of Congress contains a full set.

35. See *What to Eat,* prior to 1906; after 1906, *National Food Magazine,* published by the Pierce Publishing Co., Chicago, Illinois.

36. See, for example, *Hampton's,* 10 February 1910, 234–42; *Outlook,* 7 September 1912; *Collier's Weekly,* 6 April 1912.

37. Dow to Wiley, 12 February 1909; Wiley to Dow, 14 February 1909; Dow to Wiley, 23 February 1909; Box 74, WP.

38. Francis Hamilton, a New York lawyer, headed up the effort to get Wiley the Nobel Prize. A record of the effort is in the boxes containing correspondence for 1909 in the Wiley Papers. See also Lamb, "The Devil's Candle," 102.

39. Wiley's report was not supposed to be published, but it slipped into print while Wilson was out of town. F.I.D. 104; Anderson, *The Health of a Nation,* 214–15; "The Influence of Sodium Benzoate on the Nutrition and Health of Man," Department of Agriculture, Report 88, Office of the Secretary of Agriculture, Washington, D.C., 1909.

40. Williams Bros. et al., "Testimony," 6 vols., contains the best assessments on all sides of this issue.

41. Wilson's careful preparation for this meeting is revealed in the correspondence between Remsen Board members in the Ira Remsen Papers, Milton S. Eisenhower Library, Johns Hopkins University; Wilson to Taft, 22 August 1909, Series 5, File 1, WHT Papers.

42. Dow to Wiley, 1 July 1909, Box 73, WP; Dow to Wiley, 14 July 1909, Box 314, AKW; Dow to Wiley, 28 July 1909, Box 245, AKW; Dow to Wiley, 3 August 1909, Box 72, WP; Dow to Wiley, 6 August 1909, Box 72, WP; Wiley to Reed, 6 August 1909, Box 72, WP; Dow to Wiley, 9 August 1909, Box 72, WP.

43. Wilson to Taft, 27 August 1909, Series 5, File 1, WHT Papers. The *American Food Journal* (15 September 1909) contains official proceedings of the convention.

44. Taft to Wilson, 31 August 1909, #20 Series 8, WHT Papers.

45. Barnard to Wiley, 24 January 1907; Wiley to Barnard, 2 February 1907; Wiley to Downey, 29 January 1907; Downey to Wiley, 2 February 1907; Hurty to Wiley, 18 March 1907; Wiley to Hurty, 18 March 1907; all RG 97, Entry 8, File 794.

46. Anderson, *The Health of a Nation,* 231. An injunction was also requested in the state court in Muncie, Indiana, but the federal court became the center of action. Wiley gives his account of the Indiana case in *History of a Crime.* Copies of the six volumes of testimony in "Williams Bros. et al." are in Boxes 234–36, WP.

47. Wiley to Barnard, 3 July 1909, Box 245, AKW; Barnard to Wiley, 27 December 1909; Box 85, WP. Wiley testimony, Williams Bros. et al., vol. 4, 3548; Dow to Wiley, 3 February, Box 85, WP. Barnard to Wiley, 14 January 1910, Box 316, AKW.

48. Ira Remsen to J. H. Long, 14 January 1910, RP. The other insurgent referred to was Gifford Pinchot. Remsen thought since the administration had survived dismissing Pinchot they could survive getting rid of Wiley; Confidential letter, Wilson to Ira Remsen, 12 February 1910, RP.

49. Remsen to Long, 11 May 1910, RP.

50. Remsen to Long, 11 May 1907, RP; Memorandum for Wiley from McCabe, 17 June 1910; Barnard to Wiley, 24 June 1910; Wiley to Barnard, 30 June 1910, all Box 85, WP; Wiley to Bingham, 6 July 1910, Memorandum for Solicitor from Wiley, 30 July 1910, Box 87, WP.

51. Edward Kremers to President C. R. Van Hise, 1 June 1910 (copy), Box 82, WP; Wiley to Magnus Swenson, 17 July 1910, Box 82, WP.

52. Williams Brothers et al., Wiley Testimony, vol. 4, 3, 212–13, 548; Williams Bros. et al., Testimony, Arvill Bitting, vol. 3, 2608–65.

53. Williams Bros. et al., Testimony, Katherine Bitting, vol. 3, 2665–2711. Burton J. Howard and Charles Henry Stephenson, *Microscopical Studies on Tomato Products* (Washington, D.C.: General Printing Office, 1917), 1–24.

54. Willams Brothers et al., Sebastian Mueller, Testimony, vol. 4, 2988; Loudon, Testimony, vol. 3, 2293–2301.

55. Lamb, "The Devil's Candle," 124.

Chapter 9

1. James Harvey Young, "From Oysters to After-Dinner Mints," 32; Clayton Coppin, "Sweeter Manners, Purer Laws: A Regulatory History of the Corn Syrup Industry," *Market Process* (spring 1990): 61–68.

2. Visser, 45; Harold Mcgee, *On Food and Cooking* (New York: Scribner's, 1984), 394–96; Arthur S. Dewing, *Corporate Promotions and Reorganizations* (Cambridge: Harvard University Press, 1914), 72–73.

3. Ibid., 74–75; Okun, *Fair Play in the Marketplace*, 226–30; U.S. Internal Revenue, *Report on Glucose* (Washington, D.C.: Government Printing Office, 1884), 228–29; Heitmann, *Sugar.*

4. Dewing, *Corporate Promotions,* 76–77, 81–85, 104–9.

5. *Journal of Proceedings of the Seventh Annual Convocation of State Dairy and Food Departments* (Washington, D.C., 1903) 553–56.

6. See, for example, *Puck,* 1 January 1908. Other cartoons are in the Wiley papers but sources are not always identified.

7. Victor S. Clark, *History of Manufacturers in the United States,* vol. 3 (New York, McGraw-Hill, 1929), 269–70; State Dairy and Food Departments, 1903, 553–56.

8. U.S. House of Representatives, "Brief Submitted to The Board of Food and Drug by Corn Products Refining Co. in the Matter of Labeling Corn Products," *Hearings on Expenditures in the Department of Agriculture, April 24–August 22, 1911* (Washington, D.C.: Government Printing Office, 1911), 1171.

9. Ibid., 1174.

10. Ibid., 1152–53.

11. Ibid., 1156–57.

12. Ibid., 1171–94.

13. Ibid., 1171–79.

14. Hearing No. 36, 30 September 1907.

15. "Hearing on the Subject of Labeling of Corn Products," 5 December 1907, RG 16, "Corn Syrup," 1907–8; Wiley had considered glucose an adulterant since his days at Purdue; see James Harvey Young, *Pure Food,* 101.

16. Wiley to William Frear, 27 December 1907, Box 62, Wiley Papers, Manuscripts Division, Library of Congress (hereafter cited as WP); William Frear to Wiley, 8 January 1908, Box 313, Anna Kelton Wiley Papers, Manuscripts Division, Library of Congress (hereafter cited as AKW).

17. Wiley to William Frear, 27 December 1907, William Frear Papers, Pennsylvania State University, State College; Frear to Wiley, 8 January 1908, Box 313, AKW.

18. Wiley Brief, *Expenditures*, 1911, Part 2, 1336–37; Dewing, *Corporate Promotions*, 79–80. For Bedford's response denying Wiley's accusations, see U.S. House of Representatives, *Expenditures*, 1372–73.

19. Circular letter, 11 December 1907, 17 Entry, RG 16, "Corn Syrup"; 1907–8, Charles Baskerville to Wiley, 18 January 1908, quoted in U.S. House of Representatives, *Expenditures*, 1411.

20. U.S. House of Representatives, 1351–71.

21. Quote is based on recollections of Secretary of Agriculture James Wilson, U.S. House of Representatives, 890.

22. Roosevelt to H. H. Rusby, 7 January 1909, Box 72, WP.

23. *Washington Evening Star,* 14 March 1908.

24. Mark Sullivan to Wiley, 9 November 1908, Box 312, AKW; Wiley to T. C. Hendley, 2 December 1910, Box 83, WP.

25. A series of letters written on Chicago Food and Drug Inspection Laboratory stationery with the signature block removed details spying on the *American Food Journal* during February and March 1912, Box 90, AKW. For Wiley's view of the *American Food Journal,* see Wiley to Dr. Paul M. Pilcher, 18 December 1911, Box 90, WP.

26. Department of Agriculture, Food Inspection Decision 66; for a summary of the Corn Products Refining Company's position see E. T. Bedford to Secretary of Agriculture Wilson, 25 January 1912, RG 16, Record of the Secretary of Agriculture, Correspondence, "Corn Syrup."

27. Harvey W. Wiley, *Good Housekeeping,* December 1926, 920; Harvey W. Wiley, *Good Housekeeping,* January 1930, 90.

28. *United States v. 40 Barrels and 20 Kegs of Coca-Cola.* 431: N.J. No. 1455.

29. See Box 200, WP.

30. Wiley, *History of a Crime against the Food Law,* 377.

31. Lamb, "The Devil's Candle," 149.

32. Charles Howard Candler, *Asa Griggs Candler* (Atlanta: Emory University Press, 1950), 144–55. Candler believed that the assault on his company began in 1909. Wiley, however, had begun gathering evidence and speaking out against the product as early as 1907.

33. Richard S. Tedlow, *New and Improved: The Story of Mass Marketing in America* (New York: Basic Books, 1990), 29; James Harvey Young, "Three Southern Food and Drug Cases," *Journal of Southern History* 49, no. 1 (1983): 5–6.

34. Young, "Three Southern Food Drug Cases," 6; Tedlow, *New and Improved,* 32–35.

35. *American Food Journal* (15 April 1911): 10–15.

36. Young, "Southern Food and Drug Cases," 7; Adjutant General F. L. Ainsworth to James Wilson, 18 July 1907, Series 8, File 82, RG 97.

37. Wiley to Coca-Cola, 13 February 1906, Letterbook, Wiley to G. H. Simmons, 23 March 1906, Letterbooks, RG 97.

38. Young, "Southern Food and Drug Cases," 10.
39. See, for example, Wiley to James E. Tower, 19 February 1909, Box 76, WP.
40. Asa Candler to Wiley, 25 February 1907, Series 8, File 2719, RG 97.
41. Wiley to Coca-Cola Company, 28 February 1907, Series 8, File 2719, RG 97. In April, Wiley sent an article to Edward Bok, editor of the *Ladies' Home Journal,* on the dangers of temperance drinks. While not naming the firm directly, there is little doubt that Coca-Cola was one of his targets. See Box 190, WP.
42. Wiley to John J. Abel, 4 May 1907, Entry 8, File 101, RG 97.
43. For letters sent to Bureau of Chemistry see Series 8, 1907, Files 2303, 2719; 3858; RG 97, Kebler to C. S. Hallowell, 3 July 1907, Series 8, File 2303, RG 97.
44. W. M. Hays to Coca-Cola, 20 July 1907; John S. Candler to Hays, 1 August 1907, W. M. Hays to John S. Candler, 10 August 1907; John S. Candler to Hays, 15 August 1907, Series 8, File 2719, RG 97. A copy of this rare "illegal" label is in this file.
45. John S. Candler to George McCabe, 19 September 1907, Entry 17, File 757, RG 16.
46. Candler, *Asa Griggs Candler,* 123–24. Mark Pendergrast, *For God, Country, and Coca-Cola: The Unauthorized History of the Great American Soft Drink and the Company That Makes It* (New York: Charles Scribner's Sons, 1993), 110–11. On Arbuckle, see Clayton A. Coppin, "John Arbuckle," 11–15.
47. Wilson to Wiley, 15 October 1907, Series 8, File 1, RG 97, BAIC; Wiley to James Wilson, 16 October 1907, Box 64, WP.
48. Wiley to James Wilson, 16 October 1907 Box 64, WP.
49. Pendergrast, *For God, Country, and Coca-Cola,* 114–15.
50. Forrestal, *Faith, Hope and $5,000,* 15–25.
51. A copy of this news report is in Box 85, WP.
52. Wiley to Moffett and Son, 22 January 1910, Box 85, WP.
53. Wiley to Edwin B. Pillsbury, 22 January 1910, Box 86, WP.
54. Wiley to F. N. Barrett, 22 January 1910, Box 87, WP.
55. Acetphenetidin (phenacetin) was considered a derivative of acetanilide and was required on labels. This ruling was challenged by the Antikamnia Company, and Monsanto supported the challenge. It was another reason for Wiley to dislike Monsanto. See William C. Fiedler, "Antikamnia: The Story of a Pseudo-ethical Pharmaceutical," *Pharmacy in History,* 21, no. 2 (1979): 60–71. Wiley to Secretary Wilson, 8 February 1910, Box 86, WP. It was Wiley's practice to send an inspector to investigate any company that was critical of him. When the secretary of agriculture or the president received a letter complaining about enforcement of the food law, they usually forwarded the letter to the Bureau of Chemistry. Wiley would then send an inspector to investigate the company.
56. Frederick Dunlap to Wiley, 3 November 1908, Box 205, WP.
57. Wiley to Board of Food and Drug Inspection, 12 May 1909, Entry 45, File 966, RG 16. Young, "Southern Food and Drug Cases," 10.
58. Memoranda between members of the Board of Food and Drug Inspection, 12, 15, 27 March, 10, 12, 17 May, 2 August 1909, Entry 45, File 966, RG 16, OSA.
59. Clayton Coppin, "James Wilson," 174–75.
60. Young, "Southern Food and Drug Cases," 13–15; *American Food Journal* (15 April 1911): 10–15.
61. Anderson, *The Health of the Nation,* 237.
62. Wiley to Norman Hapgood, 31 March 1911, Box 98, WP.

63. The transcripts of the trial are available in *Plaintiff in Error vs. Forty Barrels and Twenty Kegs of Coca-Cola, The Coca-Cola Company of Atlanta, Georgia, Claimant and Intervener,* U.S. Supreme Court, Transcripts of Records File Copies of Briefs 1915, Vols. 79 and 80, Case No. 562. Queeny's testimony appears on 1062–66. Members of the Remsen board were excluded from testifying at the trial.

64. Young, "Southern Food and Drug Cases," 17; *Records of the Solicitor of the Department of Agriculture,* Entry 45, File 966, RG 16. The file contains copies of the reports of the undercover agents; they make for some interesting reading. Coca-Cola was probably aware of the government's undercover activity. The company had its own agents in Chattanooga to spy on the government's agents, most of whom stayed in a hotel owned by J. T. Lupton, a Coca-Cola associate. See Pendergrast, *For God, Country, and Coca-Cola,* 119.

65. Wiley to Norman Hapgood, 31 March 1911; Hapgood to Wiley, 5 April 1911, Box 88, WP.

66. Young, "Southern Food and Drug Cases," 18.

Chapter 10

1. Harvey W. Wiley, "What Is the Most Important Task Before the New Administration Under President Taft," Box 191, Wiley Papers, Manuscripts Division, Library of Congress (hereafter cited as WP).

2. Samuel Hopkins Adams, "What Has Become of Our Pure Food Law?" *Hampton's* (10 February 1910), 234–42.

3. J. H. Long to Ira Remsen, 27 January 1910, James Wilson to Remsen, 12 February 1910, J. H. Long to Remsen, 2 September 1910, Ira Remsen Papers, Milton S. Eisenhower Library, Johns Hopkins University (hereafter cited as RP).

4. George McCabe to Wiley, 24 June 1910, Box 85, WP.

5. Ibid.

6. Frederick Dunlap, "Memorandum for the Board of Food and Drug Inspection," 8 September 1910, Box 87, WP.

7. Department of Agriculture, *General Order No. 140,* 9 June 1910.

8. George McCabe to Wiley, 30 June 1910, Box 85, WP; Memorandum for Bureau of Chemistry from Office of Solicitor, 27 July 1910 and 1 August 1910, Box 205, WP.

9. L. S. Dow to Wiley, 3, 5, 14 February 1910, Box 85, WP.

10. Lamb, "The Devil's Candle," 103–4; L. S. Dow to Wiley, 31 December 1909, L. S. Dow to Wiley, 3 February 1910, Box 85, WP.

11. George McCabe to Harvey W. Wiley, Farmer, 5 November 1910, Box 83, WP.

12. *American Food Journal* (15 January 1911).

13. The correspondence with Rusby is reprinted in House of Representatives, *Hearings on Expenditures in the Department of Agriculture,* 62d Cong., 1st Sess., 1911, 109–59; Anderson, *The Health of a Nation,* 244–45.

14. Anderson, op. cit., 245–46.

15. Ibid., 246.

16. Copies of the letters to President Taft and Secretary Wilson are in Records of the Secretary of Agriculture, Correspondence, 1911, "Wiley," RG 16; *Oil, Paint, and Drug Reporter* (17 July 1911): 42; *Oil, Paint, and Drug Reporter* (24 July 1911): 7; *Washington Herald,* 17 July 1911, clippings, Box 227, WP.

17. House of Representatives, *Hearings on Expenditures,* 1911, passim; Wiley to H. E. Barnard, 1 May 1911, Box 94, WP; H. E. Barnard to Wiley, 3 August 1911, Box 100, WP.

18. House of Representatives, *Hearings on Expenditures,* 1911, especially the testimony of George McCabe; *Oil, Paint, and Drug Reporter* (21 August 1911): 7, 25; *Oil, Paint, and Drug Reporter* (25 September 1911): 25–26. For the pro-Wiley attitude of the press, see Jon S. Mosby Jr. to Wiley, 15 September 1911, Box 90, WP.

19. House of Representatives, Report No. 249, 62d Cong., 2d sess., 1912; Wiley to Richard H. Waldo, 2 December 1911, Box 90, WP; Wiley to John Arbuckle, 22 December 1911, Box 94, WP.

20. *Congressional Record,* 62d Congress, 2d session, 2525, 2562, 2633.

21. Ibid., 2634–36. The Mann quotation is from 2641.

22. William H. Taft to Wiley, 14 September 1911, Box 100, WP.

23. A copy of Taft's statement is in Box 100, WP; Anderson, *The Health of a Nation,* 249.

24. *American Food Journal* (15 December 1911).

25. Wiley to Richard H. Waldo, 2 December 1911, Box 90, WP; Wiley to John Arbuckle, 22 December 1911, Box 94, WP; Message delivered to United Press, 27 February 1912 (copy), Box 103, WP; Wiley to James Wilson, 29 February 1912, Box 102, WP; Anderson, *The Health of a Nation,* 252 and note 17, 317.

26. "Statement for the Press," 14 March 1912, Box 103, WP.

27. Harvey W. Wiley, "Why I Support Wilson and Marshall," speech given 3 October 1912, Box 109, WP.

28. *American Food Journal* (15 July 1912); H. E. Barnard to Wiley, 18 July 1912, R. M. Allen to James E. Tower (copy), 28 July 1912, R. M. Allen to Wiley, 30 July 1912, Box 107, WP.

Conclusion

1. Harvey Levenstein, *Paradox of Plenty: A Social History of Eating in America* (Oxford: Oxford University Press, 1993), 16–17.

2. Pendergrast, *For God, Country, and Coca-Cola,* 109–24; Paul Van Riper, "Harvey W. Wiley, Pioneering Consumer Advocate," in *Exemplary Public Administrators: Character and Leadership in Government* (San Francisco: Jossey-Bass Publishers, 1992), 30–56.

3. Thomas K. McCraw, *Prophets of Regulation,* 306.

Bibliography

Unpublished Sources

Browne, Charles A. "A History of the New York Sugar Trade Laboratory." Papers. Library of Congress, Washington, D.C.

Fox, William Lloyd. "Harvey W. Wiley: The Formative Years." Ph.D. diss., George Washington University, 1960.

Frear, William. Papers. Pennsylvania State University, State College.

Hoing, Willard. "James Wilson as Secretary of Agriculture, 1897–1913." Ph.D. diss., University of Wisconsin, Madison, 1964.

Lamb, Ruth DeForest. "The Devil's Candle." Ph.D. diss., Vasser College Library. Poughkeepsie, New York, c. 1940.

Remsen, Ira. Papers. Milton S. Eisenhower Library. Johns Hopkins University, Baltimore, Maryland.

Roosevelt, Theodore. Papers. Manuscripts Division. Library of Congress, Washington, D.C.

Taft, William Howard. Papers. Manuscripts Division. Library of Congress, Washington. D.C.

Wiley, Anna Kelton. Papers. Manuscripts Division. Library of Congress, Washington, D.C.

Wiley, Harvey Washington. Papers. Manuscripts Division. Library of Congress, Washington, D.C.

Government Records

National Association of State Food and Dairy Officials. *Proceedings*. Washington, D.C., 1898–1904.

Record Group 16, Records of the Office of the Secretary of Agriculture (OSA), National Archives.

Record Group 97, Records of the Bureau of Agriculture and Industrial Chemistry (BAIC), National Archives.

Record Group 88, Records of the Food and Drug Administration, National Archives.

U.S. Congress. House. *Hearings on Expenditures in the Department of Agriculture*. Brief Submitted to the Board of Food and Drug by Corn Products Refining Co. in the Matter of Labeling Corn Products. 1907, 2. 62nd Cong., 1st sess., 1911.

Congressional Record. 62d Congress. 1912.

U.S. Department of Agriculture. *The Influence of Sodium Benzoate on the Nutrition and Health of Man*. Report 88. Washington, D.C.: General Printing Office, 1909.

U.S. House. Committee on Agriculture Appropriations. *Expenditures in the Department of Agriculture: Hearings before the Committee on Expenditures in the Department of Agriculture, April 24–August 22, 1911*. Washington, D.C.: General Printing Office, 1911.

U.S. House. Committee on Agriculture. *Hearings on Agriculture Appropriations*. 59th Cong., 1st sess., 1906.

U.S. House. Committee on Interstate and Foreign Commerce. *Hearings on Pure Food.* 59th Cong. 1st sess., 1906.

U.S. House. *Hearings Before the Committee on Agriculture.* 59th Cong., 2d sess., 1907.

U.S. Department of Agriculture. Board of Food and Drug Inspection. *Food Inspection Decision 76. Dyes, Chemicals, and Preservatives in Foods.* Washington, D.C.: General Printing Office, 1907.

U.S. House. *Hearings on Expenditures in the Department of Agriculture.* 62nd Cong., 1st sess., 1911.

U.S. President's Commission. *Proceedings Before and by the Direction of the President Concerning the Meaning of the Term "Whisky."* Washington, D.C.: Government Printing Office, 1909.

U.S. Department of Agriculture. Bureau of Chemistry. *Chemistry Bulletin 38: Proceedings of the Tenth Annual Convention of The Association of Official Agricultural Chemists.* Washington, D.C.: General Printing Office, 1893.

U.S. Department of Agriculture. Bureau of Chemistry. *Bulletin 13:* Washington, D.C.: General Printing Office, 1887.

U.S. Department of Agriculture. Bureau of Chemistry. *Bulletin 84.* Washington, D.C.: General Printing Office, 1904–8.

U.S. Department of Agriculture. Office of the Secretary. *Circular 21.* Washington, D.C.: General Printing Office, 1967.

U.S. Internal Revenue. Department of the Treasury. *Report on Glucose.* Washington: General Printing Office, 1884.

Union Distilling Co. v. Bernard Bettmann et al., U.S. Circuit Court, Southern District of Ohio, Case No. 6407, National Archives, Great Lakes Region.

United States vs. 40 Barrels and 20 Kegs of Coca-Cola. 431: United States, Plaintiff in Error vs. Forty Barrels and Twenty Kegs of Coca Cola, The Coca Cola Company of Atlanta, Georgia, Claimant and Intervener, U.S. Supreme Court. 1915. Transcripts of Records File Copies of Briefs 1915, Vols. 79 and 80, Case No. 562 N.J. No. 1455. Washington, D.C.: Supreme Court Library.

Journals, Articles, and Newspapers

Adams, Samuel Hopkins. "What Has Become of Our Pure Food Law?" *Hampton's,* 10 February 1910, 234–42.

Advertising Age. 20 January 1990, 58.

American Food Journal. 1906–11.

Bailey, Thomas A. "Congressional Opposition to Pure Food Legislation." *American Journal of Sociology* 36 (July 1930): 52–64.

Baily, Martin N., and Clifford Winston. *Brookings Papers on Economic Activity.* Washington, D.C.: The Brookings Institution, 1989.

Barkan, Ilyse D. "Industry Invites Regulation: The Passage of the Pure Food and Drug Act of 1906." *American Journal of Public Health* 75, no. 1 (January 1985): 18–25.

Bartel, A. P., and L. G. Thomas. "Direct and Indirect Effects of Regulation: A New Look at OSHA's Impact." *Journal of Law and Economics* 28 (April 1985): 1–25.

Baumol, William J. "Entrepreneurship in Economic Theory." *American Economic Review* (May 1968).

Becker, Gary S. "A Theory of Competition Among Pressure Groups for Political Influence." *Quarterly Journal of Economics* 98 (August 1983): 371–400.

Braeman, John. "The Square Deal in Action." In *Change and Continuity in Twentieth-Century America,* ed. John Braeman, Robert H. Bremner, and Everret Walters. Columbus: Ohio State University Press, 1964.

Breton, Albert, and Raymond Breton. "An Economic Theory of Social Movements." *American Economic Review* (May 1969): 198–205.

Buchanan, James. "What Should Economists Do?" *Southern Economic Journal* (30 January 1964): 213–22.

Buchanan, James, and Gordon Tullock. "Polluter's Profits and Political Response: Direct Controls versus Taxes." *American Economic Review* 65 (March 1975): 139–47.

Carson, Gerald. "Who Put the Borax in Dr. Wiley's Butter?" *American Heritage* 7 (1956): 58–63.

Collier's Weekly. 6 April 1912.

Coppin, Clayton A. "James Wilson and Harvey Wiley: The Dilemma of Bureaucratic Entrepreneurship." *Agricultural History* 54, no. 2 (spring 1990): 166–79.

———. "John Arbuckle: Entrepreneur, Trustbuster, and Humanitarian." *Market Process* 7, no. 1 (spring 1989): 11–15.

———. "Sweeter Manners Purer Laws: A Regulatory History of the Corn Syrup Industry." *Market Process* (spring 1990): 61–68.

Coppin, Clayton, and Jack C. High. "Entrepreneurship and Competition in Bureaucracy: Harvey Washington Wiley's Bureau of Chemistry, 1883–1903." In *Regulation: Economic Theory and History,* ed. Jack High. Ann Arbor: University of Michigan Press, 1991.

———. "Umpires at Bat: Setting Food Standards by Government Regulation." *Business and Economic History* 2 (1992): 109–17.

DiLorenzo, Thomas. "Competition and Political Entrepreneurship." *Review of Austrian Economics* (1987).

Douglas, Mary. "Deciphering a Meal." *Daedalus* 101.

Fausold, Martin L. "James W. Wadsworth, Sr., and The Meat Inspection Act of 1906." *New York History* 51, no. 1 (1970): 42–61.

Fiedler, William C. "Antikamnia: The Story of a Pseudo-ethical Pharmaceutical." *Pharmacy in History* 21, no. 2 (1979): 60–71.

Good Housekeeping, December 1926, 92.

Good Housekeeping, January 1930, 90.

Hampton's. 10 February 1910.

Hayek, F. A. "The Use of Knowledge in Society." In *Individualism and Economic Order,* 77–91. Chicago: University of Chicago Press, 1948.

Hidy, Ralph. 1970. "Business History: Present Status and Future Needs." *Business History Review* 44 (winter 1970).

High, Jack. "Can Rents Run Uphill?" *Public Choice* 65 (1990): 229–37.

———. "A Tale of Two Disciplines." In *Regulation: Economic Theory and History,* ed. Jack High, 1–17. Ann Arbor: University of Michigan Press, 1991.

High, Jack C., and Clayton Coppin. "Wiley and the Whiskey Industry: Strategic Behavior in the Passage of the Pure Food Act." *Business History Review* 62 (summer 1988): 287–309.

Kane, R. James. "Populism, Progressivism, and Pure Food." *Agricultural History* 38 (1964): 155–69.

Keuchel, Edward F. "Chemicals and Meat: The Embalmed Beef Scandal of the Spanish-American War." *Bulletin of the History of Medicine* 48 (1974).

Lévi-Strauss, Claude. "The Culinary Triangle." *Partisan Review* 33.

Lowery. "The Senate Plot Against Pure Food." *World's Work* 10 (1905).

Lusk, Graham. "The Remsen Board and Dr. Wiley." *Medical Record* (9 December 1911).

Marcus, Alan I. "Setting the Standard: Fertilizers, State Chemists, and Early National Commercial Regulation, 1880–1887." *Agricultural History* no. 1 (1987).

McChesney, Fred S. "Rent Extraction and Rent Creation in the Economic Theory of Regulation." *Journal of Legal Studies* 16 (January 1987).

McCormick, Richard. "The Discovery that Business Corrupts Politics: A Reappraisal of the Origins of Progressivism." *American Historical Review* 86, no. 2 (April 1981).

McCraw, Thomas K. "Regulation in America." *Business History Review* 49 (summer 1975): 159–83.

McKenzie, William D. "The Consumers' League and Its Work for Pure Food." *The American Pure Food and Drug Journal* 1, no. 8 (August 1908): 8–12.

National Food Magazine. Chicago, Ill.: Pierce Publishing Company, 1906.

Needham, Henry Beach. "Senate of Special Interests." *World's Work* 2 (1905): 7206–11.

Newsweek. 1 July 1991, 45.

Newsweek. 27 May 1991, 46–53.

The New York Herald. 27 August 1905.

Nye, Ronald L. "Federal vs. State Agricultural Research Policy: The Case of California's Tulare Experiment Station, 1889–1909." *Agricultural History* 57, no. 4 (1983): 436–49.

Outlook. 7 September 1912.

Parmenter, W. "The Jungle and Its Effects." *Journalism History* 10, nos. 1–2 (1983): 14–34.

Peltzman, Sam. "The Economic Theory of Regulation a Decade after Deregulation." In *Brookings Papers of Economic Activity,* ed. Martin Neal Bailey and Clifford Winston. Washington, D.C.: Brookings Institute, 1989.

Pinkett, Harold T. "The Keep Commission, 1905–1909: A Rooseveltian Effort for Administrative Reform." *Journal of American History* 52, no. 2 (1965): 297–312.

Posner, Richard. "Theories of Economic Regulation." *Bell Journal of Economics and Management Science* 5 (autumn 1974): 335–58.

Reynolds, Terry S. "Defining Professional Boundaries: Chemical Engineering in the Early Twentieth Century." *Technology and Culture* 27 (1986): 694–716.

Rosenberg, Charles E. "Rationalization and Reality in Shaping American Agriculture Research, 1875–1914." In *The Sciences in the American Context: New Perspectives,* ed. Nathanial Reingold. Washington, D.C.: Smithsonian Institute Press, 1979.

Salisbury, Robert. "An Exchange Theory of Interest Groups." *Midwest Journal of Political Science* (1969): 1–32.

Sokolov, Raymond. "Sauce for the Masses." *Natural History* 93 (May 1984): 90ff.

Stigler, George J. "The Economics of Information." *Journal of Political Economy* (June 1961): 213–25.

———. "The Theory of Economic Regulation." *Bell Journal of Economics and Management* 2 (spring 1971).

Time. July 15, 1991.

Temin, Peter. *Taking Your Medicine: Drug Regulation in the United States.* Cambridge: Harvard University Press, 1980.

Tinker, Jackson. "Who Killed the Pure Food Bill?" *Public Opinion* (15 April 1905): 572–73, 590.

Tollison, Robert. "Regulation and Interest Groups." In *Regulation: Economic Theory and History.* Ann Arbor: University of Michigan Press, 1991.

Van Riper, Paul. "Harvey W. Wiley, Pioneering Consumer Advocate." In *Exemplary Public Administrators: Character and Leadership in Government.* San Francisco: Jossey-Bass Publishers, 1992.

Vietor, Richard H. K. "Businessmen and the Political Economy: The Railroad Rate Controversy of 1905." *Journal of American History* 64 (June 1977): 47–66.

Wagner, Richard. "Agency, Economic Calculation, and Constitutional Construction." In *The Political Economy of Rent Seeking,* ed. Charles Rowley. Boston: Kluwer Academic Publishers, 1988.

———. "Pressure Groups and Political Entrepreneurs." *Papers on Non-Market Decision Making* (1966).

Walker, Francis A. "The Meat Inspection Act of 1906." *Quarterly Journal of the Royal Economic Society* 16 (December 1906): 491–511.

Washington Evening Star. March 14, 1908.

Washington Post. May 6, 1991, A10.

Washington Post. June 5, 1991, A3.

Weingast, Barry R., and Mark J. Moran. "Bureaucratic Discretion or Congressional Control?" *Journal of Political Economy* 91 (October 1983): 765–800.

Wirtschafter, Jonathan. "The Genesis and Impact of the Medical Lobby, 1898–1906." *Journal of the History of Medicine and Allied Sciences* 13, no. 1 (1958): 15–49.

Wood, Donna J. "The Strategic Use of Public Policy: Business Support for the 1906 Pure Food and Drug Act." *Business History Review* 59 (autumn 1985): 403–32.

Yeager, Mary A. "Bureaucracy." *Encyclopedia of American History,* ed. Glenn Parker (New York: Charles Scribner's Sons, 1980): 894–926.

Young, James Harvey. "From Oysters to After-Dinner Mints: The Role of the Early Food and Drug Inspectors." *Journal of the History of Medicine and Allied Sciences* 47 (1987).

———. "The Long Struggle for the 1906 Law." *FDA Consumer* (12 June 1981): 12–16.

———. "The Pig that Fell into the Privy: Upton Sinclair's *The Jungle* and the Meat Inspection Amendment of 1906." *Bulletin of the History of Medicine* 59 (1984).

———. " 'This Greasy Counterfeit': Butter Versus Oleomargarine in the United States Congress, 1886." *Bulletin of the History of Medicine* 53, no. 3 (1970).

———. "Three Southern Food and Drug Cases." *The Journal of Southern History* 49, no. 1 (1983).

Zamula, Evelyn. 1984. "Tale of the Tomato: From 'Poison' to Pizza." *FDA Consumer* (July–August 1984): 24+.

Books

Adams, Henry. *The Education of Henry Adams.* Boston: Massachusetts Historical Society, 1918.

Alberts, Robert C. *The Good Provider: H. J. Heinz and His 57 Varieties.* Boston: Houghton Mifflin, 1973.

Anderson, Oscar. *The Health of a Nation.* Chicago: University of Chicago Press, 1958.

Armelagos, George, and Peter Farb. *Consuming Passions: The Anthropology of Eating.* New York: Washington Square Press, 1980.

Baron, Stanley. *Brewed in America: The History of Beer and Ale in the United States.* Boston: Little Brown, 1962.

Belasco, Warren J. *Appetite for Change: How the Counter Culture Took on the Food Industry, 1966–1988.* New York: Pantheon Books, 1989.

Bishop, Joseph Bucklin. *Charles Joseph Bonaparte.* New York: Charles Scribner's Sons, 1922.

Bitting, A. W. *Appertizing or the Art of Canning; Its History and Development.* San Francisco: The Trade Pressroom, 1937.

Boorstin, Daniel J. *The Americans: The Democratic Experience.* New York: Random House, 1973.

Breyer, Stephen. *Regulation and Its Reform.* Cambridge: Harvard University Press, 1982.

Braemen, John, Robert H. Brenner, and Everett Walters. *Change and Continuity in Twentieth-Century America.* Columbus: Ohio State University Press, 1964.

Burrow, James G. *AMA: Voice of American Medicine.* Baltimore: Johns Hopkins University, 1963.

Candler, Charles Howard. *Asa Griggs Candler.* Atlanta: Emory University Press, 1950.

Carson, Gerald. *Cornflake Crusade.* New York: Rinehart, 1957.

Casson, Mark. *The Entrepreneur.* New York: Barnes and Noble, 1982.

Caswell, Julie A., ed. *Economics of Food Safety.* New York: Elsevier Science, 1991.

Chandler, Alfred. *The Visible Hand.* Cambridge: Harvard University Press, 1977.

Clark, Victor S. *History of Manufacturers in the United States.* Vol. 3. New York: McGraw-Hill, 1929.

Crandall, Robert. *Controlling Industrial Pollution: The Economics and Politics of Clean Air.* Washington, D.C.: The Brookings Institution, 1983.

Crunden, Robert M. *Ministers of Reform: The Progressive Achievement in American Civilization.* New York: Basic Books, 1982.

Cummings, Richard Osborn. *The American and His Food.* Chicago: University of Chicago Press, 1940.

Dewing, Arthur S. *Corporate Promotions and Reorganizations.* Cambridge: Harvard University Press, 1914.

Downs, Anthony. *An Economic Theory of Democracy.* New York: Harper and Row, 1957.

Dupree, A. Hunter. *Science in the Federal Government: A History of Policies and Activities to 1940.* Cambridge: Harvard University Press, 1957.

The Early Years of Federal Food and Drug Control. Madison, Wisc.: American Institute of the History of Pharmacy, 1982.

Ewen, Elizabeth. *Immigrant Women in the Land of Dollars: Life and Culture on the Lower East Side, 1890–1925.* New York: Monthly Review Press, 1985.

Fitzell, Philip B. *Private Labels: Store Brands and Generic Products.* Westport, Connecticut: AVI Publishing Company, 1982.

Forrestal, Dan J. *Faith, Hope and $5,000: The Story of Monsanto.* New York: Simon and Schuster, 1977.

Frolich, Norman, Joe A. Oppenheimer, and Oran Young. *Political Leadership and Collective Goods.* Princeton, N.J.: Princeton University Press, 1971.

Goldman, Eric F. *Charles J. Bonaparte, Patrician Reformer.* Baltimore: Johns Hopkins Press, 1943.

Gwinn, Chester A. *Food and Drugs Act, June 30, 1906.* Washington, D.C.: General Printing Office, 1914.

Hayter, Earl W. *The Troubled Farmer, 1850–1900: Rural Adjustment to Industrialism.* Dekalb: Northern Illinois University Press, 1968.

Heitmann, John Alfred. *The Modernization of the Louisiana Sugar Industry, 1830–1910.* Baton Rouge: Lousiana State University Press, 1987.

Helrich, Kenneth. *The Great Collaboration.* Arlington, Va: AOAC, 1984.

Herbert, Robert, and Albert Link. *The Entrepreneurs.* New York: Praeger, 1982.

Hess, John L., and Karen Hess. *The Taste of America.* New York: Grossman Publishers, 1977.

High, Jack. *Regulation: Economic Theory and History.* Ann Arbor: University of Michigan Press, 1991.

Hinich, Melvin J., and Richard Staelin. *Consumer Protection Legislation and the U.S. Food Industry.* New York: Pergamon Press, 1980.

Hise, Charles van. *Concentration and Control.* New York: Macmillan, 1912.

Horwitz, Robert Britt. *The Irony of Regulatory Reform.* Oxford: Oxford University Press, 1989.

Houston, David. *Eight Years with Wilson's Cabinet, 1913–1920.* New York: Doubleday, 1926.

Howard, Burton J., and Charles Henry Stephenson. *Microscopical Studies on Tomato Products.* Washington, D.C.: General Printing Office, 1917.

Howe, Irving. *World of Our Fathers.* New York: Simon and Schuster, 1976.

Kallett, Arthur, and F. J. Schlink. *100,000,000 Guinea Pigs: Dangers in Everyday Foods, Drugs, and Cosmetics.* New York: Grosset and Dunlap, 1935.

Katzman, David M. *Seven Days a Week: Women and Domestic Service in Industrializing America.* New York: Oxford University Press, 1978.

Keats, John. *What Ever Happened to Mom's Apple Pie?* Boston: Houghton Mifflin, 1976.

Kerr, K. Austin. *American Railroad Politics.* Pittsburgh: University of Pittsburgh Press, 1968.

Kirzner, Israel. *Competition and Entrepreneurship.* Chicago: University of Chicago Press, 1973.

———. *Discovery and the Capitalist Process.* Chicago: University of Chicago Press, 1985.

Kolko, Gabriel. *Railroads and Regulation.* Princeton, N.J.: Princeton University Press, 1965.

———. *The Triumph of Conservatism.* New York: Macmillan, 1963.

Langworthy, C. F. *Food and Diet in the United States. Yearbook of the Department of Agriculture.* Washington, D.C.: USDA, 1907.

Leech, Margaret. *In the Days of McKinley.* New York: Harper Brothers, 1959.

Levenstein, Harvey. *Paradox of Plenty: A Social History of Eating in America.* Oxford: Oxford University Press, 1993.

———. *Revolution at the Table: The Transformation of the American Diet.* New York: Oxford University Press, 1988.

Lewis, Eugene. *Public Entrepreneurship: Toward a Theory of Bureaucratic Political Power.* Bloomington: Indiana University Press, 1980.

Link, Arthur S. *American Epoch.* New York: Alfred A. Knopf, 1955.

Lord, Walter. *The Good Years.* New York: Harper and Row, 1960.

MacAvoy, Paul. *The Economic Effects of Regulation: The Trunk-line Railroad Cartels and the Interstate Commerce Commission before 1900.* Cambridge: MIT Press, 1965.

Matthews, Glenna. *Just a Housewife: The Rise and Fall of Domesticity in America.* New York: Oxford University Press, 1987.

McChesney, Fred S. *Money for Nothing.* Cambridge: Harvard University Press, 1997.

McCraw, Thomas K. *Prophets of Regulation.* Cambridge: Harvard University Press, 1984.

———. *Regulation in Perspective.* Cambridge: Harvard University Press, 1981.

Mcgee, Harold. *On Food and Cooking.* New York: Charles Scribner's Sons, 1984.

Mennell, Stephen. *All Manners of Food: Eating and Taste in England and France from the Middle Ages to the Present.* Oxford and New York: Basil Blackwell, 1985.

Mises, Ludwig von. *Bureaucracy.* New Haven: Yale University Press, 1944.

———. *Human Action.* New Haven: Yale University Press, 1949.

More, Louise Boland. *Wage-Earners' Budgets.* New York: Henry Holt, 1907.

Morgan, Dan. *The Merchants of Grain.* New York: Viking Press, 1979.

Natenberg, Maurice. *The Legacy of Dr. Wiley.* Chicago: University of Chicago Press, 1957.

Niskanan, William A. *Bureaucracy and Representative Government.* Chicago: Aldine-Atherton Press, 1971.

Okun, Mitchell. *Fair Play in the Marketplace: The First Battle for Pure Food and Drugs.* Dekalb: Northern Illinois University Press, 1986.

Pabst, William R., Jr. *Butter and Oleomargarine: An Analysis of Competing Commodities.* New York: Columbia University Press, 1937.

Penick, James, Jr. *Progressive Politics and Conservation: The Ballinger-Pinchot Affair.* Chicago: University of Chicago Press, 1968.

Pendergast, Mark. *For God, Country, and Coca-Cola: The Unauthorized History of the Great American Soft Drink and the Company That Makes It.* New York: Charles Scribner's Sons, 1993.

Pinchot, Gifford. *Breaking New Ground.* New York: Harcourt, Brace, 1947.

Ricardo, David. *Principles of Political Economy and Taxation.* London: E. P. Dutton and Sons, 1933.

Ridell, Robert W. *All the World's a Fair: Visions of Empire at American International Expositions, 1876–1916.* Chicago: University of Chicago Press, 1984.

Robins, William. *A Plot against the People.* Ontario: Hiram Walker and Sons, 1911.

Root, Waverly, and Richard de Rochemont. *Eating in America: A History.* New York: Ecco Press, 1981.

Schlesinger, Arthur M. *Paths to the Present.* New York: Macmillan, 1949.

Schumpeter, Joseph. *Capitalism, Socialism, and Democracy.* New York: Harper and Row, 1942.

———. *The Theory of Economic Development.* Cambridge: Harvard University Press, 1934.

Shapiro, Laura. *Perfection Salad: Women and Cooking at the Turn of the Century.* New York: Farrar, Straus and Giroux, 1986.

Simkhovitch, Mary Kingsbury. *The City Worker's World in America.* New York: Macmillan Company, 1917.

Stephenson, Nathaniel W. *Nelson W. Aldrich.* Port Washington, N.Y.: Kennikat Press, 1930.

Strasser, Susan. *Satisfaction Guaranteed: The Making of the American Mass Market.* New York: Pantheon Books, 1989.

Sullivan, Mark. *Our Times.* 6 vols. New York: Charles Scribner's Sons, 1926–35.

Tannahill, Reay. *Food in History.* New York: Crown, 1973.

Tedlow, Richard S. *New and Improved: The Story of Mass Marketing in America.* New York: Basic Books, 1990.

Temin, Peter. *Taking Your Medicine: Drug Regulation in the United States.* Cambridge: Harvard University Press, 1980.

Turner, James. *The Chemical Feast.* New York: Grossman Publishers, 1970.

Vietor, Richard K. *Environmental Politics and the Coal Coalition.* College Station: Texas A&M University Press, 1980.

Visser, Margaret. *Much Depends on Dinner: The Extraordinary History and Mythology, Allure and Obsessions, and Taboos, of an Ordinary Meal.* New York: Grove Press, 1986.

Washburn, Malcolm E. *The Cosmos Club of Washington: A Centennial History, 1878– 1978.* Washington, D.C.: Cosmos Club, 1978.

Whitnah, Donald. *A History of the United States Weather Bureau.* Urbana: University of Illinois Press, 1961.

Whorton, James C. *Crusaders for Fitness: The History of American Health Reformers.* Princeton, N.J.: Princeton University Press, 1982.

Wilcox, Claire. *Public Policies Towards Business.* 3d ed. Homewood, Ill.: Richard D. Irwin, 1966.

Wilcox, Earley Vernon. *Tama Jim.* Boston: Stratford, 1930.

Wiley, Harvey Washington. *An Autobiography.* Indianapolis: Bobbs-Merrill, 1930.

———. *History of a Crime against the Food Law: The Amazing Story of the National Food and Drugs Law Intended to Protect the Health of the People, Perverted to Protect Adulteration of Food and Drugs.* Washington, D.C.: Harvey W. Wiley, 1929.

Wilson, Steven. *Food and Drug Regulation.* Washington, D.C.: American Council on Public Affairs, 1942.

Wood, Donna J. *Strategic Uses of Public Policy: Business and Government in the Progressive Era.* Marshfield, Mass.: Pitman Publishing, 1986.

Yeager, Mary. *Competition and Regulation: The Development of Oligopoly in the Meat Industry.* Greenwich, Conn.: JAI Press, 1981.

Young, James Harvey. *The Medical Messiahs.* Princeton, N.J.: Princeton University Press, 1967.

———. *Pure Food: Securing the Federal Food and Drugs Act of 1906.* Princeton, N.J.: Princeton University Press, 1989.

———. *The Toadstool Millionaires.* Princeton, N.J.: Princeton University Press, 1961.

———, ed. *The Early Years of Federal Food and Drug Control.* Madison, Wisc.: American Institute of the History of Pharmacy, 1982.

Index